In the name of God, the Compas

Sayyid Quṭb

❦

IN THE SHADE OF
THE QUR'ĀN

Fī Ẓilāl al-Qur'ān

VOLUME IV
❦
SŪRAH 5

Al-Mā'idah

———— ❦ ————

Translated and Edited by
Adil Salahi & Ashur Shamis

———— ❦ ————

THE ISLAMIC FOUNDATION
AND
ISLAMONLINE.NET

Published by

THE ISLAMIC FOUNDATION,

Markfield Conference Centre,
Ratby Lane, Markfield, Leicester LE67 9SY, United Kingdom
Tel: (01530) 244944, Fax: (01530) 244946
E-mail: i.foundation@islamic-foundation.org.uk
Website: www.islamic-foundation.org.uk

Quran House, PO Box 30611, Nairobi, Kenya

PMB 3193, Kano, Nigeria

ISLAMONLINE.NET,
P.O. Box 22212, Doha, Qatar
E-mail: webmaster@islam-online.net
Website: www.islamonline.net

British Library Cataloguing-in-Publication Data
Qutb, Sayyid, 1903–1966
    In the shade of the Qur'an: fi zilal al-Qur'an,
    Vol. 4: Surah 5: Al-Ma'idah
    1. Koran
    I. Title
    II. Salahi, Adil
    III. Shamis, Ashur
    297.1'227

ISBN 0 86037 351 7
ISBN 0 86037 346 0 pbk

Typeset by: N.A.Qaddoura
Cover design by: Imtiaze A. Manjra

Printed and bound in Great Britain by Antony Rowe Ltd., Chippenham, Wiltshire

Contents

iii

Transliteration Table

Consonants. Arabic

initial: unexpressed medial and final:

ء	ʼ	د	d	ض	ḍ	ك	k
ب	b	ذ	dh	ط	ṭ	ل	l
ت	t	ر	r	ظ	ẓ	م	m
ث	th	ز	z	ع	ʽ	ن	n
ج	j	س	s	غ	gh	ـﻫ	h
ح	ḥ	ش	sh	ف	f	و	w
خ	kh	ص	ṣ	ق	q	ي	y

Vowels, diphthongs, etc.

Short:	◌َ	a	◌ِ	i	◌ُ	u
long:	ـَا	ā	◌ُو	ū	ـِي	ī
diphthongs:			◌َوْ	aw		
			◌َىْ	ay		

SŪRAH 5

Al-Mā'idah

(The Repast)

Prologue

The Qur'ān was bestowed from on high to Muḥammad, God's Messenger, so that he might, by means of it, establish a state, bring a community into being, organise a society, cultivate minds and consciences and set moral values. The Qur'ān was also to set the bonds that would operate within the Muslim community, as also define the international relations the Muslim state might have. All these were to be firmly joined together, so that all their parts would form one coherent whole, stemming from a single source and referring to a single authority. This is, in fact, the nature of religion, as defined by God and practised by Muslims in the days when they were indeed truly Muslims.

Hence, we find in this *sūrah*, as we found in the three long ones preceding it, a whole host of topics interlinked by the main goal the Qur'ān was revealed to achieve, namely, social organisation on the basis of a well-defined concept formulated by faith. Such a concept looks up to God for all its laws, values, standards and code of living and maintains that all Godhead, Lordship and authority belong to God alone.

We also find in this *sūrah* a clear effort to formulate concepts of belief, pure, purged of all traces of idolatrous superstition, and distortion perpetrated by followers of earlier Divine religions. Moreover, the Muslim community is made fully aware of its true nature, its role, the course it must follow and the difficulties that it involves. It is also alerted to the wicked designs of its enemies who are certainly hostile

1

to its faith. The *sūrah* also includes rulings concerning some of its worship rituals, specifically those which aim to give the Muslim individual and the Muslim community spiritual purification, consolidating their relations with their Lord. Other legislation included in the *sūrah* aims to regulate relations within the Muslim community, as well as inter-community relations. Furthermore, the *sūrah* includes legislation permitting or prohibiting certain types of food, drink, marriages and other practices. All these form a complete unit, in a single *sūrah*, confirming the true meaning of religion, as God intended it and as understood by Muslims who are true to their faith.

In this *sūrah*, as well as in the two preceding *sūrahs*, this idea is not given implicitly but is rather stated explicitly and emphatically. Furthermore, the *sūrah* makes clear that all these together form the religion of Islam, that accepting it all means faith, and that putting it all into practice is the meaning of submission to God or Islam. It further states that those who do not judge according to God's revelations are unbelievers, wrongdoers and transgressors. Indeed, by refusing to judge in accordance with God's revelations, they prefer the judgement of ignorance, and this is something that a Muslim believer simply cannot do.

This fundamental principle is given prominence in the *sūrah* together with the pure concept of faith on which it is based. It is pertinent to show here how the two are intertwined.

As it emphasises that making God's revelation the basis of all judgements is the true meaning of Islam, and that what God has pronounced as lawful or unlawful is the true meaning of religion, the Qur'ān relies on the fact that God is the only deity in the universe and has no partner to share in His Divinity; God the only Creator has no partner in His creation; the only Owner has no partner in His dominion. Hence, it is both logical and inevitable that nothing should be decided except on the basis of His law and by His permission. The One who creates all and owns all has all authority to determine the constitution to be followed by His creatures in His dominion. He is the One to legislate and to be obeyed whatever He may rule. Whoever disputes this is guilty of disobedience, rebellion and disbelief. It is He who defines the true concept of faith as well as the proper code of living. Those who believe in Him embrace the faith He has revealed and implement the system He has outlined. The two go hand in hand. They worship Him through offering the worship rituals and through implementing the code He has legislated, drawing no distinction between a ritual and a legal provision. Both come from God, who alone holds all sovereignty and all authority. This is the essence of the belief in Him as the only God, who has all dominion and who knows all that takes place anywhere in the heavens and the earth. Hence, implementing God's law is at the core of every prophet's religion. Indeed, it is Divine religion which cannot take any other form.

Thus, statements come thick and fast in the *sūrah* emphasising God's oneness and repudiating all forms of polytheism, trinity and association of partners with God or equals to Him. Such statements also establish the characteristics of Godhead and servitude to God in absolute clarity. (See verses 15–17 and 72–3)

Because God is the only Lord, Creator and Sovereign, then He is the only one who legislates and defines what is lawful and what is forbidden. He is the one to be obeyed in what He legislates in the same way as He is the one to whom people should address their worship. He has concluded a covenant with His servants to this effect. Hence, He requires believers in Islam to fulfil their covenant, and warns them against the consequences of breaching it as did the Israelites before them. (Verses 1–2, 7–8, 12–14)

The *sūrah* includes a host of legislative rulings on a wide variety of subjects, such as which animals are lawful to eat when slaughtered or hunted; what is permissible or restricted during the period of consecration, or *ihrām*, in pilgrimage and in the Sacred Mosque at the Ka'bah; what is permissible or forbidden in marriage; purification for worship and prayer; judgement and the administration of justice; mandatory punishment for theft and rebellion against a lawful Islamic government; wines and intoxicants, gambling, idols and divining arrows; atonement for breached oaths and hunting when in the state of consecration; making a will; cattle marked out by superstition and set aside from man's use; and penal provisions in the Torah that have been incorporated in Islamic law. Thus, we see how legal provisions throughout the *sūrah* are presented hand in hand with teachings concerning worship, this without any separating format between them.

Side by side with such rulings and legal provisions, varied as they are, we are commanded to obey God and observe what He has legislated and ordered. We are also commanded not to make any verdict of permissibility or prohibition which is not sanctioned by God. We also

3

have a statement that Islam is the faith God has laid down for the community that submit to Him in all its affairs. It is the faith He has perfected in order to make His grace bestowed on the Muslim community complete. (Verses 2, 87, 92 and 3)

The *sūrah* does not express in general terms the commandment of absolute obedience with respect to prohibition and permissibility. Rather, it makes an absolutely clear statement requiring people to make all judgements based on what God Himself has revealed. To place such judgement on any other basis is tantamount to disbelief, wrongdoing and transgression. The *sūrah* includes many decisive statements in this respect. (Verses 41–50)

Thus the whole issue is made abundantly clear: there is one God who is the Creator and the Owner of all. Hence, there is one judge, legislator and master commanding all authority. This, by necessity, means that there is only one legal code and one approach. The result of all this is that there can be either obedience and judgement in accordance with God's law, which is the prerequisite of faith, or there can be disobedience, rebellion and judgement on some other basis, which is the mark of disbelief, wrongdoing and transgression. This is the essence of the Divine religion, the following of which is the subject matter of God's covenant with mankind. It is the same religion preached by all God's messengers to all believing communities and the community of Muḥammad's followers.

It is, then, imperative that Divine religion means that all judgement should be in accordance with what God has revealed from on high, paying no regard to any other consideration. It is only on the basis of such reality that God's authority and sovereignty are seen to operate fully and the declaration of "there is no deity other than God" takes practical effect.

The mutual association between Divine religion and making God's revelation the basis of all judgement is not merely due to the fact that God's revelation is infinitely better than all the laws and regulations human beings may devise and enact. This is only one, though not the main, reason for it. The main reason is found in the fact that judgement in accordance with God's revelation is the practical meaning of attributing all Godhead to God alone and denying all others any attribute of Godhead. This is the meaning of Islam, both linguistically, i.e. submission, and religiously, i.e. self-surrender to God alone.

It is not sufficient, therefore, that human beings should adopt legislation similar to Divine law, or indeed that they should adopt Divine law itself but label it as their own, without attributing it to Him and implementing it in acknowledgement of His sovereignty. What is important here is that people must not claim for themselves any authority or sovereignty except in the form of implementing God's law and establishing His authority on earth.

It is on this principle that the judgement made in the *surah* is based: "*Those who do not judge in accordance with what God has revealed are indeed unbelievers ... wrongdoers ... transgressors*". (Verses 44, 45 and 47) This is because those people who have taken for their judgement a basis other than what God has revealed are in effect rejecting God's position as the only God in the universe. They express their rejection through their actions and practices, even though they may not declare it verbally. Actions truly speak louder than words. Hence, the Qur'ān describes them as unbelievers, wrongdoers and as iniquitous. These are apt descriptions for their rejection of Godhead as they refuse to acknowledge God's absolute sovereignty, and claim for themselves the most essential quality of Godhead, namely enacting legislation for people which is at variance with God's law. This concept is repeatedly emphasised in several clear statements made in this *surah*.

Another main theme running throughout the *surah* is the outline which is given of the nature of the Muslim community, its true role in human life on earth, its attitude towards its enemies, and at the same time an exposé of those enemies, their deviant beliefs as also what they scheme against Islam. As it did in the previous three *surah*s, here again we see the Qur'ān leading the Muslim community in battle against hostile forces.

The book that has been revealed to this community is the final message God sends to mankind. It confirms previous messages in the essence of faith and the main concepts they outline. However, since it is God's final message, it is the final and governing text. It provides the ultimate version of the Divine law God wants mankind to implement for the whole duration of human life on earth. Whatever it endorses of past law remains part of God's law, and whatever it abrogates loses this status, even though it is stated in one or the other of God's revealed books. "*This day I have perfected your religion for you and bestowed on you the full measure of My blessings and have chosen Islam as a religion for you.*" (Verse 3) "*And to you We have revealed the Book, setting forth the truth, confirming the Scriptures which had already been revealed before it and superseding them.*" (Verse 48)

The role assigned to the Muslim community, then, is that of a trusteeship over mankind: it must ensure justice for all, unaffected by feelings of friendship or hostility, or by what difficulties others place in its way. To endure difficulties and hardships is part and parcel of the discharge of its trust, as is the dismissal of other people's deviation, caprice and desire. The Muslim community must always endeavour not to allow even the slightest deviation from its course or its legal code to curry favour with, or win the support of anyone. It must always seek to win God's pleasure and implement His law. (Verses 2, 8, and 48–9)

A consequence of the fact that the Muslim community is the heir to all Divine messages, the recipient of God's final message to mankind and the trustee over mankind on the basis of the last religion is that it must never have a patronage relationship with those who reject this religion or those who mock its duties and acts of worship. Its patrons are only God, His Messenger, and true believers. The bond that makes this community is not its race, geographical location or national heritage; its only bond is that of faith, the Divine code and final message. (Verses 3, 51, 55, 57–8 and 105)

The enemies of the Muslim community are those who reject Divine guidance and take a hostile attitude towards the system revealed by God. They remain unwilling to see the truth or to moderate their long-standing attitude of hardened hostility to it. The Muslim community must always be able to identify them on the basis of their past attitude towards God's messengers and their recent one towards Islam, its Messenger and followers. (Verses 12–14, 20–6, 32, 41–3, 59–64, 68, 70–1, and 78–82)

This sustained attack that exposes the enemies of the Muslim community, with particular emphasis on the hostility of the Jews and idolaters and some references to the hypocrites and Christians, lead us to another theme the *sūrah* highlights. This theme portrays an attitude that was very much alive in the Muslim community of Madinah at the time when the Qur'ān was revealed. It also deals with the attitude of the Muslim community throughout its history towards hostile forces, which remain the same at all times.

It is, then, pertinent to ask: at what stage in the history of the Muslim community in Madinah was this *sūrah* revealed? A number of reports suggest that this *sūrah* was revealed after *Sūrah* 48, Al-Fatḥ, or The Conquest. It is well known that *Sūrah* 48 was revealed shortly after the Prophet concluded the Peace Treaty of al-Ḥudaibiyah in Year 6 after his migration to Madinah. Some of these reports also suggest that the whole *sūrah*, with the exception of verse 3, was revealed on one occasion. Verse 3, according to these reports, was revealed later, during the Prophet's pilgrimage in Year 10.

However, a careful review of this *sūrah's* themes and the events that took place during the Prophet's lifetime tends to refute this report. Indeed, one of the events that took place shortly before the Battle of Badr conclusively proves that the verses that speak about the attitude of the Israelites towards entering the Holy Land with Moses were known to the Muslims before that Battle which took place in Year 2 AH. Indeed, one report suggests that Sa'd ibn Mu'ādh, and another report says that al-Miqdād ibn 'Amr, quoted one of these verses, as one or the other said to the Prophet: "We will not say to you what the Israelites said to Moses, 'Go forth, you and your Lord, and fight. We will stay here'. Rather we say: 'Go forth, you and your Lord, and fight; we will indeed fight with you.'"

Furthermore, in reviewing the themes of the *sūrah* it is clear that when the verses speaking about the Jews were revealed, they still commanded a position of strength and influence in Madinah, and this could have had a bearing on the Muslim community. Hence, the need for this campaign to expose their reality and to render their scheming ineffective. It is well known that the position and influence of the Jews in Madinah was at a very low ebb after the siege and punishment of the Jewish tribe of Qurayzah that followed the Battle of the Moat. By the end of that siege, the three main Jewish tribes of Qaynuqā', al-Nadīr and Qurayzah had been evacuated from Madinah. All this took place before the signing of the Treaty at al-Ḥudaibiyah with the Arab idolaters. Hence, once that Treaty came into effect, there was no need to give the Jews such importance whereby a whole *sūrah* was devoted to them. Moreover, the time of peaceful coexistence with the Jews was over, and could not be reinstated after they had violated their pledges time after time. Hence, some verses in the *sūrah* must have been revealed before their evacuation. Examples of these are verses 13 and 42.

All this tends to indicate that the opening of the *sūrah* and one or two passages of it were most probably revealed after *Sūrah* 48, while several of its passages were revealed much earlier. Moreover, verse 3 which includes the statement, "*This day I have perfected your religion for you and have bestowed on you the full measure of My blessings and have chosen Islam as a religion for you*", was revealed much later. In fact, this statement was the last of all Qur'ānic revelations, according to the most accurate reports. This means that the *sūrah* could not have been revealed all at once, as one report suggests.

We need to re-emphasise here what we said in the Prologues to *Sūrahs* 2, 3 and 4. As it was being revealed, the Qur'ān was providing leadership for the Muslim community in its battle against its enemies who rejected and opposed its faith, including the Jews, the idolaters and hypocrites. At the same time and using the same approach, it was formulating a proper concept of faith for the believers and giving the Muslim community directives and legislation for its internal organisation. This was all done by means of the same integrated approach.

The most basic and important aspect of building this structure was to purge the monotheistic faith of all confusion, while making it clear that religion means a system for life. It was also intended to illustrate that making God's revelations the basis of all judgement and to be guided in all matters of life by God's message is the true meaning of faith, and that this is Islam in practice. In fact, without all this, the concept of God's oneness will not materialise. As we have already said, the real meaning of God's oneness is to attribute all Godhead, with its essential qualities to God alone. Sovereignty and legislation are among these qualities, just like offering worship rituals. Hence, they must all be attributed and addressed to God alone. This *sūrah* emphasises this point most strongly.

As is clear from this quick preview, the themes discussed in this *sūrah* are closely related to those discussed in the previous three *sūrahs*. However, each *sūrah* has its own distinctive character, approach and style. Each is distinguished by the focus it maintains, the aspects it highlights and the effects it seeks to achieve. This gives each *sūrah* its own quintessential and distinctive style.

The style that distinguishes this *sūrah* is its decisiveness whether in the legal provisions it outlines, which must naturally be free of ambiguity, or in the principles and directives it lays down. These may be given in different styles in other *sūrahs*. However, in the present *sūrah* they are given in full detail and in a distinctively decisive phraseology.

—·—·—

A word should be added about God's statement in the third verse of the *sūrah*: "*This day I have perfected your religion for you and have bestowed on you the full measure of My blessings and have chosen Islam as a religion for you.*" This statement implies the oneness of the source from which the Muslim community receives its code of living, social system and the law that governs its relations and ties with others for all time. It also implies the completeness of this religion with all its details of belief, worship and legal code. None of these may be changed or amended. This religion is now completed and finalised. To amend any part of it is tantamount to rejecting it altogether, because it implies a contradiction of what God has stated about its perfection. To deny or contradict that is to deny the faith altogether. To turn away from it and to adopt a different system or legal code need not be described by us; it has been fully described by God in this *sūrah*. Hence, it needs no further elaboration from us.

This verse states most decisively that Islam is a religion and a legal code for all time; that this version which God has approved as a religion for Muslims is the final one. It is the faith and the religion for that time and all time. There need not be a new religion for every period of time. What we have is a final message, completed and perfected by God who has approved it as a faith for all mankind. Whoever wants to change, amend, alter, replace, or develop any part of it is better advised to seek for himself a faith other than Islam: "*He who seeks a religion other than self-surrender to God, it will not be accepted from him, and in the life to come he will be among the lost.*" (3: 85)

This Divine constitution that includes a concept of belief, worship rituals and a legal code is meant to govern all human life. It allows life to develop and progress without any need to breach any part of the

9

constitution or its detailed provisions. It is meant to be like this, because it is God's final message to mankind.

This constitution has all the necessary elements that facilitate life's development without breaching any of its fundamental or detailed principles. It also means that the constitution has made the necessary provisions for such life development. We must remember that as God devised this constitution, with all its details, He was fully aware of future developments in life and of the emerging needs and requirements of mankind. Hence, when God declares that He has perfected this faith and approved it as a religion for mankind, He has made it able to meet all such requirements. Whoever thinks otherwise does not give God His due respect and status.

Now we will begin looking at the text of the *sūrah* in detail.

I

Contracts and Their Fulfilment

Al-Mā'idah (The Repast)

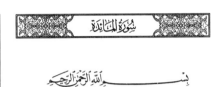

In the Name of God, the Merciful, the Beneficent

Believers, be true to your contracts. Lawful to you is the [flesh of the] beasts of cattle, other than that which is announced to you herein. But you are not allowed to hunt while you are in the state of consecration. God decrees what He will. (1)

Believers, do not offend against the symbols set up by God, or against the sacred month, or the offerings or the garlands, or against those who repair to the Sacred House, seeking God's grace and pleasure. Only when you are clear of the Sacred Precincts and released from the state of consecration may you hunt. Do not let your hatred of people who would debar you

11

from the Sacred Mosque lead you into aggression; but rather help one another in furthering righteousness and piety, and do not help one another in furthering evil and aggression. Have fear of God, for God is severe in retribution. (2)

الْبِرِّ وَالتَّقْوَىٰ وَلَا تَعَاوَنُوا عَلَى الْإِثْمِ وَالْعُدْوَٰنِ وَاتَّقُوا اللَّهَ إِنَّ اللَّهَ شَدِيدُ الْعِقَابِ ۝

Forbidden to you are carrion, blood, the flesh of swine; and that over which any name other than God's has been invoked; and the animal that has been strangled, or beaten to death, or killed by a fall, or gored to death, or savaged by a beast of prey, except that which you may have slaughtered when it is still alive; and [forbidden to you are] animals that have been slaughtered on idolatrous altars. And [forbidden also] is the division [of meat] by raffling with arrows; for all this is sinful. Today, the unbelievers have lost all hope of your religion. Have no fear of them, then, but fear Me alone. This day I have perfected your religion for you and have bestowed on you the full measure of My blessings and have chosen Islam as a religion for you. He who is forced by hunger [to eat of what is forbidden], with no inclination to commit sin, [will find] God Much-Forgiving, Merciful. (3)

حُرِّمَتْ عَلَيْكُمُ الْمَيْتَةُ وَالدَّمُ وَلَحْمُ الْخِنزِيرِ وَمَا أُهِلَّ لِغَيْرِ اللَّهِ بِهِ وَالْمُنْخَنِقَةُ وَالْمَوْقُوذَةُ وَالْمُتَرَدِّيَةُ وَالنَّطِيحَةُ وَمَا أَكَلَ السَّبُعُ إِلَّا مَا ذَكَّيْتُمْ وَمَا ذُبِحَ عَلَى النُّصُبِ وَأَن تَسْتَقْسِمُوا بِالْأَزْلَٰمِ ذَٰلِكُمْ فِسْقٌ الْيَوْمَ يَئِسَ الَّذِينَ كَفَرُوا مِن دِينِكُمْ فَلَا تَخْشَوْهُمْ وَاخْشَوْنِ الْيَوْمَ أَكْمَلْتُ لَكُمْ دِينَكُمْ وَأَتْمَمْتُ عَلَيْكُمْ نِعْمَتِي وَرَضِيتُ لَكُمُ الْإِسْلَٰمَ دِينًا فَمَنِ اضْطُرَّ فِي مَخْمَصَةٍ غَيْرَ مُتَجَانِفٍ لِّإِثْمٍ فَإِنَّ اللَّهَ غَفُورٌ رَّحِيمٌ ۝

They ask you what is lawful to them. Say: Lawful to you are all good things of life. As for those hunting animals which you train by imparting to them something of the knowledge God has imparted to you, you may eat of what they catch for you. But mention God's name over it and have fear of God; indeed, God is swift in reckoning. (4)

يَسْـَٔلُونَكَ مَاذَآ أُحِلَّ لَهُمْ قُلْ أُحِلَّ لَكُمُ ٱلطَّيِّبَٰتُ وَمَا عَلَّمْتُم مِّنَ ٱلْجَوَارِحِ مُكَلِّبِينَ تُعَلِّمُونَهُنَّ مِمَّا عَلَّمَكُمُ ٱللَّهُ فَكُلُوا۟ مِمَّآ أَمْسَكْنَ عَلَيْكُمْ وَٱذْكُرُوا۟ ٱسْمَ ٱللَّهِ عَلَيْهِ وَٱتَّقُوا۟ ٱللَّهَ إِنَّ ٱللَّهَ سَرِيعُ ٱلْحِسَابِ ٤

Today, all the good things of life have been made lawful to you. The food of those who were given revelations is lawful to you, and your food is lawful to them. And the virtuous women from among the believers and the virtuous women from among those who were given revelations before you (are also lawful to you) when you give them their dowers, taking them in honest wedlock, not in fornication, nor as mistresses. Anyone who rejects the faith (will find that) all his works will be in vain. In the life to come he shall be among the losers. (5)

ٱلْيَوْمَ أُحِلَّ لَكُمُ ٱلطَّيِّبَٰتُ وَطَعَامُ ٱلَّذِينَ أُوتُوا۟ ٱلْكِتَٰبَ حِلٌّ لَّكُمْ وَطَعَامُكُمْ حِلٌّ لَّهُمْ وَٱلْمُحْصَنَٰتُ مِنَ ٱلْمُؤْمِنَٰتِ وَٱلْمُحْصَنَٰتُ مِنَ ٱلَّذِينَ أُوتُوا۟ ٱلْكِتَٰبَ مِن قَبْلِكُمْ إِذَآ ءَاتَيْتُمُوهُنَّ أُجُورَهُنَّ مُحْصِنِينَ غَيْرَ مُسَٰفِحِينَ وَلَا مُتَّخِذِىٓ أَخْدَانٍ وَمَن يَكْفُرْ بِٱلْإِيمَٰنِ فَقَدْ حَبِطَ عَمَلُهُۥ وَهُوَ فِى ٱلْءَاخِرَةِ مِنَ ٱلْخَٰسِرِينَ ٥

Believers, when you are about to pray, wash your faces, and your hands and arms up to the elbows, and pass your wet hands lightly over your heads, and wash your feet up to the ankles. If you are in a state of ceremonial impurity,

يَٰٓأَيُّهَا ٱلَّذِينَ ءَامَنُوٓا۟ إِذَا قُمْتُمْ إِلَى ٱلصَّلَوٰةِ فَٱغْسِلُوا۟ وُجُوهَكُمْ وَأَيْدِيَكُمْ إِلَى ٱلْمَرَافِقِ وَٱمْسَحُوا۟ بِرُءُوسِكُمْ وَأَرْجُلَكُمْ إِلَى ٱلْكَعْبَيْنِ

purify yourselves. But if you are ill, or on a journey, or if one of you has come from the toilet, or if you have been in intimate contact with women and can find no water, then have recourse to pure dust, passing therewith lightly over your faces and your hands. God does not want to impose any hardship on you, but He wants to purify you, and to bestow on you the full measure of His blessings, so that you may be grateful. (6)

وَإِن كُنتُمْ جُنُبًا فَٱطَّهَّرُواْ وَإِن كُنتُم مَّرْضَىٰ أَوْ عَلَىٰ سَفَرٍ أَوْ جَآءَ أَحَدٌ مِّنكُم مِّنَ ٱلْغَآئِطِ أَوْ لَٰمَسْتُمُ ٱلنِّسَآءَ فَلَمْ تَجِدُواْ مَآءً فَتَيَمَّمُواْ صَعِيدًا طَيِّبًا فَٱمْسَحُواْ بِوُجُوهِكُمْ وَأَيْدِيكُم مِّنْهُ مَا يُرِيدُ ٱللَّهُ لِيَجْعَلَ عَلَيْكُم مِّنْ حَرَجٍ وَلَٰكِن يُرِيدُ لِيُطَهِّرَكُمْ وَلِيُتِمَّ نِعْمَتَهُۥ عَلَيْكُمْ لَعَلَّكُمْ تَشْكُرُونَ ٦

Remember always the blessings God has bestowed on you and the covenant with which He has bound you when you said: "We have heard and we obey." Hence, remain God-fearing. Surely God has full knowledge of the secrets of people's hearts. (7)

وَٱذْكُرُواْ نِعْمَةَ ٱللَّهِ عَلَيْكُمْ وَمِيثَٰقَهُ ٱلَّذِى وَاثَقَكُم بِهِۦ إِذْ قُلْتُمْ سَمِعْنَا وَأَطَعْنَا وَٱتَّقُواْ ٱللَّهَ إِنَّ ٱللَّهَ عَلِيمٌ بِذَاتِ ٱلصُّدُورِ ٧

Believers, be steadfast in your devotion to God, bearing witness to the truth in all equity. Never allow your hatred of any people to lead you away from justice. Be just, this is closer to righteousness. And remain God-fearing. Surely, God is aware of all that you do. (8)

يَٰٓأَيُّهَا ٱلَّذِينَ ءَامَنُواْ كُونُواْ قَوَّٰمِينَ لِلَّهِ شُهَدَآءَ بِٱلْقِسْطِ وَلَا يَجْرِمَنَّكُمْ شَنَـَٔانُ قَوْمٍ عَلَىٰٓ أَلَّا تَعْدِلُواْ ٱعْدِلُواْ هُوَ أَقْرَبُ لِلتَّقْوَىٰ وَٱتَّقُواْ ٱللَّهَ إِنَّ ٱللَّهَ خَبِيرٌۢ بِمَا تَعْمَلُونَ ٨

God has promised those who believe and do good works that they shall have forgiveness of sins and a rich reward. (9)

وَعَدَ ٱللَّهُ ٱلَّذِينَ ءَامَنُوا۟ وَعَمِلُوا۟ ٱلصَّٰلِحَٰتِ لَهُم مَّغْفِرَةٌ وَأَجْرٌ عَظِيمٌ ٩

As for those who disbelieve and deny Our revelations – they are the ones destined for Hell. (10)

وَٱلَّذِينَ كَفَرُوا۟ وَكَذَّبُوا۟ بِـَٔايَٰتِنَآ أُو۟لَٰٓئِكَ أَصْحَٰبُ ٱلْجَحِيمِ ١٠

Believers, remember the blessings God has bestowed on you, when certain people designed to stretch against you their hands, but He stayed their hands from you. Remain, then, God-fearing. In God let the believers place their trust. (11)

يَٰٓأَيُّهَا ٱلَّذِينَ ءَامَنُوا۟ ٱذْكُرُوا۟ نِعْمَتَ ٱللَّهِ عَلَيْكُمْ إِذْ هَمَّ قَوْمٌ أَن يَبْسُطُوٓا۟ إِلَيْكُمْ أَيْدِيَهُمْ فَكَفَّ أَيْدِيَهُمْ عَنكُمْ وَٱتَّقُوا۟ ٱللَّهَ وَعَلَى ٱللَّهِ فَلْيَتَوَكَّلِ ٱلْمُؤْمِنُونَ ١١

Overview

There must be controls and constraints in life. These may apply to man's inner life, to what he does in his own affairs, and to his life with other human beings, whether related to him or not, members of his extended family, clan or tribe, community or nation, friends or enemies. These controls and constraints may also govern man's relations with other creatures, whether God has made these subservient to man or not, and to inanimate objects which man finds in the world at large. Furthermore, there must be controls and constraints to govern man's life and his relationship with his Lord, which is the essence of all life.

Islam sets up these controls in human life, defines them with clarity and accuracy, and imparts to them an authority derived from God, ensuring that they remain well respected, observed and obeyed. They are not subject to changing tendencies or temporary interests which may be given prominence by an individual, a group, a nation or a generation. Indeed, these controls and restraints, set up and defined by God, themselves represent the overall "interest", since they have God's authority. Man's interest lies clearly in observing them even though an individual, a community, a nation or a whole generation may feel otherwise, for it is God who knows best, while human beings have, at best, a defective knowledge. What God decides is better than what they may decide for themselves. Indeed, if people were to maintain the lowest degree of politeness in their relationship with God, they would question their own definition of their interest if it were seen to be in conflict with God's definition. True politeness requires that man should have no definition of his interest other than that given by God, which he should accept and obey willingly, always assured and content that it will work for his benefit.

These controls and constraints are what is termed by God here as "contracts". He commands those who believe in Him to remain true to these contracts.

This *sūrah* opens with a clear order to fulfil these contracts before it proceeds to explain what is lawful and what is unlawful of slaughtered animals, types of food and drink, and also of family relations. It also explains a large number of legal provisions and rules of worship, as well as the true nature of faith, submission to God and the nature of Godhead. The *sūrah* also clarifies the type of relations which exist between the nation of Islam and other nations and beliefs. It explains the obligations of the community of believers in remaining true to their faith, bearing witness in all fairness, maintaining a position of leadership among mankind by virtue of their revealed Book. Theirs is the Book that supersedes all earlier revelations, establishing the rule of God as He has revealed it. They must always be on their guard lest they overlook some of what God may have revealed. They must also ensure that their personal feelings of love or hostility are not allowed to influence the way they administer full justice.

That the *sūrah* follows this pattern after giving a clear opening gives the term "contracts" a much wider sense than what immediately springs to mind. It is evident that "contracts" in this particular context means all the controls God has set up for human life, the most important of which is the contract of believing in God, acknowledging His overall Lordship and submitting to His will. This is the basic contract from which all the other contracts and controls in life are derived.

This contract of believing in God, with all that it entails of total submission and absolute obedience to Him, is the contract God made with Adam (peace be upon him) when He placed him in charge of the earth according to an agreement stating, as we are told in the Qur'ān: *"We said: You shall all descend from it [Paradise]. Guidance shall reach you from Me. Those who follow My guidance shall have nothing to fear, nor shall they grieve. But those who deny and gainsay Our revelations shall have the fire, wherein they shall abide."* (2: 38–9) It is, then, an authority given to man on the condition that he follows God's guidance as revealed in His Books which He has vouchsafed to His messengers. Otherwise, the very contract which places man in charge of the earth is violated.

Such a violation essentially makes every action that contravenes God's orders invalid and irremediable. Everyone who believes in God and wants to fulfil his contract with Him is obliged to repel this evil and refuse to deal with it in principle. Otherwise, he is not true to his contract.

The same contract or covenant was made again with all mankind when they were still within the loins of their parents. This is again stated in the Qur'ān: *"Your Lord has brought forth their offspring from the loins of the children of Adam and called on them to bear witness about themselves, 'Am I not your Lord?' – to which they answered: 'Yes, we do bear witness to this.' (Of this We remind you) lest you say on the Day of Resurrection, 'We were indeed unaware of this'; or lest you say, 'Indeed, it was but our forefathers who, in times gone by, began to associate partners with God; and we were but their late offspring: will You, then, destroy us for the doings of falsehood inventors?'"* (7: 172–3)

This is another contract made with every individual. God states that He has made this contract with every one of the children of Adam when they were within the loins of their parents. It is not for us to ask how this happened. God knows His creation best and He knows how to address them in every stage of their lives in a way that makes His address understood and their pledge binding. When He says that He has made a contract with them that they will always acknowledge His Lordship, then it must be so. If they do not fulfil this contract, they stand accused of being untrue to their obligations.

God also made a covenant with the Children of Israel, as is mentioned later in this *sūrah*, when He raised the mountain high above their heads as if to give them cover. They thought that it would fall on their heads. We will also learn from this *sūrah* how they were in breach of their covenant and how they were made to suffer the consequences, just as all those who break their covenants with God eventually suffer.

Those who believed in the Prophet Muḥammad (peace be upon him) also made a covenant with God, pledging themselves to: "obey the Prophet fully in times of ease and times of hardship, and in preference to our own comfort and interest. We also pledge not to dispute with rulers their authority". Some of them later made certain special contracts supplementing this general one. The second agreement of 'Aqabah which facilitated the way for the Prophet to migrate to Madinah was a contract made between the Prophet and the spokesmen of the Anṣār. In al-Ḥudaibiyah, the pact made under the tree came into force, and was later known as the "pact that pleased God".

It is on the basis of the contract to believe in God and to submit to Him that all contracts and covenants are made, whether they relate to all commandments and orders included in the Divine law, or to transactions with other people, or to relations with other creatures and inanimate objects in the universe. These are all contracts believers are required to fulfil. Their essential condition of believing in God makes these contracts binding on them and makes their fulfilment a basic duty. Hence the opening address: *"Believers, be true to your contracts."* (Verse 1)

Implementing Divine Decrees

Once the address is made to all believers to honour their contracts, some of these are stated in detail: *"Lawful to you is the [flesh of the] beasts of cattle, other than that which is announced to you herein. But you are not allowed to hunt while you are in the state of consecration. God decrees what He will. (Verse 1) Believers, do not offend against the symbols set up by God, or against the sacred month, or the offerings or the garlands, or against those who repair to the Sacred House, seeking God's grace and pleasure. Only when you are clear of the Sacred Precincts and released from the state of consecration may you hunt. Do not let your hatred of people who would debar you from the Sacred Mosque lead you into aggression; but rather help one another in furthering righteousness and piety, and do not help one another in furthering evil and aggression. Have fear of God, for God is severe in retribution. (Verse 2) Forbidden to you are carrion, blood, the flesh of swine; and that over which any name other than God's has been invoked; and the animal that has been strangled, or beaten to death, or killed by a fall, or gored to death, or savaged by a beast of prey, except that which you may have slaughtered when it is still alive; and [forbidden to you are] animals that have been slaughtered on idolatrous altars. And [forbidden also] is the division [of meat] by raffling with arrows; for all this is sinful. Today, the unbelievers have lost all hope of your religion. Have no fear of them, then, but fear Me alone. This day I have perfected your religion for you and have bestowed on you the full measure of My blessings and have chosen Islam as a religion for you. He who is forced by hunger [to eat of what is forbidden], with no inclination to commit sin, [will find] God Much-Forgiving, Merciful."* (Verse 3)

Whatever is stated here, either prohibiting or making lawful certain slaughtered animals, or certain species, or restricting places and times, is part of the "contract" believers must fulfil. It is part of the contract of faith that those who are party to it, i.e. the believers, must receive their instructions regarding what is lawful and what is unlawful only from God. In this respect, they recognise no authority other than His. Hence, they are addressed as believers at the outset of this detailed explanation of what they may and may not have.

"Lawful to you is the [flesh of the] beasts of cattle, other than that which is announced to you herein." Only because of this permission by God, not through any other authority, is it lawful and permissible for you to eat the flesh of whatever is included under the term "beasts of cattle", whether slaughtered or hunted, with the exception of the prohibitions that follow. Such prohibitions can either be temporary, restricted to certain places, or are total and applicable at all times and places. The beasts of cattle include camels, cows and sheep. Added to these are undomesticated animals like zebra, deer, bull and buffalo.

Thereafter, all other exceptions are detailed. The first pertains to hunting when believers are in the state of consecration: *"But you are not allowed to hunt while you are in the state of consecration. God decrees what He will."* (Verse 1) The prohibition here applies to the whole process of hunting. When one enters into the state of consecration as one starts pilgrimage or *'umrah*, one turns to God with one's whole being, turning one's back to familiar life practices which are a source of entertainment and pleasure. One turns one's face, and one's whole being, to the Sacred House which God has endowed with a feeling of security that applies to all those in it. Hence, it is necessary that when we are there, we do not stretch our hands to kill any living thing. Thus, one experiences during this time a necessary feeling of the bonds between all living things created by God, the giver of life. All creatures are, thus, safe from human aggression. The necessities of life, for which game and hunting have been allowed for food purposes, are thus reduced in order to impart to man a sense of elevation above what is familiar and lawful to him in ordinary days.

Before proceeding to add more details of what is excepted from the initial ruling of general permission, this contract is linked to the overall contract of faith. The believers are also reminded of the source of that covenant: "*God decrees what He will.*" (Verse 1) His will is absolute and He gives His commandments as He wishes. No one may have a say in what He decrees and no one can abrogate or overrule His judgement. What He outlines in this *sūrah* is His verdict on what is lawful and what is forbidden to us.

The address is again made to the believers to emphasise that they are not allowed to violate what God has restricted: "*Believers, do not offend against the symbols set up by God, or against the sacred month, or the offerings or the garlands, or against those who repair to the Sacred House, seeking God's grace and pleasure. Only when you are clear of the Sacred Precincts and released from the state of consecration may you hunt.*" (Verse 2) The first thing that springs to mind regarding the meaning of "*the symbols set up by God*" is that it is a reference to the rites of pilgrimage and *'umrah* and the restrictions that apply to everyone who enters into the state of consecration when he starts his pilgrimage or *'umrah* and which remain in force until the main part of the pilgrimage is over and when animals intended for sacrifice are slaughtered. During the state of consecration, a pilgrim does not offend against these restrictions, because such an offence represents a desecration of the sanctity imparted to them by God. The *sūrah* describes these rites as being set up by God in order to emphasise their sanctity and to warn against their desecration.

Other Restrictions

The term "*the sacred month*" as it occurs in this Qur'ānic verse refers to the four months of sanctity in the lunar calendar which are: Rajab, Dhu'l-Qa'dah, Dhu'l-Ḥijjah and al-Muḥarram. God has forbidden fighting in these four months, which used to be given special sanctity by Arabian tribes prior to Islam. However, they manipulated them as they wished, delaying certain months according to a ruling given by certain monks or a decree issued by the chiefs of powerful tribes. When Islam was revealed, their sanctity was endorsed by God's legislation. This sanctity is based on a Divine order made when God created the heavens and the earth, as mentioned in *Sūrah* 9, Repentance: *"The number of months, in God's sight, is twelve months [laid down] in God's decree on the day when He created the heavens and the earth. Of these four are sacred."* (9: 36) The Qur'ān also states that delaying the sacred months and manipulating them is an indication of compounded disbelief. Thus, the correct order has been re-established according to God's decree. These months remain sacred unless aggression is waged during them against the Muslims, when they are permitted to repel such aggression, without giving the aggressor a chance to escape, making use of the sanctity of these months which they do not recognise. The Islamic view of fighting in these months is mentioned in *Sūrah* 2, The Cow. (*In the Shade of the Qur'ān*, Vol. I, pp. 257–60)

The offerings mentioned in the *sūrah* refer to sacrificial animals which pilgrims slaughter during pilgrimage as part of its rites. This may be a camel, a cow or a sheep. To offend against these is to slaughter them for any reason other than the one for which they have been consecrated. Nor may they be slaughtered until the day of sacrifice during pilgrimage or after the end of *'umrah*. The major part of any sacrificial animal is distributed to the poor of the Ḥaram area. Those who offer such a sacrifice are encouraged to partake of it.

The term "the garlands" mentioned in the *sūrah* refers to cattle which are adorned with garlands to denote that they have been pledged for sacrifice. They are then left alone to graze as they wish until the day when the pledge falls due for their sacrifice. Included among these are cattle intended for sacrifice during pilgrimage and which are given a special sign to indicate the purpose for which they have been pledged. Once such cattle are adorned with garlands, they are no longer available for ordinary slaughter. They are slaughtered only for the purpose for which they have been pledged. It is also said that the garlands refer to a special type of band or necklace worn by those who want to be safe from an enemy or a person who wants to kill them for revenge or for any other purpose. They take some leaves or branches from the trees of the Ḥaram area to make bands and wear them. They then move freely, fearing no aggression from anyone. Scholars who advance this view say that the immunity given to such people was later abrogated when the verse was revealed which states: *"The idolaters are impure; let them not come near the Sacred Mosque after this year."* (9: 28) And by the verse which states: *"Take them and kill them wherever you find them."* (4: 91) The first view which says that the garlands denote the cattle intended for sacrifice is the weightier one, especially since they are mentioned after the offerings normally sacrificed during pilgrimage.

Similarly, God has given special sanctity to those who flock to the Sacred House, seeking a share of God's bounty and grace and aiming to please Him. They come to the House to do some legitimate business and to seek God's pleasure, whether at the time of pilgrimage or at other times. When they come to God's Sacred House, they are given security.

Having explained all these restrictions, this verse makes it clear that once the period of consecration is over, hunting becomes lawful again, provided that it takes place outside the Ḥaram area: *"Only when you are clear of the Sacred Precincts and released from the state of consecration may you hunt."* (Verse 2) This is an area of security which God establishes in His Sacred Mosque, as He has indeed established a time of security during the Sacred Months. People, animals, birds and trees in this area are immune from human aggression. This makes it an area of absolute peace, in response to the prayer of Abraham, the noble father of this nation. This period of peace is extended to the whole planet for four complete months every year, under the guardianship of Islam. People who enjoy the sweetness of this real sense of security will be keen to maintain it according to its provisions and to fulfil their covenants with God. They will try to extend it so that it encompasses human life throughout the year and the whole world over.

Justice for Friend and Foe

With the emphasis placed here on sanctity and security, God calls on those who believe in Him to fulfil their contracts with Him and to rise to the level which enables them to assume the leadership of mankind that has been assigned to them. To fulfil this role they must not allow themselves to be influenced by personal feelings, emotions or temporary circumstances. God calls on them not to transgress even against those who debarred them from entering the Sacred Mosque when they sought to visit it in the year known as "the year of al-Ḥudaibiyah" and earlier. The actions of those people left deep scars in the Muslims' hearts, which were bound to arouse emotions of hatred. But all this notwithstanding, the actions of the Muslim community must not be guided by such feelings. Its duty fits its great role: *"Do not let your hatred of people who would debar you from the Sacred Mosque lead you into aggression; but rather help one another in furthering righteousness and piety, and do not help one another in furthering evil and aggression. Have fear of God, for God is severe in retribution."* (Verse 2)

This is the ultimate standard of self-control and compassion. But it is this very ultimate standard that must be attained by the community entrusted by its Lord with the task of being the guide and guardian of humanity. Here it is called upon to attain a sublime horizon. This is part of the responsibility of leadership. It means that believers must overlook what happens to them personally and what they may have to endure of harm caused by others, in order to give to mankind a great model of righteous behaviour that can be achieved only by following Islam. In this way, they give a positive testimony for Islam which is certain to make it appealing to the rest of mankind.

The task outlined here is a great one, but as it is put in this *sūrah* it does not represent a great burden that will weigh heavily on man. There is a recognition that a human being may be angry and may harbour feelings of hatred. But human beings are not entitled, as a result of fury or hatred, to transgress and be unjust to others. Moreover, cooperation within the ranks of the community of believers must further righteousness and piety, not evil or aggression. The believers are commanded to have fear of God and are reminded that His punishment may be very severe. Such a reminder, together with the commandment to fear God, helps the Muslim community to control its hatred and to rise above the desire to exact revenge, because it is a community always seeking God's pleasure. How Islam works on people is best illustrated by the spectacular results it achieved in moulding the Arabs such that this noble behaviour became characteristic of them and, hence, they abided by its requirements. Prior to Islam they were far removed from such lofty standards. Their unchallenged motto was: "Support your brother, whether he is the victim or the perpetrator of injustice." Tribal loyalty was of paramount importance. To cooperate in furthering evil and aggression was more natural to them than cooperation in furthering piety and righteousness. They forged alliances, but their purpose was more to support evil than to support right. Rare were the pacts made in pre-Islamic days which supported what was and is right. This was only natural in an environment where traditions, customs and morals were not derived from God's constitution. Perhaps the best expression of this principle was the motto we have just quoted. A pre-Islamic poet has also put it in a nutshell when he says: "I am only a man of the tribe of Ghuzayyah: I go with my tribe, whether it follows the right way or the wrong one."

Then the Islamic constitution was revealed to establish new values and to remould people's way of thinking. Islam tells the believers: *"Do not let your hatred of people who would debar you from the Sacred Mosque lead you into aggression; but rather help one another in furthering righteousness and piety, and do not help one another in furthering evil and aggression. Have fear of God, for God is severe in retribution."* (Verse 2) Thus, a new bond linking hearts to God was established. Values and morals were given a new Divine standard. The Arabs, and mankind as a whole, were led out of blind fanaticism and the control of personal and tribal feelings in determining who is a friend and who is a foe. Man was reborn in the Arabian Peninsula. The new man derives his moral standards from God. This heralded the rebirth of man throughout the world. Prior to this, there was nothing in Arabia but blind loyalties which say: "Support your brother, whether he is the victim or the perpetrator of injustice." The same blind loyalties were known throughout the world.

It is a great divide that separates a community governed by such blind loyalty and fanaticism and a community governed by a constitution stating: *"Do not let your hatred of people who would debar you from the Sacred Mosque lead you into aggression; but rather help one another in furthering righteousness and piety, and do not help one another in furthering evil and aggression. Have fear of God, for God is severe in retribution."* (Verse 2) That great divide was removed by the only force that could remove it, namely, Islam.

Prohibited Meat

The *sūrah* now begins to give the details of the exceptions made in the first verse of cattle that are lawful to eat: *"Forbidden to you are carrion, blood, the flesh of swine; and that over which any name other than God's has been invoked; and the animal that has been strangled, or beaten to death, or killed by a fall, or gored to death, or savaged by a beast of prey, except that which you may have slaughtered when it is still alive; and [forbidden to you are] animals that have been slaughtered on idolatrous altars. And [forbidden also] is the division [of meat] by raffling with arrows; for all this is sinful. Today, the unbelievers have lost all hope of your religion. Have no fear of them, then, but fear Me alone. This day I have perfected your religion for you and have bestowed on you the full measure of My blessings and have chosen Islam as a religion for you. He who is forced by hunger [to eat of what is forbidden], with no inclination to commit sin, [will find] God Much-Forgiving, Merciful."* (Verse 3)

The first three types: carrion, blood and the flesh of swine are mentioned as forbidden in verse 173 of *Sūrah* 2, The Cow. We commented on this prohibition in our discussion of this verse: Vol. I, pp. 167–9. Whether human knowledge will eventually be able to determine the reasons for this prohibition or not, Divine knowledge has made it clear that these types of food are unwholesome. This is all that we need to know, because God only forbids what is evil and what harms human life in one way or another, whether such harm is known to man or not. Human knowledge remains limited. It does not know everything that causes harm and all that is useful.

Animals on which a name other than that of God has been invoked are forbidden to eat because such a practice is essentially contrary to faith, which is based on the fact that Godhead belongs to God alone. The first thing that follows from this acknowledgement is that the purpose behind every intention and action must be the pursuit of God's pleasure and that every step is made in His name, which is invoked before every action. Therefore, when the name of anyone other than God is invoked at the slaughtering of an animal, and indeed when no name is mentioned at such slaughter, the flesh of that animal is forbidden to eat because such an action is basically contrary to faith. It is in this moral respect that it is unwholesome and, therefore, added to what is physically unwholesome such as carrion, blood and pork.

Animals strangled in one way or another, or beaten or gored to death, or killed by a fall, or savaged by a beast of prey, are all types of carrion. Unless these are caught when still alive and slaughtered in the proper Islamic manner, they are forbidden meat. These details are given here in order to remove any suspicion that these may have a separate ruling. Scholars have spoken in detail on these and given different rulings with regard to "slaughter", and when an animal is deemed to have been slaughtered. Some scholars consider that if an animal has suffered an injury inevitably leading to its death, it cannot be made lawful even when it is slaughtered before it dies. Other scholars consider that such a slaughter, when the animal is still alive, is appropriate, regardless of the type of injury. These details may be referred to in books of Islamic jurisprudence, or *Fiqh*.

Before Islam, there were idols in the Ka'bah where the unbelievers used to slaughter their animals. They also used to throw some of the blood of their slaughtered animals on these idols. Animals slaughtered on such idolatrous altars, wherever they may be, are forbidden because of the place of their slaughter, even though the name of God may have been mentioned at the time of slaughter. The action itself is idolatrous.

Of the types of meat that are made forbidden in this verse there remains the one concerned with the divining of arrows. These arrows were used in pre-Islamic Arabia in order to decide whether to undertake a certain action or not. Different reports suggest that either three or seven arrows were used, with each indicating a different action. The same arrows were also used in gambling, and to divide the meat of the camel offered for gambling. Every one of the gamblers had an arrow. The arrows were mixed and one is drawn. The person whose name was given to that arrow would take the amount of meat apportioned to it. God has forbidden resorting to arrows for dividing anything and using these arrows for any division because it is just a type of gambling, and all gambling is strictly forbidden. He has also prohibited eating the meat divided in this manner.

"He who is forced by hunger [to eat of what is forbidden], with no inclination to commit sin, [will find] God Much-Forgiving, Merciful." A person who is so hungry that he fears for his life may eat of any of these forbidden types, as long as he does not intend to do what is forbidden and commit a sin. Scholars have given different rulings on how much one is allowed to eat: is it only what is sufficient for someone to stay alive, or is one allowed to eat one's fill? Alternatively, can people in this predicament save something for other meals if they fear that they may not find food that is permissible? We need not go into these details here. It is sufficient for our purpose to understand that this religion of ours always allows for what is easy, and always gives situations of necessity the sort of rulings ensuring that no affliction is caused to its followers. In the end, matters are left to clear intention and to being conscious of what God requires of us. A person who is driven by an extreme situation to eat of these forbidden types, having no intention to commit a sin, will suffer no punishment. Instead, they will find that God is certainly Much-Forgiving, Merciful.

Perfection at its Best

So far we have discussed the details of forbidden food as detailed in this verse. The verse, however, also includes other statements that require proper discussion.

Today, the unbelievers have lost all hope of your religion. Have no fear of them, then, but fear Me alone. This day I have perfected your religion for you and have bestowed on you the full measure of My blessings and have chosen Islam as a religion for you. (Verse 3)

This statement, which comes in the middle of a detailed account of which meat is forbidden to eat, was the last statement of the Qur'ān to be revealed. It declares the completion of the message of Islam and that its blessings have been brought to their full. 'Umar, the Prophet's Companion endowed with a keen insight, felt that the Prophet's remaining days on earth were numbered. He had discharged all his duties and conveyed his message. He was certain to be called to his appointment with God. 'Umar's eyes were tearful as he felt the approach of that departure.

These great words come within a verse which has as its subject matter the prohibition of certain types of animal food, and within a *sūrah* which has the detailed purposes we have already mentioned. What we understand from this is that Divine law is a single and complete whole that cannot be split into separate parts. Its provisions may tackle the concept of faith, or acts of worship, or permissions and prohibitions, or social regulations and international relations, but they are all of equal value. In their totality they constitute the religion God describes in this verse as having been perfected by Him. Moreover, it is the blessing of which He has bestowed a full measure on the believers. They represent the code of living God has chosen to be implemented by His servants. To reject any part of this code is to reject it all, and to reject the Divine faith altogether.

We have previously stated that to reject any part of this code, which God has been pleased to vouchsafe to the community of believers, and to substitute for it something made by man has only one clear meaning, namely, that Godhead is denied to God and its attributes are given to human beings. This is a rebellion against God's authority on earth and a claim of Godhead, since its main quality, i.e. the authority to legislate, is given to someone other than God. This means a rejection of Islam altogether.

"Today, the unbelievers have lost all hope of your religion." (Verse 3) They have reached a point of despair and realised that they cannot distort or detract from this religion or invalidate it when God has made it perfect and guaranteed to preserve it. They may defeat the Muslims in battle or

gain mastery over them for a period of time, but they can never vanquish this religion. It is the only religion that has been preserved against all factors of corruption and distortion. Its enemies have tried very hard to distort and to scheme against it, and its people were at times totally ignorant of its truth. But God never allows the earth to be without a group of true believers who recognise the truth of this faith and who dedicate themselves to its advocacy. Islam remains with them fully understood and preserved until they hand it over to the next generation of true believers. God's promise that the unbelievers' despair of vanquishing this religion will always come true.

The believers are then addressed, *"Have no fear of them, then, but fear Me alone."* (Verse 3) The unbelievers can never detract from the essence of this religion. Nor can they gain the upper hand against its advocates, unless these deviate from it and no longer give, through their action and behaviour, a practical translation of its method of living. In other words, they abandon the duties it assigns to them and neglect to fulfil its provisions in their way of life.

This Divine directive given to the Muslim community in Madinah does not apply only to their generation. It is addressed to the believers at all times and in all places. It is a directive to the believers who willingly accept the religion God has chosen for them, in its totality, and implement it as a constitution covering all aspects of life. It is these who are the true believers.

"This day I have perfected your religion for you and have bestowed on you the full measure of My blessings and have chosen Islam as a religion for you." (Verse 3) The day on which God revealed this verse during the Prophet's pilgrimage of farewell was the day when this religion attained its perfection and no room was left for any further improvement. The greatest Divine blessings were bestowed on the believers in full measure by giving them this all-embracing and comprehensive code. Islam as a faith and religion was chosen for them by God. Therefore, anyone who finds it unacceptable as a way of life actually rejects what God has determined to be the proper faith.

Grace Abounding

This is a highly inspiring statement. We may contemplate it for a long while without exhausting the essential facts and profound directives it contains or the duties and obligations it assigns.

The first thought that flashes in our minds dwells on the perfection of this religion. What does a believer see when he looks at the procession of faith that started ever since the early days of human life, led by God's messengers, the first of whom was Adam (peace be upon him), down to Muḥammad, the last of all Prophets conveying God's final message to mankind? He sees a noble procession enlightened by Divine guidance and bringing light to mankind. He also sees clear landmarks defining the way. But he realises that every one of God's Messengers was sent to his own community and every message was meant for a certain period of time, with the exception of the last Messenger and the last message. Each message was addressed to a particular community living in a particular environment. Hence, each was adapted to certain conditions. It is true that all of them called for submission to God alone, because that is the essence of the Divine faith. They all required that Divine instructions be faithfully followed, in an attitude of complete obedience to God alone, because this is the essence of Islam in its broader meaning of surrender to God. But each one of them had its own code suitable to the prevailing conditions of its community at the particular time in which it was revealed.

When it was God's will to conclude His messages to human beings, He sent the last Prophet with a message to mankind, not to a particular community or a particular period. This message addresses the very nature of man which remains the same in all periods and across all communities: *"This is the natural disposition which God has instilled into man. No change shall be made in God's creation. This is the ever true faith."* (30: 30) This message contains a law addressing all aspects of human life and lays down basic principles and guidelines for those aspects which change according to the time and the environment, as well as detailed regulations for those that remain constant throughout all periods and communities. With such general principles and detailed regulations, this law regulates human life from the time of the revelation of this message to the end of human life. All directives, laws and controls required to help human life to develop and prosper are given within this framework.

When all this has been established, God tells the believers: *"This day I have perfected your religion for you and have bestowed on you the full measure of My blessings and have chosen Islam as a religion for you."* (Verse 3) Thus, the faith and the law have been brought to perfection, since the combination of both constitutes religion. No believer may then imagine that religion, in this sense, requires any addition or complement to improve on it, or needs some modification or adaptation to suit local conditions. No one who entertains such thoughts is a true believer; for a believer accepts what God says and is satisfied with His choice. The law of the particular time in which the Qur'ān was revealed applies to all time because, according to God's own statement, it is the law of the religion revealed to mankind to be implemented by all communities for the rest of time. The detailed regulations and laws will remain the same, while the basic principles constitute the framework within which human life develops and progresses. When the framework is broken, man abandons faith altogether.

This religion, including this particular legal code, has been chosen for man by God, man's Creator who knows His creation well. Anyone who says that yesterday's law cannot be implemented today claims to know man's needs better than God. Secondly, a believer is bound to reflect on the fact that God has bestowed the full measure of His blessings on believers when He perfected their religion for them. This blessing represents not only a rebirth of man, but also the fulfilment and purpose of his existence. Man led a life of insignificance prior to knowing his Lord and Creator, the universe and his position and role in it. All these are defined for him by Islam, the religion his Lord has chosen for him. Before man's liberation from submission to other creatures to attain the state of submission to God alone, and before the attainment of true equality in human life through a law devised by God and supported by His authority, man could only lead a life next to non-existence.

Indeed, his new knowledge of these great facts as established by this religion of Islam was the herald of man's new birth. Without this knowledge man could be no more than an animal or, at best, a prospective human being still in the process of formation and moulding. Only through acquiring this knowledge does man attain his most perfect position which is far removed from all man-made concepts that might have prevailed during different periods of human history.

Blessings in Full Measure

Islam gives man a concept of faith which requires him to believe in God, His angels, revelations, messengers and the Day of Judgement. As he formulates this concept, he leaves the realm of animals which comprehend nothing beyond the extent of their senses to an area which extends well beyond the realm of human perception. Thus, man can comprehend the physical and the metaphysical, the perceptible and the imperceptible. As man acknowledges God's oneness, he is liberated from submission to any authority other than that of God. He feels that he cannot be enslaved by any power other than that of God. He is equal to, if not nobler than, any other creature. It is to God alone that man addresses his worship, from God alone he receives his laws, systems and constitution, on God alone he relies, and Him alone he fears. Through the Divine way of life, laid down by Islam, all human power is dedicated to achieve goodness and to improve life. Thus, he is elevated above the standard of animals, or the fulfilment of desires.

Only a person who has known the true nature of the life of darkness, or *jāhiliyyah*, (which is the Islamic term for any system not based on Divine revelations) and its oppressive concepts and chaos can appreciate the fact that only through the implementation of Islam does man enjoy the full measure of God's blessings. A person who has experienced a life of error, loss and chaos following hollow concepts can fully appreciate the blessing of faith. When one reflects on the suffering that results from tyranny, confusion and total lack of balance in all sorts of systems human beings devise for themselves, one can state with absolute conviction that life with faith and with the implementation of the Islamic system is the greatest blessing we may enjoy in this world.

The Arabs who were first addressed by the Qur'ān were quick to appreciate its significance, because it told them of their own experience. In matters of faith, they were at the lowest depth of ignorance, believing in idols and considering angels, *jinn*, stars and forefathers as deities equal to the Supreme Lord. With Islam, they came to know what it meant to believe in the One God who has power over all things, who sees all and knows all, and who is at the same time fair, compassionate and merciful. He is close to everyone and answers everyone. There is no intermediary between Him and any one of His servants. In this way all of us have been liberated from all forms of tyranny, whether that of chiefs, priests or superstition.

The Arab social make-up established a distinction between different classes and allowed everyone with power to tyrannise others. Indeed, to all Arabian chiefs, regardless of their relevant positions in the strict tribal hierarchy, oppression was synonymous with dignity and high position. An Arabian poet described the weakness of someone he was castigating in these terms: "His tribe are never unfaithful to their trust and never try to take the smallest of articles unfairly". 'Amr ibn Hind was an Arab chief when he imposed his rule that he would only talk to people from behind a screen. He further considered it impudent for tribal chiefs to refuse that their mothers serve in his palace. Al-Nu'mān ibn al-Mundhir, another Arabian king, was so dictatorial in his rule that he chose a day for pleasure when he gave his bounty to all and sundry, and chose a day for displeasure when he killed everyone he met that day from morning till evening. Examples of such class tyranny in Arabia abound.

In the days prior to Islam, infant girls were buried alive in Arabia; women suffered much injustice; drinking, gambling and indecent sexual practices were common. Abuse of women, revenge killings, assault, stealing, and looting were characteristics of Arabian life; but these went hand in hand with disunity and weakness before any external enemy. Arabian tribes were quick to fight one another, but when the Abyssinians launched an attack with the aim of destroying the Ka'bah, all tribes took a defeatist attitude.

It is from such depths of iniquity that Islam rescued the Arabs, moulding them into a nation, one capable of assuming the leadership of all mankind. It was the same generation of Arabs which lived in the depths of ignorance and darkness, before it experienced life at the top as envisaged by Islam. Hence, they were quick to fully appreciate the significance of the Qur'ānic statement: *"This day I have perfected your religion for you and have bestowed on you the full measure of My blessings and have chosen Islam as a religion for you."* (Verse 3)

The Choice Religion

Finally, a believer is bound to reflect on the fact that it was God who chose Islam as a faith for him. This then is a manifestation of God's care and love for this nation. It is He Himself who has laid down its code of living for it.

These words place a heavy burden on the shoulders of this nation whereby it must prove itself equal to this great Divine care. No! I pray God for forgiveness. Nothing that this nation in all its generations can give will match the care God has taken of it. People can only do their utmost in acknowledging God's grace and praising Him for it. In this way, they show that they are aware of their duty and try to fulfil it as best they can, seeking God's forgiveness at the same time for any slips or failures.

The fact that God Himself has chosen this religion for the Muslim nation requires Muslims to appreciate the value of this choice and to exert every effort to implement God's choice in their lives. How foolish and miserable it would be of anyone to ignore, or indeed reject, what God has chosen for him and to try to establish for himself a way of life different from that laid down by God. Such an attitude is nothing short of a ghastly and punishable crime. Its perpetrator cannot escape scot-free when he rejects God's choice. God may leave those who have never known Islam to do what they like for a period of time. As for those who have known Islam and rejected or abandoned it, choosing for themselves other methods of life, these will deservedly suffer the results of their choice.

Nothing Wholesome is Forbidden

They ask you what is lawful to them. Say: Lawful to you are all good things of life. As for those hunting animals which you train by imparting to them something of the knowledge God has imparted to you, you may eat of what they catch for you. But mention God's name over it and have fear of God; indeed, God is swift in reckoning. (Verse 4) Today, all the good things of life have been made lawful to you. The food of those who were given revelations is lawful to you, and your food is lawful to them. And the virtuous women from among the believers and the virtuous women from among those who were given revelations before you (are also lawful to you) when you give them their dowers, taking them in honest wedlock, not in fornication, nor as mistresses. Anyone who rejects the faith (will find that) all his works will be in vain. In the life to come he shall be among the losers. (Verse 5)

This question from the believers about what is lawful describes the frame of mind the chosen community adopted by virtue of the honour of being addressed by God Himself. It gives us an impression of the sort of reluctance they had in approaching anything that was practised in pre-Islamic days lest it be unacceptable to Islam. They felt that they needed to ask about everything to make sure that it fitted with their new way of life.

When we look into the history of that period we cannot fail to recognise the profound change Islam brought about in the Arabian mentality. Islam shook the Arabs into eradicating all traces of ignorance that might have been left behind. It gave the Muslims, whom it had picked up from the depths of darkness to elevate into light and a high level of humanity, a feeling that they were reborn and that they were living a completely new life. It imparted to them a profound sense of the great divide between their present and their past. They recognised the great bounty God had bestowed on them and, therefore, they were keen to adapt their lives to the new Divine method, the benefits of which they were able to discern in their own lives. They were conscious of God's grace and keen not to violate His orders. The net result of all this was their constant reluctance to continue with their old practices, unless they made sure that they were acceptable to Islam.

It is in this context that we should read their question to the Prophet (peace be upon him) about lawful food, after they had heard the verses which outlined what was forbidden to them: *"They ask you what is lawful to them."* The answer was especially significant: *"Say: Lawful to you are all good things of life."* This imparts to them the true feeling that they have not been forbidden anything good or wholesome. Indeed, all the good things of life have been made lawful to them. Only bad or evil things are forbidden. Needless to say, everything that God forbids mankind is either something physically repugnant to uncorrupted human nature, such as carrion, blood and the flesh of swine, or something a believer's heart finds nauseating, such as the flesh of animals on which the name of someone other than God has been invoked, or what has been slaughtered over idolatrous altars, or something that has been divided with the help of arrows, which is a type of gambling.

To the good things mentioned here in general, a special type is also added to emphasise that which is good. These are animals caught by beasts and birds of prey which have been trained for that very purpose, such as a hawk or a falcon, and hunting dogs and lions which have been trained to overpower game animals: *"As for those hunting animals which you train by imparting to them something of the knowledge God has imparted to you, you may eat of what they catch for you. But mention God's name over it and have fear of God; indeed, God is swift in reckoning."* (Verse 4)

The condition which makes what is caught by such trained hunting animals lawful to eat is that they should leave their prey for their master. That is, the hunting beast or bird must not eat of the animal it has killed, except when the master has gone away. If they eat of their prey at the time of the catch, they have not been properly trained. They are simply killing other animals for themselves not for their masters. As such, the master may not eat of the game they kill, even if most of it is left, and even if they bring the prey back alive to him. Once they have eaten of it, it cannot be made lawful, not even by proper methods of slaughter.

God reminds the believers of this aspect of His grace, which is manifested in their ability to train their beasts and birds of prey. It is He who has made these hunting animals subservient to them and given them the knowledge to train them. This is a fine touch, typical of the Qur'ānic method of cultivating believers' minds. The Qur'ān makes use of every occasion and opportunity to impress on people's hearts the fundamental truth that everything we have has been given to us by God. God has created us, given us all the knowledge we have and made everything on earth subservient to us. It is He whom we should thank for whatever we achieve, every gain we make and ability we develop. Thus, in every moment of his life, a believer is fully aware that everything within himself and around him is God's gift to him. He does not allow himself to overlook, even for the briefest moment, the fact that he is indebted to God for everything he may enjoy, all that he possesses, every action he makes. This is what makes him a properly devout person.

God teaches the believers to mention His name over all game animals caught for them by their beasts and birds of prey. This should be done when the hunting animal or bird is set free. Since it may kill its prey with its claws or teeth, this killing is considered as the slaughter of the animal. As God's name is mentioned at the time of slaughter, it is also mentioned when the beast or bird of prey is set on its hunting spree.

The believers are finally reminded to continue to fear God and that His reckoning is very swift. Hence, they should always be on their guard. The question of permissibility or prohibition is thus closely related to the more important feeling of being conscious of God and of fearing Him. It is the pivot round which every intention and every action in the life of a believer turns. Thus, it transforms human life into a relationship with God, a recognition of His greatness and a consciousness of His presence and power in all situations, whether we are alone or with others: *"and have fear of God; indeed, God is swift in reckoning."* (Verse 4)

Good Relations with Other Religions

The *sūrah* goes on to outline more types of food made permissible for believers, and adds to that what is permissible in marriage. *"Today, all the good things of life have been made lawful to you. The food of those who were given revelations is lawful to you, and your food is lawful to them. And the virtuous women from among the believers and the virtuous women from among those who were given revelations before you (are also lawful to you) when you give them their dowers, taking them in honest wedlock, not in fornication, nor as mistresses."* (Verse 5)

Again the variety of permissible pleasures are initially described as good: *"Today all the good things of life have been made lawful to you."* This emphasises the meaning we have already stressed, explaining that only evil things have been forbidden to Muslims. Within the framework of making good things lawful, we witness a genuine manifestation of Islamic tolerance when it comes to dealing with non-Muslim communities living side by side with Muslims in the land of Islam, or perhaps having a relationship based on a peace treaty or one of simple loyalty.

Islam does not merely extend religious freedom to these communities allowing them to live a life of isolation from the rest of society. It creates a social set-up based on partnership and mutual friendship. Their food is lawful to Muslims and the food of Muslims is also lawful to them, so that visits and hospitality can be exchanged. The whole society will thus enjoy an air of tolerance and friendship. Moreover, chaste, virtuous women from among these communities who had previously received revelations from God are lawful for Muslims to marry. Indeed, these women are mentioned side by side with chaste, virtuous Muslim women. Only the followers of Islam show such a degree of tolerance and friendliness towards other communities. A Christian Catholic may feel very reluctant at marrying a Christian Orthodox or Protestant woman, despite the fact that all these belong to Christianity. Only those who are not strictly religious may enter such a marriage.

This is clear evidence that Islam provides the only system which allows for the establishment of a world community where Muslims do not live in isolation from the followers of other revealed religions and where barriers are not erected between the followers of different religions which exist side by side in Muslim lands. This also applies to social relations. As for loyalty and patronage, these are covered by different rules which will be outlined later in this *sūrah*.

The same conditions apply to lawful marriages with either virtuous Muslim women or virtuous women of the followers of other Divine religions: *"When you give them their dowers, taking them in honest wedlock, not in fornication, nor as mistresses."* (Verse 5) This means that a dower must be paid for a serious, lawful marriage by which a man provides his wife with a home, security and protection. The money paid must never be used for an illegitimate relationship that makes a woman available to any man as a prostitute or only to one man as a mistress. Both types were known in pre-Islamic Arabia and recognised by Arabian society prior to its purification by Islam.

These rulings are followed by a comment which carries an added emphasis together with a strong warning against their violation: *"Anyone who rejects the faith [will find that] all his works will be in vain. In the life to come he shall be among the losers."* (Verse 5) All these regulations are related to faith. To implement them as they are is faith, or at least is evidence of faith. A person who abandons them rejects the faith altogether. Hence, all his actions will be to no avail. Indeed, whatever good he may do will be rejected by God. This state of affairs, i.e. the rejection of the actions of one who denies the faith, is described in the Qur'ān in terms of what may happen to an animal which grazes in a poisonous area. Its belly is greatly swollen and it dies. This is a perfect description of what is rejected of man's actions. It swells, but it comes to nothing. In the life to come, such a person suffers a loss that comes on top of his vain actions.

It is to be noted that this stern warning comes by way of comment on rulings outlining what is permissible and what is forbidden in matters of food and marriage. This is indicative of the fact that all details of this religion of Islam are closely interwoven in one whole. Nothing that is in conflict with its principles and regulations, whether relevant to fundamentals or matters of detail, is at all acceptable.

Getting Ready for Prayer

This discourse about good food and good, virtuous women is followed by a reference to prayer and regulations governing purification in preparation for prayer. *"Believers, when you are about to pray, wash your faces, and your hands and arms up to the elbows, and pass your wet hands lightly over your heads, and wash your feet up to the ankles. If you are in a state of ceremonial impurity, purify yourselves. But if you are ill, or on a journey, or if one of you has come from the toilet, or if you have been in intimate contact with women and can find no water, then have recourse to pure dust, passing therewith lightly over your faces and your hands. God does not want to impose any hardship on you, but He wants to purify you,*

37

and to bestow on you the full measure of His blessings, so that you may be grateful." (Verse 6)

It is not by mere coincidence that regulations on purification are mentioned together with regulations on hunting, consecration and dealing with those who turned the Muslims away from the Sacred Mosque. Nor is it unrelated to the general context of this *sūrah*. Indeed, it comes at the right place to serve a definite purpose. Firstly, this is a reference to another aspect of the good things of life: a pure enjoyment of the spirit which is mentioned together with good food and virtuous women. In prayer, a believer finds enjoyment that surpasses that of all material luxuries. It is the enjoyment of a meeting with God in an atmosphere of purity and total devotion. When the pleasures of food and marriage have been outlined, reference is made to a higher level of enjoyment, namely, purification and prayer. Together, both types of enjoyment are necessary for man.

Secondly, the regulations governing purification and prayer are the same as other regulations outlined in the *sūrah*, whether relating to food and marriage, permissible and forbidden hunting, or to human relations in times of peace and war: all these regulations are devotional. In their totality, they constitute the religion acceptable to God. In Islam, there is no difference between what is termed as "rulings on worship" and "rulings governing human transactions". This division has been established by scholars to serve the requirements of classification. It is not essential to the Divine way of life or to Islamic law. The Divine way of life comprises both aspects which together form the religion and the law God has laid down for people to follow. Neither category has any precedence over the other. Indeed, neither can be properly fulfilled without the other. Islam cannot be properly implemented in the life of the Muslim community unless both sets of rulings are strictly followed.

All these regulations are "contracts" which the believers are ordered by God to fulfil. All of them are devotional in the sense that a Muslim fulfils them in order to earn God's pleasure. They are all manifestations of a Muslim's submission to God. We cannot separate worship from transactions except in scholarly classification. Both types indicate aspects of worship, duties and contracts made with God. To violate any of them is to violate the basic contract of believing in God. It is to this fundamental fact that the Qur'ānic ordering of the regulations outlined in this *sūrah* refers.

Too Valuable an Obligation

"Believers, when you are about to pray…" Prayer is a meeting with God. Anyone who is about to offer a prayer stands up in front of God Himself, makes his supplication to Him, and addresses Him in a highly intimate manner. Therefore, it is important to prepare for it properly. In this respect, it is necessary to undergo a physical purification to help with the spiritual preparation. Perhaps this is the reason, as we understand it – though God alone knows the truth – for the requirement of ablution, the essential parts of which are detailed in this Qur'ānic verse: to wash one's face, hands and arms to the elbows, to wipe one's head lightly with one's wet hand and to wash one's feet up to the ankles. These requirements are the subject of very minor differences among scholars, perhaps the most important of which is whether they should be done in the order they are mentioned in this verse or done without following any particular order. This type of ablution is required for a minor invalidation of purity, such as going to the toilet or releasing wind. A shower or a bath in which one washes all one's body is required to remove a state of ceremonial impurity which happens as a result of ejaculation whether through a wet dream or when awake, sexual intercourse and also women's menstruation.

Having outlined the requirements of ablution in both ordinary and total situations, the Qur'ānic verse speaks of dry ablution which may replace either type. This is a concession of which Muslims may avail themselves in the following situations: when water is not available; when a person is ill and needs to have an ordinary ablution, i.e. *wuḍū'*, or when he is required to have a grand ablution, i.e. *ghusl*, but where water may be harmful to him; and when a person is travelling and needs to perform either type of ablution.

The *sūrah* refers to the reasons requiring ordinary ablution by the phrase: *"or if one of you has come from the toilet"*, which indicates answering a call of nature in any way. As for what requires total ablution, washing one's whole body, the *sūrah* uses a gentle expression indicating sexual contact: *"Or if you have been in intimate contact with women."* In any of these situations, a person who cannot find or use water may not offer his prayer until he has performed dry ablution. He should select a clean surface, on the earth itself or anything associated with it, even if it is the saddle of his horse or mule, or a wall. He must make sure that the surface is free from impurity. He strikes it with both hands, shakes it and wipes it over his face, and then wipes it over his hands up to the elbows. Some scholars say that one strike is sufficient to wipe over the face and both hands, while others say two strikes are required, one to wipe the face and the other to wipe the hands. There are other differences among scholars about what is meant by *"or if you have been in intimate contact with women"*. Is it any touch or contact? Or is it sexual intercourse? Or is it any touch associated with sexual thoughts? Similarly, scholars speak about whether any illness allows dry ablution, or whether it is only an illness that makes the use of water harmful. Moreover, it is perhaps more correct to say that if water is too cold or if the person fears that using the water may cause him harm, then dry ablution is permissible.

The verse concludes with this comment: *"God does not want to impose any hardship on you, but He wants to purify you, and to bestow on you the full measure of His blessings, so that you may be grateful."* (Verse 6)

As we have already said, purification is an essential requirement before a meeting with God. In both ordinary and total ablution, i.e. washing certain parts of one's body or the whole of one's body, the requirement of purification is met physically and spiritually. In dry ablution, only the spiritual part is fulfilled. It is considered sufficient when water is not available or can be harmful. God does not want to afflict people or to overburden them or cause them any difficulty in meeting their religious duties. He simply wants them to be blessed with the grace of purification and to make them feel His grace so that they show their gratitude to Him. When they do, He increases and even multiplies His grace. This clearly illustrates how the easy Islamic code of living combines a gentle and practical approach with Divine blessings.

This Qur'ānic verse states clearly the Divine purpose behind the requirements of ablution, ordinary and total: *"He (God) wants to purify you, and to bestow on you the full measure of His blessings, so that you may be grateful."* When we reflect on this statement, we are bound to see the thread of unity and complementarity Islam establishes between worship and other legislation. Washing some parts of our bodies as we do in ablution, *wuḍū'*, or having a full bath, *ghusl*, as we do in total ablution, are not merely meant for physical cleanliness. Otherwise, some pedantic people these days might claim that we have no need for the rituals of the primitive Arabs, since our standards of civilization mean that we take a bath regularly and keep our bodies clean. The fact is that this is a double-fronted exercise to unite the cleanliness of the body with the purification of the soul in the same act of worship a believer addresses to his Lord. The spiritual side is certainly stronger because when it is not possible or inadvisable to use water, dry ablution, which fulfils only this stronger aspect, is deemed sufficient. Moreover, this religion of Islam is a complete way of life which addresses all situations in all societies and stages with a unified and consistent system. In this way, its purpose is realised in all situations in one way or another. Let us then make sure that we fully understand the purpose of Islam before passing a judgement that may not be based on sound knowledge or Divine guidance. We must also maintain an attitude of propriety when we speak about God and His legislation.

Talking about dry ablution as a substitute for ablution with water leads us to consider the fact that Islam is especially keen that obligatory prayer be regularly attended to, in other words without fail. This provision added to similar ones relating to offering prayer in times of fear, or in the case of illness, when it can be offered in seated or reclining positions, shows that every impediment preventing anyone from offering prayers is removed. Islam takes extra care that prayer is offered at its defined times. Indeed, Islam relies heavily on this particular aspect of worship to achieve its educational and reform purposes, so as to mould human nature in a satisfactory shape. As prayer is a meeting with God, a believer feels that when he stands in front of God, this contact is so profoundly important to him that he would not wish to lose it even in the most critical of situations. No difficulty should prevent a Muslim from this meeting with his Lord. He derives from it reassurance, happiness and a contented heart. To him, this is a treasure too valuable to lose.

Justice Even When Dealing with Enemies

So far, the *surah* has outlined a number of instructions concerning the types of food believers are permitted to eat, purification and other matters. By way of commenting on these instructions, the *surah* reminds the believers of the blessings God has bestowed on them when they have accepted the faith and the covenant He has made with them that they will listen and obey. It is indeed this covenant that admits them into the fold of Islam. The next verses remind them to have fear of God and that He is aware of all thoughts people may entertain.

Remember always the blessings God has bestowed on you and the covenant with which He has bound you when you said: "We have heard and we obey." Hence, remain God-fearing. Surely God has full knowledge of the secrets of people's hearts. (Verse 7) Believers, be

41

steadfast in your devotion to God, bearing witness to the truth in all equity. Never allow your hatred of any people to lead you away from justice. Be just, this is closer to righteousness. And remain God-fearing. Surely, God is aware of all that you do. (Verse 8)

The first generation to be addressed by the Qur'ān were fully aware of the extent of God's blessings bestowed on them by His revealing this religion. They felt the change within themselves, in their lives, community, and in the position they occupied among mankind. A simple reference to this blessing was always sufficient to turn their attentions to a great, undeniable fact of life. Similarly, a reference to the covenant with which God bound them to listen and to obey aroused in them feelings of dignity, since they were the other party in a contract made with God, the Almighty. To a believer who contemplates such a relationship, this is something great indeed. Hence, it is sufficient to remind them of their duty to remain God-fearing. They were ever conscious of God: *"Hence, remain God-fearing. Surely God has full knowledge of the secrets of people's hearts."* (Verse 7)

The Qur'ān often uses the highly expressive and evocative statement that God has full knowledge of people's innermost thoughts, or the secrets of their hearts. In Arabic, this expression combines accuracy with inspiring beauty. It speaks of something that is always present in the heart. This is a reference to secret feelings and thoughts. Deep as a person may bury these secrets, they are known fully to God.

A Gulf Too Wide

Part of the covenant with which God has bound the Muslim community requires it to deal with other people on the basis of absolute justice, which is never affected by feelings of love or hatred, or by feelings, interests, or relations of any kind. It is justice based on the duty of remaining steadfast in devotion to God alone. No influences are ever allowed to tilt the balance of justice, especially when believers are mindful that God watches over them and knows what lies at the bottom of their hearts. They fully understand this address: *"Believers, be steadfast in your devotion to God, bearing witness to the truth in all equity. Never allow your hatred of any people to lead you away from justice. Be just, this is closer to righteousness. And remain God-fearing. Surely, God is aware of all that you do."* (Verse 8)

Earlier in this *sūrah*, God forbade the believers to allow their hatred of those who prevented them from entering the Sacred Mosque in Makkah to turn into an act of aggression against them. This is indeed a tough standard of self-restraint and tolerance to which they were elevated by the Divine system. Now they are ordered that hatred must never lead them away from justice. This is an even higher standard which is much more difficult to attain. The first was a stage requiring them not to launch aggression. Here, they are required to maintain justice despite their feelings of hatred and hostility. The first stage stopped at a passive attitude requiring self-restraint. The second is a proactive attitude ensuring justice to people who are hostile to the believers and detested by them.

This Divine system, which brings out the best in man, realises that this is a very difficult objective. Hence, it gives a helping introduction: *"Believers, be steadfast in your devotion to God..."* The instructions are also concluded with a comment that helps in achieving the objective: *"Remain God-fearing. Surely, God is fully aware of all that you do."*

No human being can attain this standard unless he deals in such a matter directly with God. This is the result that comes about when people are steadfast in their devotion to God, addressing their feelings purely to Him, fearing none but Him, and realising that He knows their innermost thoughts. No earthly consideration can lift human beings to such a high standard and keep them there. It is a standard achievable only through absolute dedication to God. Similarly, no faith or system on earth guarantees absolute justice to detested enemies in the same way as this religion does. This is because Islam addresses those who believe in it, making it clear to them that even when they have to administer justice to their enemies, they are dealing with God and they must rid themselves of any other consideration. With these basic elements in it, Islam has maintained its role as the last universal religion for humanity. Its system guarantees to all mankind, whether they believe in it or not, that they will have justice. For absolute justice is a duty incumbent on all Muslims and they fulfil this duty to God, no matter what hatred is shown to them by other people.

Difficult and hard as this duty is, it is binding on the Muslim community because of its leading role amongst mankind. The role of leadership was fulfilled by this community and all its conditions were met when the believers in this faith implemented it. To them, these instructions were not mere recommendations or ideals, but a reality they should practise in their daily lives. The history of mankind has never before, nor indeed ever since, witnessed any such standard being put into practice, becoming a reality, except during the shining periods in history when Islam was implemented as a way of life. History gives us numerous cases and examples which testify that these duties and commandments outlined by God were transformed into a practical system, fully implemented in the daily life of the Muslim community. They were not mere ideals to which homage was paid. Nor were they individual examples. They left their mark on life practices to the extent that people felt that that was the only way to live.

When we look from that high summit on human life in all periods of darkness, everywhere on earth, including the type of darkness we see in modern times, we realise how great is the gulf between a system devised by God to be implemented in human life and man-made systems. The gap between the effects on people's lives of these man-made systems on the one hand and the Divine system on the other is too wide to bridge.

People may advocate certain principles, but such advocacy is one thing and practising these principles in reality is another. Indeed, it is often the case that people do not put into effect the principles they call on others to adopt. It is not merely that people should be told to implement certain principles, but more importantly where this call comes from and what kind of authority it has over consciences and feelings. Another hugely instrumental factor is people's knowledge of the ultimate arbiter on the net result of the efforts they put into practising these principles. The true value of the call made by religion on people to implement its principles comes from the sway religion exercises over people. But when a call is only made by a certain person, we have to ask what support such a call has, and what authority it has over people's minds, and what reward it can promise those who work hard to implement these principles? Thousands of people may call for justice, purity, liberation, self-denial, tolerance, love, sacrifice and so on. Their call, however, motivates no one because it lacks the proper support. It is not the call itself that is most important, but rather the power behind the call.

People may listen to others advocating certain ideals, but what is the practical outcome of all this? The fact is that they know by nature that the advocacy comes from people like them, who share with them the same degree of ignorance and weakness and who have similar prejudices of their own. At the end of the day, such advocacy has only a minimum effect on their lives.

Religious directives, on the other hand, are complemented by practical steps which aim to shape life in a certain fashion. If religion were to be confined to directives and rituals, then the directives would remain unimplemented, as we see today everywhere. A complete way of life on the basis of religion is necessary to allow its directives to be put into practice in life situations where directives and practices complement one another. This is the Islamic view of religion which makes it a complete system regulating all aspects of life.

When this concept of religion was put into practice by the Muslim community, that community occupied the top position in human society. It will do the same today, reducing this latter day ignorance to the same lowly level as it did the Arabian ignorance of the past. Conversely, when religion was reduced to mere directives given on a pulpit, and rituals practised in mosques, and when it no longer regulated the system of life, it lost its very existence in human life.

A Promise That Never Fails

Moreover, there must be a reward given by God to the believers, who deal with Him alone. This reward is needed to give encouragement to people to fulfil their obligations and to discharge their trust. The end of those who disbelieve and deny God's revelations must be different from that of those who believe and do well: *"God has promised those who believe and do good works that they shall have forgiveness of sins and a rich reward. As for those who disbelieve and deny Our revelations – they are the ones destined for Hell."* (Verses 9–10)

This is a reward to compensate good believers for what they miss of the luxuries and riches of this life when they fulfil their trust. It is a reward that reduces to insignificance all the hardship faced by the believers as they face up to human obstinacy and determined denial of the truth. It is only fair that Divine justice will not deliver to the good and the bad the same treatment.

Believers need to look up to this Divine system of justice and reward, so that they are able to overcome all temptations and impediments when they deal with God. Certain people only need to feel that God is pleased with them to appreciate its value, as well as the value of discharging their trust. But the Divine system deals with all people and with human nature itself. God knows that by nature man needs this promise of forgiveness and rich reward and needs to know the end of the disbelievers and their punishment. This reassures the believers and enables them to face up to the schemes of the evil ones, especially since they are commanded to deal justly with those whom they hate because of all the hardship they may have suffered at their hands.

The *sūrah* continues to cultivate this spirit of justice and tolerance among the Muslim community, and to weaken feelings of hostility, prejudice and revenge. It reminds Muslims of God's grace which manifested itself in restraining the hands of the unbelievers when they intended to make a determined assault against the Muslims: *"Believers, remember the blessings God has bestowed on you, when certain people designed to stretch against you their hands, but He stayed their hands from you. Remain, then, God-fearing. In God let the believers place their trust."* (Verse 11)

Reports give different explanations as to whom this verse refers to. It is perhaps more correct to say that it refers to a group of unbelievers who tried to attack the Prophet and the Muslims during the days which led to the peace agreement at al-Ḥudaibiyah, but God foiled their design and enabled the Muslims to take them captive instead. The event itself is not as important as the lessons learnt from it. The Qur'ān draws on these lessons to reduce the Muslims' hatred of these people, so that they would feel reassured as they reflected on the fact that God Himself takes care of them and protects them. In such an atmosphere, self-restraint, tolerance and the administration of justice become so much easier. Muslims would be ashamed of themselves if they were not to fulfil their covenant with God, especially when it is He who protects them from their enemies.

Perhaps we should say here very briefly that the idea of God's protection of the believers from aggression by their enemies is expressed in an image of hands being stretched to launch an aggression and then being stayed by a higher power. This charges the expression to its highest, as if the image of the events is placed in front of those who listen to the Qur'ānic verse and as if they witness these events right here and now. The Qur'ān employs this most expressive way in order to get its message to people in the clearest possible way.

2

Broken Pledges

Indeed, God made a covenant with the Children of Israel and We appointed among them twelve captains. God said: I shall be with you. If you attend to your prayers, practise regular charity, believe in My messengers and support them and offer up to God a generous loan, I shall forgive you your sins and admit you into gardens through which running waters flow. But any of you who, after this, rejects the faith will indeed have strayed from the right path. (12)

﷽ وَلَقَدْ أَخَذَ ٱللَّهُ مِيثَٰقَ بَنِىٓ إِسْرَٰٓءِيلَ وَبَعَثْنَا مِنْهُمُ ٱثْنَىْ عَشَرَ نَقِيبًا ۖ وَقَالَ ٱللَّهُ إِنِّى مَعَكُمْ ۖ لَئِنْ أَقَمْتُمُ ٱلصَّلَوٰةَ وَءَاتَيْتُمُ ٱلزَّكَوٰةَ وَءَامَنتُم بِرُسُلِى وَعَزَّرْتُمُوهُمْ وَأَقْرَضْتُمُ ٱللَّهَ قَرْضًا حَسَنًا لَّأُكَفِّرَنَّ عَنكُمْ سَيِّـَٔاتِكُمْ وَلَأُدْخِلَنَّكُمْ جَنَّٰتٍ تَجْرِى مِن تَحْتِهَا ٱلْأَنْهَٰرُ ۚ فَمَن كَفَرَ بَعْدَ ذَٰلِكَ مِنكُمْ فَقَدْ ضَلَّ سَوَآءَ ٱلسَّبِيلِ ﴿١٢﴾

Then for having broken their covenant, We rejected them and caused their hearts to harden. They now distort the meaning of [revealed] words, taking them out of their context. Moreover,

فَبِمَا نَقْضِهِم مِّيثَٰقَهُمْ لَعَنَّٰهُمْ وَجَعَلْنَا قُلُوبَهُمْ قَٰسِيَةً ۖ يُحَرِّفُونَ ٱلْكَلِمَ عَن

they have forgotten much of what they have been told to bear in mind. From all but a few of them you will always experience treachery. But pardon them, and forbear. God loves those who do good. (13)

مَوَاضِعِهِۦ وَنَسُواْ حَظًّا مِّمَّا ذُكِّرُواْ بِهِۦ وَلَا تَزَالُ تَطَّلِعُ عَلَىٰ خَآئِنَةٍ مِّنْهُمْ إِلَّا قَلِيلًا مِّنْهُمْ فَٱعْفُ عَنْهُمْ وَٱصْفَحْ إِنَّ ٱللَّهَ يُحِبُّ ٱلْمُحْسِنِينَ ۝

Likewise, from those who said, "We are Christians," We have accepted a firm covenant, but they, too, have forgotten much of what they had been told to bear in mind. Therefore, We have given rise among them to enmity and hatred to last until the Day of Resurrection. God will make clear to them what they have done. (14)

وَمِنَ ٱلَّذِينَ قَالُوٓاْ إِنَّا نَصَٰرَىٰٓ أَخَذْنَا مِيثَٰقَهُمْ فَنَسُواْ حَظًّا مِّمَّا ذُكِّرُواْ بِهِۦ فَأَغْرَيْنَا بَيْنَهُمُ ٱلْعَدَاوَةَ وَٱلْبَغْضَآءَ إِلَىٰ يَوْمِ ٱلْقِيَٰمَةِ وَسَوْفَ يُنَبِّئُهُمُ ٱللَّهُ بِمَا كَانُواْ يَصْنَعُونَ ۝

People of earlier revelations, Our Messenger has come to you to make clear to you much of what you have been concealing of the Scriptures, and to forgive you much. There has come to you from God a light and a clear Book (15)

يَٰٓأَهْلَ ٱلْكِتَٰبِ قَدْ جَآءَكُمْ رَسُولُنَا يُبَيِّنُ لَكُمْ كَثِيرًا مِّمَّا كُنتُمْ تُخْفُونَ مِنَ ٱلْكِتَٰبِ وَيَعْفُواْ عَن كَثِيرٍ قَدْ جَآءَكُم مِّنَ ٱللَّهِ نُورٌ وَكِتَٰبٌ مُّبِينٌ ۝

Through which God guides those who seek His good pleasure to the paths of peace. By His grace, He leads them out of darkness into light and guides them to a straight way. (16)

يَهْدِي بِهِ ٱللَّهُ مَنِ ٱتَّبَعَ رِضْوَٰنَهُۥ سُبُلَ ٱلسَّلَٰمِ وَيُخْرِجُهُم مِّنَ ٱلظُّلُمَٰتِ إِلَى ٱلنُّورِ بِإِذْنِهِۦ وَيَهْدِيهِمْ إِلَىٰ صِرَٰطٍ مُّسْتَقِيمٍ ۝١٦

Unbelievers indeed are they who say: "God is the Christ, son of Mary." Say: Who could have prevailed with God in any way had it been His will to destroy the Christ, son of Mary, and his mother, and everyone on earth? To God belongs the kingdom of the heavens and the earth and all that is between them. He creates what He wills and God has power over all things. (17)

لَّقَدْ كَفَرَ ٱلَّذِينَ قَالُوٓا۟ إِنَّ ٱللَّهَ هُوَ ٱلْمَسِيحُ ٱبْنُ مَرْيَمَ قُلْ فَمَن يَمْلِكُ مِنَ ٱللَّهِ شَيْئًا إِنْ أَرَادَ أَن يُهْلِكَ ٱلْمَسِيحَ ٱبْنَ مَرْيَمَ وَأُمَّهُۥ وَمَن فِي ٱلْأَرْضِ جَمِيعًا وَلِلَّهِ مُلْكُ ٱلسَّمَٰوَٰتِ وَٱلْأَرْضِ وَمَا بَيْنَهُمَا يَخْلُقُ مَا يَشَآءُ وَٱللَّهُ عَلَىٰ كُلِّ شَىْءٍ قَدِيرٌ ۝١٧

Both the Jews and the Christians say: "We are God's children and His loved ones." Say: Why then does He punish you for your sins? You are only human beings of His creation. He forgives whom He will and punishes whom He will. To God belongs the kingdom of the heavens and the earth and all that is between them, and to Him all shall return. (18)

وَقَالَتِ ٱلْيَهُودُ وَٱلنَّصَٰرَىٰ نَحْنُ أَبْنَٰٓؤُا۟ ٱللَّهِ وَأَحِبَّٰٓؤُهُۥ قُلْ فَلِمَ يُعَذِّبُكُم بِذُنُوبِكُم بَلْ أَنتُم بَشَرٌ مِّمَّنْ خَلَقَ يَغْفِرُ لِمَن يَشَآءُ وَيُعَذِّبُ مَن يَشَآءُ وَلِلَّهِ مُلْكُ ٱلسَّمَٰوَٰتِ وَٱلْأَرْضِ وَمَا بَيْنَهُمَا وَإِلَيْهِ ٱلْمَصِيرُ ۝١٨

People of earlier revelations! Now after an interval during which no messengers have appeared, Our Messenger has come to you to make things plain to you, lest you say: "No one has come to give us good news or to warn us." Now there has come to you a bearer of good news and a warner. God has power over all things. (19)

يَـٰٓأَهۡلَ ٱلۡكِتَـٰبِ قَدۡ جَآءَكُمۡ رَسُولُنَا يُبَيِّنُ لَكُمۡ عَلَىٰ فَتۡرَةٍ مِّنَ ٱلرُّسُلِ أَن تَقُولُواْ مَا جَآءَنَا مِنۢ بَشِيرٍ وَلَا نَذِيرٖ فَقَدۡ جَآءَكُم بَشِيرٞ وَنَذِيرٞۗ وَٱللَّهُ عَلَىٰ كُلِّ شَيۡءٖ قَدِيرٞ ١٩

And so Moses said to his people: "My people, remember the favours which God has bestowed upon you when He raised up prophets among you, made you kings and granted you what He has not granted to any other community. (20)

وَإِذۡ قَالَ مُوسَىٰ لِقَوۡمِهِۦ يَـٰقَوۡمِ ٱذۡكُرُواْ نِعۡمَةَ ٱللَّهِ عَلَيۡكُمۡ إِذۡ جَعَلَ فِيكُمۡ أَنۢبِيَآءَ وَجَعَلَكُم مُّلُوكٗا وَءَاتَىٰكُم مَّا لَمۡ يُؤۡتِ أَحَدٗا مِّنَ ٱلۡعَٰلَمِينَ ٢٠

My people, enter the holy land which God has assigned to you. Do not turn your back, for then you will be lost." (21)

يَـٰقَوۡمِ ٱدۡخُلُواْ ٱلۡأَرۡضَ ٱلۡمُقَدَّسَةَ ٱلَّتِي كَتَبَ ٱللَّهُ لَكُمۡ وَلَا تَرۡتَدُّواْ عَلَىٰٓ أَدۡبَارِكُمۡ فَتَنقَلِبُواْ خَٰسِرِينَ ٢١

"Moses", they answered, "mighty people dwell in that land, and we will surely not enter it unless they depart from it. If they do depart, then we will enter". (22)

قَالُواْ يَـٰمُوسَىٰٓ إِنَّ فِيهَا قَوۡمٗا جَبَّارِينَ وَإِنَّا لَن نَّدۡخُلَهَا حَتَّىٰ يَخۡرُجُواْ مِنۡهَا فَإِن يَخۡرُجُواْ مِنۡهَا فَإِنَّا دَٰخِلُونَ ٢٢

Thereupon two men who were God-fearing and on whom God had bestowed His grace said: "Go in upon them through the gate. As soon as you enter it, you shall be victorious. In God you should place your trust, if you are true believers." (23)

قَالَ رَجُلَانِ مِنَ ٱلَّذِينَ يَخَافُونَ أَنْعَمَ ٱللَّهُ عَلَيْهِمَا ٱدْخُلُوا۟ عَلَيْهِمُ ٱلْبَابَ فَإِذَا دَخَلْتُمُوهُ فَإِنَّكُمْ غَٰلِبُونَ وَعَلَى ٱللَّهِ فَتَوَكَّلُوٓا۟ إِن كُنتُم مُّؤْمِنِينَ ۝

They said, "Moses, we will never go in so long as they are in it. Go forth, then, you and your Lord, and fight, both of you. We shall stay here." (24)

قَالُوا۟ يَٰمُوسَىٰٓ إِنَّا لَن نَّدْخُلَهَآ أَبَدًا مَّا دَامُوا۟ فِيهَا فَٱذْهَبْ أَنتَ وَرَبُّكَ فَقَٰتِلَآ إِنَّا هَٰهُنَا قَٰعِدُونَ ۝

"Lord", he said, "I am master of none but myself and my brother. Do, then, draw a dividing line between us and these wrong-doing folk." (25)

قَالَ رَبِّ إِنِّى لَآ أَمْلِكُ إِلَّا نَفْسِى وَأَخِى فَٱفْرُقْ بَيْنَنَا وَبَيْنَ ٱلْقَوْمِ ٱلْفَٰسِقِينَ ۝

He replied, "This land shall, then, be forbidden to them for forty years, during which they will wander aimlessly on earth. Do not grieve for these wrong-doing folk." (26)

قَالَ فَإِنَّهَا مُحَرَّمَةٌ عَلَيْهِمْ أَرْبَعِينَ سَنَةً يَتِيهُونَ فِى ٱلْأَرْضِ فَلَا تَأْسَ عَلَى ٱلْقَوْمِ ٱلْفَٰسِقِينَ ۝

Overview

In the first passage of this *sūrah*, God reminds the Muslims of their covenant with Him and directs them to always remember the blessings He has bestowed on them when He accepted their covenant and bound them to it. The reminder serves as further encouragement to them to fulfil their pledges and to beware of breaking God's covenant. This new passage outlines the attitudes different groups of those formerly given Divine revelations had taken towards their covenants with God. The passage explains what punishment befell earlier communities as a result of their violation of their covenants. This serves as a reminder to the Muslim community, pointing out that God's law never fails and admits no favouritism. It also reveals the true nature of the people of earlier revelations and their attitude towards Islam. It, thus, enables the Muslims to see through them and to counter their wicked designs against Islam which they treacherously work out under the guise of following the teachings of their religions. In truth, they had turned their backs on their faith and violated their pledges to God.

This passage firstly discusses the covenant God made with the followers of Moses, when He saved them from subjugation in Egypt and their subsequent violations of this covenant. As a result, they were cursed and rejected by God. They were also denied His blessings and guidance. It also refers to the covenant God made with those who claimed to be Christians. As a result of their following a course contrary to their covenant with God, the seeds of enmity were sewn among them. Hostility among their different sects will continue until the Day of Judgement. The passage also refers to the attitude of the Jews when they cowardly refused to enter the Holy Land, although God had promised them that they would have it for themselves. They said to Moses: *"Go forth, then you and your Lord, and fight, both of you. We shall stay here."* (Verse 24)

This exposition of these pledges and covenants, and the attitudes of those who were previously given revelations, also reveals the distortion that had crept into the Jewish and Christian faiths. Included in their covenants was a condition that they would continue to believe in God's oneness and fully submit to Him. By so doing, they would fulfil their part of the bargain and earn all the blessings God had bestowed on them and the guarantees of victory He had given them. They refused all this and, consequently, incurred the scourge of God's curse and ended up in disunity, suffering persecution by others.

This passage also calls on them anew to follow the Divine guidance embodied in the final message from God, conveyed by Muḥammad, His last Messenger. It refutes their argument that it had been a very long time since the last of their prophets had died and, hence, they had subsequently forgotten everything. A new Messenger who warns and gives happy news has now been sent to all mankind. Their argument is thus refuted by undeniable evidence.

Through this new call to them, the unity of the Divine faith becomes clearly apparent. God accepts the same covenant from all His servants, which binds them to believe in Him alone, and to believe in, and support, His messengers, making no distinction between them. It calls upon them to attend regularly to their prayers, to regularly pay charity and so financially support God's cause. These are the terms of the covenant with God laying down the essentials of the true faith, defining proper worship and outlining the main features of a social system that is suitable to man and acceptable to God.

The Terms of Covenants Made with God

Indeed, God made a covenant with the Children of Israel and We appointed among them twelve captains. God said: I shall be with you. If you attend to your prayers, practise regular charity, believe in My messengers and support them and offer up to God a generous loan, I shall forgive you your sins and admit you into gardens through which running waters flow. But any of you who, after this, rejects the faith will indeed have strayed from the right path. (Verse 12) Then for having broken their covenant, We rejected them and caused their hearts to harden. They now distort the meaning of [revealed] words, taking them out of their context. Moreover, they have forgotten much of what they have been told to bear in mind. From all but a few of them you will always experience treachery. But pardon them, and forbear. God loves those who do good. (Verse 13)

Likewise, from those who said, "We are Christians," We have accepted a firm covenant, but they, too, have forgotten much of what they had been told to bear in mind. Therefore, We have given rise among them to enmity and hatred to last until the Day of Resurrection. God will make clear to them what they have done. (Verse 14)

The covenant God had accepted from the Children of Israel stated a specific condition and stipulated certain penalties in case of default. After explaining the circumstances leading to the confirmation of this covenant, the *sūrah* mentions its terms, conditions and penalties. It was a covenant made with the twelve captains of the Israelites, representing all twelve tribes descending from Jacob, or Israel. Each tribe descended from one of Jacob's sons. The terms of the covenant are outlined as follows: *"God said: I shall be with you. If you attend to your prayers, practise regular charity, believe in My messengers and support them and offer up to God a generous loan, I shall forgive you your sins and admit you into gardens through which running waters flow. But any of you who, after this, rejects the faith will indeed have strayed from the right path."* (Verse 12)

When God says to any group of people, *"I shall be with you"*, He gives them a great promise. He who has God on his side suffers no opposition. Whoever and whatever stands against him is of no consequence. Moreover, whoever is with God will not go astray. To be with God is sufficient to ensure the right guidance and the proper support. Anyone who is sure to be on God's side will never suffer worry or misery. He is reassured and blessed with unfailing happiness. He need not ask for anything better than what he already has.

But God does not give this blessing of being with them as a special favour or a personal gift. This comes only after its conditions are fulfilled. It is, indeed, a contract that outlines conditions and specifies penalties. The first condition is to attend to prayer. This is more than merely offering prayers. It means that prayers should become a manifestation of a true relationship between man and his Lord. This makes prayer an educative element which purifies man's behaviour and dissuades him from committing any blatant sin or gross indecency.

Second is charitable payment, in recognition of God's favour for having given us what we have and by way of acknowledgement of the fact that whatever we may own actually belongs to God. The payment of *zakāt*, or charity, is a manifestation of our obedience to God with regard to how to dispense with the money He has given us and specified the conditions of our ownership of it. Moreover, a perfect system of social security can thus be implemented in a society established on faith. Thus, the social economy becomes free of the shackles which result from the concentration of national wealth in the hands of a small minority. This leads to a situation where the overwhelming majority of the population is unable to buy its needs while a small minority enjoys all the wealth. This leads to all sorts of social corruption which can he prevented by the *zakāt* system which ensures the proper distribution of wealth.

The next condition is to believe in God's Messengers making no distinction between them. Every single one of them was sent by God to preach the same message. Therefore, to deny any single one of them is to deny them all and to disbelieve in God, who had sent them all. Moreover, believing in them must not be a mere mental exercise. To truly believe in them is to be actively involved in supporting them in order to ensure that they succeed in their mission. Believing in the Divine faith requires that a believer is always ready to do what is necessary and within his power to support his faith and to see it well established in human life. The Divine faith is not confined merely to a set of beliefs or acts of worship. It is a practical system which organises human life in a certain fashion. Hence, it requires the support of all its followers to establish and protect it. Otherwise, a believer does not fulfil his covenant with God.

In addition to *zakāt*, giving generously to support God's cause is mentioned as a loan given to God. It should be pointed out here that it is God who owns what we have, but He gracefully describes what we pay to further His cause as a loan given to Him.

These were the conditions of the covenant God accepted from the Children of Israel. The reward for the fulfilment of these conditions was to forgive them their sins. Human beings will always err, no matter how keen they are to do what is right. Therefore, the forgiveness of sins is a great reward and a manifestation of God's endless grace. The reward also includes admission into Heaven which is described in the Qur'ān as *"gardens through which running waters flow."* (Verse 12) This is again a reward which God bestows on human beings out of His grace. No man can earn this reward through his own actions. God, however, has promised this reward to those who do their utmost to fulfil their pledges to Him.

The penalty for failing to honour one's pledges is specified at the end of this verse: *"But any of you who, after this, rejects the faith will indeed have strayed from the right path."* (Verse 12) Hence, he can have no guidance and no way of return. The pledge had already been made, the guidance already provided, the way shown and the penalty specified. Nothing can be of any benefit any more.

Such was the covenant God accepted from the captains of the Children of Israel on behalf of their communities. They all accepted it, which made it a covenant applicable to every single individual among them, and one with the whole nation they constituted. How, then, did the Israelites subsequently fare?

Hardened Hearts

They have indeed broken their covenant with God; they killed their prophets for no legitimate reason, and they plotted to kill and crucify Jesus (peace be upon him) the last of their Prophets. They also distorted their revealed Scriptures, i.e. the Torah, and abandoned its laws. They adopted a hostile attitude towards the last of all Prophets, Muḥammad (peace be upon him). They schemed against him and betrayed him and adopted an uncompromising attitude of hostility towards his message, not hesitating to violate the treaty they signed with him. As a result, God denied them His guidance and rejected them. Their hearts were caused to harden so that they could no longer be the recipients of Divine guidance: *"Then for having broken their covenant, We rejected them and caused their hearts to harden. They now distort the meaning of [revealed] words, taking them out of their context. Moreover, they have forgotten much of what they have been told to bear in mind."* (Verse 13)

Indeed, God tells the truth. These were the distinctive features of the Israelites; a curse clearly apparent in their faces and deeply entrenched in their evil character, a hardness that left no room for a compassionate smile, and actions that took no heed of human feelings. They may appear gentle when they have something to fear or an interest to further, or when they try to sow the seeds of discord among people, but their hardness will nevertheless surface revealing how, deep at heart, they are cruel, devoid of mercy. Such was their essential nature that they distorted revealed words, took it all out of context. They distorted their revealed Book and presented it in a light different from that given to Moses (peace be upon him). They did this in more ways than one. They added to their Book much of what served their devious goals and gave them religious justification for pursuing their wicked ends, which they falsely attributed to God. They also interpreted such original statements as remained in their Book according to their prejudices, this to fit them to their wicked designs. Furthermore, they deliberately abandoned or forgot the tenets of their faith and left them unimplemented in their society because such implementation would have required them to adhere to a clean and pure method, one acceptable to God.

"From all but a few of them you will always experience treachery." (Verse 13) This is an address to the Prophet (peace be upon him), describing the attitude of the Jews towards the Muslim community in Madinah. They never hesitated to try to betray God's Messenger (peace be upon him). Their treacherous attempts came fast and furious, one after the other. Indeed, that was their standard practice during the years when they were with the Prophet in Madinah, then in the whole of Arabia. It has continued to be their practice whenever they live within a Muslim community, despite the fact that the Muslim community has been the only one to provide them with safe refuge, allow them a life free of persecution and extend to them kindly treatment and a prosperous life. Nonetheless, they have continued to show the same attitude they adopted towards the Prophet; characteristics more suited to stealthy snakes and cunning foxes. If they are unable to level a direct blow to destroy the Muslims, they resort to tricks and wicked designs instead. They scheme with every enemy of the Muslims until they find a chance to hit them hard, without mercy or compassion, paying no heed to any covenant or treaty. This is true of the great majority of them, as God described them in His Book and as He has told us of their nature which they acquired as a consequence of their breaking their covenant with God early on in their history.

The Qur'ānic description of the situation of the Jews in Madinah and their attitude towards God's Messenger (peace be upon him) is very interesting: *"From all but a few of them you will always experience treachery."* (Verse 13) Treacherous actions, intentions, words and looks are all grouped together in an Arabic expression stating the adjective and deleting the noun it qualifies. For "treachery" in the English translation we read "treacherous" in the Arabic original, which is a mode of expression suggesting a situation so rampant that it is perpetrated by every single one of them. This is part of their nature. It is also the essence of their attitude towards the Prophet and the Muslim community.

The Qur'ān is the teacher and the guide of the Muslim nation, and it marks the road the Muslims are required to follow throughout history. The Qur'ān tells the Muslims about their enemies and their historical attitude towards God's guidance. Had this nation of believers referred to the Qur'ān and listened to its directives and implemented its instructions, their enemies would never have been able to win the upper hand in any fight against Islam. But when the Muslims broke their covenants with their Lord and abandoned the Qur'ān, they suffered the setbacks and calamities known to everyone. It is true that they continue to be enchanted with musical recitations of the Qur'ān and may use these as charms, but this is not the purpose for which the Qur'ān was revealed. Indeed, when the Qur'ān is not implemented in the lives of the Muslim community, it is effectively abandoned by it, regardless of how much lip service is paid to it.

God tells the Muslim community what happened to the Children of Israel and how they were cursed, rejected and suffered hardened hearts as a result of breaking their covenants with God. Thus, the Muslim community is warned against breaking its own covenant with Him lest it should suffer the same fate. It is because Muslims have disregarded this warning and followed a way different from that of Islam that God has taken away from them the role of humanity's leadership, leaving them at its tail end. They will continue to be in this losing position until they return to their Lord, adhere to their covenant, and fulfil their pledges. Then and only then will God fulfil His promise to them, give them power and return them to the leadership of humanity. God's promise never fails.

At the time when this Qur'ānic verse was revealed, God instructed His Messenger in these terms: *"But pardon them, and forbear. God loves those who do good."* (Verse 13) To pardon their evil act is to do good, and to forgive their treachery is to do good. But a time came when forgiveness and pardon could no longer be extended. God subsequently instructed the Prophet to evacuate them from Madinah and later from the Arabian Peninsula altogether. These instructions were carried out.

The Origins of Enmity Among the Christians

God also relates to His Messenger (peace be upon him) and to the Muslim community that He accepted a covenant from those who described themselves as Christians, but they, too, were unfaithful to their covenant and suffered the consequences: *"Likewise, from those who said, 'We are Christians', We have accepted a firm covenant, but they, too, have forgotten much of what they had been told to bear in mind. Therefore, We have given rise among them to enmity and hatred to last until the Day of Resurrection. God will make clear to them what they have done."* (Verse 14)

This verse begins with a particularly significant description: *"Likewise, from those who said: 'We are Christians', We have accepted a firm covenant."* This mode of expression tells us that they simply professed to be Christians without giving practical credence to their claims. The essence of their covenant was to believe in God's oneness. Yet it was in regard to this very issue that deviation crept into the history of Christianity. It is this central clause in their covenant which became the forgotten part of what they had enjoined. When it was forgotten, every deviation became possible and enmity broke out between the numberless sects and churches of Christianity, old and new, as we will shortly but briefly explain. God tells us that their enmity and hatred will continue until the Day of Resurrection. Moreover, they will suffer the punishment of the Hereafter, at the time when they will be shown a clear image of what they have done in this life.

Old and modern history has witnessed much conflict, hostility and enmity between those who claim to be Christians. All this gives factual endorsement to what God tells us in His truthful Book. Their wars against each other have caused much more bloodshed than the wars they fought against non-Christians throughout history. They have fought each other because of conflicts over principles of faith, disputes over religious supremacy and quarrels over political, economic and social issues. Many generations have passed but their hostility and their wars have not subsided. They will continue to flare up until the Day of Judgement as stated by the One who always says the truth. This is all a natural result of their violation of their pledges to God and their negligence of what He commanded them to do. As we have already said, the first item in their covenant is to believe in God's oneness and it is this first item that they abandoned shortly after Jesus Christ had been raised by God. Perhaps this is not the proper place to discuss the reasons for this deviation in detail.

Now that the attitude taken by the Jews and Christians towards their covenants with God has been made clear, the *sūrah* addresses both communities announcing the message of the last of all prophets and that it is addressed to them as well as to the Arabs and to all mankind. They are required to follow God's last Messenger, and this requirement is part of the firm covenant they made with God. They are told that this last Messenger has come to make public much of what they have concealed of God's revelations which were entrusted to their care, and concerning which they were unfaithful to their trust. They are also told that this last

Messenger will also forgive them much of what they have concealed, because it is no longer needed in the new message. It points out some of the deviant beliefs which the last Messenger would rectify, such as the claim by the Christians that Jesus Christ, son of Mary, was God Himself, and the assertion by both Christians and Jews that they were God's sons and beloved ones. This address is concluded with a clear statement that they would have no argument to press after the revelation of this final and clear message. Nor could they claim that a long time had lapsed after the revelation of their messages, and that this had caused them to forget and become confused.

> *People of earlier revelations, Our Messenger has come to you to make clear to you much of what you have been concealing of the Scriptures, and to forgive you much. There has come to you from God a light and a clear Book, through which God guides those who seek His good pleasure to the paths of peace. By His grace, He leads them out of darkness into light and guides them to a straight way.* (Verses 15–16)

A Messenger with an Unlikely Background

Those people who received revelations in the past found it rather hard to accept that a Prophet who did not belong to them should call on them to submit themselves to God. This Prophet belonged to a nation of illiterate people whom they used to despise, on account of their being unlettered while they themselves had Divine Scriptures. God wanted to bestow a great honour on those unlettered people and, therefore, He chose from among them the individual who was to become the last of all Prophets. He also gave them His final message, addressed to all mankind. He taught those unlettered people to become the ones with the highest standard of knowledge on earth. This transformation made them the ones with the highest beliefs, the most consistent and sound way of life, the most complete system and legal code, the soundest social set-up and the most sublime standard of morality. All this was part of the grace God bestowed on them when He chose Islam to be their faith. Those unlettered people could not have aspired to be the guides for humanity without this grace they received from God. Indeed, they never had and will never have anything to offer humanity except for what their faith gives them.

In this Divine address to the people of earlier Scriptures, it is made clear that they are called upon to accept Islam, believe in Muḥammad and support him, as this has been part of their covenant which God accepted from them. They are clearly told that God Himself is a witness that this Prophet who could not read and write was His Messenger to them as well as to the Arabs and to all mankind. There is no denying the fact that his message was given to him by God, and no claim can be admitted that his message was addressed to the Arabs only; it is, indeed, addressed also to the people of earlier revelations: *"People of earlier revelations, Our Messenger has come to you to make clear to you much of what you have been concealing of the Scriptures, and to forgive you much."* (Verse 15) He has sent a Messenger to you, and his role is to open things up to you so that you see them in their reality. You can thus see how he brings out into the open what you have conspired to suppress of the basic truth of the revelations given to you.

This applies to both the Christians and Jews. The Christians suppressed the very basic and fundamental principle of faith, namely, the concept of God's oneness, and the Jews suppressed many Divine legislations such as the punishment of adulterers with stoning and the total prohibition of usury. Both the Christians and the Jews also suppressed the news of the future mission of the unlettered Prophet, *"whom they find mentioned in the Torah and the Gospel in their hands."* (7: 157) He (peace be upon him) pardons them for much of what they had distorted or suppressed as it is not included in his revelations. God has abrogated many of the rulings of earlier Scriptures and Divine codes as these had fulfilled their purpose in the particular community to which the message had been revealed. They had no longer any role to play in human society. Now the final, comprehensive and everlasting message has been revealed and become well-established as a demonstration of the perfection of the grace God has bestowed on man, when He chose self-surrender, or Islam, as the basis of the faith acceptable to Him. No abrogation or modification can be introduced into this message.

The Nature of God's Final Message

The nature of what the last Messenger has been given, the role it is destined to play in human life and its practical effect are then explained: *"There has come to you from God a light and a clear Book."* (Verse 15) Perhaps nothing expresses the nature of the Qur'ān and the Divine message of Islam more accurately and comprehensively than stating that it is "a light". In his heart of hearts, in everything in his life, in his evaluation of things, events and people, a believer realises as soon as he accepts the truth of faith that he has a light that makes everything clear to him. Everything brightens up in front of him. No longer is he confused about anything; no longer does he suffer any hesitation before taking a serious decision; no longer is he travelling an unmarked road and no longer is he uncertain of his direction. His ultimate goal is clear. His way towards it is straight and he is certain of his footsteps. Two qualities describe the message which was given to the noble Messenger: *"a light and a clear book"*.

It has been God's pleasure to choose self-surrender, or Islam, as a religion for mankind. Anyone who follows what God has been pleased to choose for him and accepts it with pleasure will be guided by God *"to the paths of peace"*. How true and accurate this description is. What this faith imparts to life as a whole is peace, in the broadest sense of the term. It is peace within the individual, the community and the whole world. It is peace with one's conscience, with one's mind and body. It is peace within the home and family, society and the community and with humanity at large. It is peace with life, the universe and with the Creator, God. Mankind never knew or experienced this sort of peace except through following this faith and implementing its laws and systems.

It is a true fact that through this religion of Islam God guides anyone who seeks His pleasure by following it *"to the paths of peace"* in all the aforementioned aspects of life. No one can appreciate how profound a blessing this is except a person who has experienced what life is like along the paths of war in ignorant societies, old and modern, or one who has experienced the turmoil of worry and restlessness generated within man's conscience by deviant faiths, or erroneous laws and systems. Those who were the first to be addressed by these Qur'ānic revelations realised, as a result of their past experience in ignorant societies, the true meaning of this peace which brought happiness into their personal lives.

We badly need to understand this basic truth. We see ignorance all around us playing havoc with man's life, as it continues to cause wars to flare up within human conscience and human society, generation after generation. No one needs to understand this true wisdom more than us since we have lived in this state of peace for a period of our history, only to leave it for a life of war that crushes our spirits, morality, behaviour and society. We put up with being choked by the tightening grip of darkness and endure the unabating war it wages against us, all when Islam and the peace it imparts to mankind is well within our reach. We only need to accept for ourselves what God has chosen for us to enjoy this blessed peace. What a raw deal we accept for ourselves when we barter good for evil, truth for error and peace for war.

We can save mankind from the tribulations of ignorance and the war it wages on man in all its shapes and forms. But we cannot do so until we save ourselves by turning back to what God has chosen for us and seek His pleasure by following it in order to be included among those whom God guides along the paths of peace and *"leads them out of darkness into light"* (Verse 16), by His grace. Everything that results from abandoning Islam adds to the state of darkness. There is the darkness of superstition and ill-conceived beliefs, the darkness of unrestrained desire and caprice, the darkness of worry and confusion, the darkness of confused values and mistaken judgements and standards. Light on the other hand, is the sort of clarity and brightness which lightens up man's conscience, his mind and his whole life.

He *"guides them to a straight way."* (Verse 16) It is in line with human nature and with the universe as well as the laws which govern the existence of both man and the universe. It leads straight to God and allows no confusion of issues or blurring of facts or errors of direction.

It is God, the Creator of man, human nature, the universe and its laws, who has devised this system for man and chosen this religion for the believers. It is only natural, therefore, that this system should show them the straight way, for no other system can map it out for them. God always tells the truth. He is in no need of anyone. It is neither of any benefit to Him that people follow His guidance, nor of any consequence to Him that they should sink into error. It is only because He is most gracious that He has given them this faith, which maps out for them the straight way. To claim that Jesus Christ is God is a blatant blasphemy. To say that the Jews and the Christians are God's beloved sons is a false fabrication. Such claims are pressed by people of earlier revelations who have suppressed the clear essence of the concept of God's oneness. The last Messenger, Muhammad (peace be upon him), was sent to put it back in its clearest form, so that those who have strayed away from it may turn back.

False Claims Leading to Disbelief

Unbelievers indeed are they who say: "God is the Christ, son of Mary." Say: Who could have prevailed with God in any way had it been His will to destroy the Christ, son of Mary, and his mother, and everyone on earth? To God belongs the kingdom of the heavens and the earth and all that is between them. He creates what He wills and God has power over all things. (Verse 17)

The message Jesus (peace be upon him) conveyed as given to him by his Lord was the message of God's absolute oneness which has been given to every messenger. Total submission to God alone as the only God and the Lord of the universe was the attitude adopted by every messenger. This clear faith, however, later became distorted after pagans adopted Christianity, retaining some traces of their old pagan beliefs which they were keen to introduce into the faith based on God's oneness. As time passed, these deviant beliefs became an integral part of the whole faith.

These deviant beliefs were not introduced all at the same time. Ecclesiastical councils introduced them at different intervals until they eventually produced this singularly confusing mixture of legends and concepts that defies even those of its advocates who try to give a logical interpretation of it.

The basic concept of God's oneness was preached after Jesus (peace be upon him) by his disciples and their followers. The Gospel of Barnabas, one of many written at the time, speaks of Jesus Christ as a Messenger of God. Internal differences then broke out, with some maintaining that the Christ was not different from other messengers sent by God. Others acknowledged that he was a messenger but they claimed that he had a special relationship with God, while a third group said that he was the son of God because he was created without a father. Nevertheless, he was one of God's creation. A different group claimed that he was God's son, and that he was not created; he shared with the Father the quality of being eternal.

To settle their differences, a great synod met in 325 AD, attended by 48,000 patriarchs and bishops who were described by Ibn al-Baṭrīq, a historian of Christianity, as follows:

They differed greatly in views and faiths. Some of them maintained that both the Christ and his mother were gods, while others, Sabilius and his followers, viewed the relationship between the Christ and the Father as a brand of fire separated from a torch, which continued to burn unaffected by this split. A third group, Ilyan and those who followed his lead, claimed that Mary did not bear Jesus for nine months, as mothers bear their children. He only passed through her belly as water runs through gutters. The Word went through her ear and came out instantly through the passage where a child is born. Another group claimed that the Christ was a human being created from the Divine with an essence similar to that of any one of us. The beginning of the son started with Mary, and he was chosen to maintain the human essence. Divine grace was bestowed on him with love and Divine will. It is for this reason that he was called the son of God. They maintained that God is an eternal, single essence and single hypostasis who had three names. They did not believe in the Word or in the Holy Spirit. This was the view advocated by Paul Shamshati, the patriarch of Antioch and his followers who were called the Bulikanians. Yet another group believed in a trinity consisting of three deities: good, evil and a middle one in between. This view was advanced by Markiun whom they claimed to be Jesus's Chief Disciple, denying Peter. A further group maintained that Jesus Christ had a Divine nature. This was the belief advocated by St. Paul and 318 bishops who followed him.[1]

The Roman Emperor Constantine, who embraced Christianity without understanding anything of it chose this last view and supported its advocates, giving them a chance to suppress all other beliefs and views, especially those who maintained that the Divine nature belonged only to the father and that Jesus, the Christ, was a human being.

The author of the *History of the Coptic Nation* has this to say about this decision: "The holy community and the apostolic church excommunicated everyone who claimed that there was a time when the son of God did not exist, or that he did not exist before he was born, or that he was born of nothing or that he was made of a substance or an essence other than that of God, the Father. It also excommunicated

---

1. Shaikh Muḥammad Abū Zahrah, *Muḥāḍarāt fī al-Naṣrānīyah*, or "Lectures on Christianity", Cairo. All that we summarise concerning these ecclesiastical councils are based on this book and its sources.

everyone who said that Jesus Christ was created, or that he was liable to change or that his shadow differed in shape."

By taking these decisions, the ecclesiastical council did not manage to win over the Unitarian followers of Aries who managed to gain power in Constantinople, Antioch, Babylon, Alexandria and Egypt.

A new disagreement erupted over the nature of the Holy Spirit, with some people maintaining that Jesus was Divine, while others rejected this. The first Synod of Constantinople met in 381 to settle these differences. The same historian of Christianity tells us of the decisions of this council as reported by the Bishop of Alexandria: "The Patriarch of Alexandria, Thimothius said: To us the Holy Spirit does not have a meaning other than the spirit of God, and the spirit of God has no meaning other than His life. Therefore, if we were to say that the Holy Spirit was created, then we are saying that the spirit of God is created, and if we were to say that the spirit of God is created, then we are saying that His life is a creation. If we were to say that His life is a creation, then we allege that He is not the Living. If we were to allege that He is not the Living, then we disbelieve in Him. Whoever disbelieves in Him is to be cursed."

Hence, the Divinity of the Holy Spirit was established in this ecclesiastical council as the Divinity of the Christ, Jesus, was established in the earlier council. Thus the Trinity of the Father, the Son and the Holy Spirit was finally established.

Yet another dispute broke out on the issue of the combination of the Divine and the human natures in the Christ. Nestor, the Patriarch of Constantinople, was of the view that there was a hypostasis and a nature. The hypostasis of Divinity was derived from the Father, while the humanity came through Mary. Therefore, Mary was the mother of man in Jesus, not the mother of God. Of the Christ who mixed with people and addressed them, he said, as quoted by the historian of Christianity: "This man who says he is the Christ is united with the son through love. It is said that he is God and the son of God, not in actuality but through grace."

He also says: "Nestor has maintained that our Lord, Jesus Christ, was not God himself, but a man full of blessings and grace, or he was inspired by God. He was infallible and committed no sin."

His view was rejected by the Bishop of Rome, the Patriarch of Alexandria and the Bishops of Antioch. They agreed to hold a fourth summit, the Afsis Council. Held in 431, this Council concluded that

"Mary the Virgin was the mother of God and that Jesus was a true God and a man at the same time, with two natures united in the hypostasis." The Council cursed Nestor.

The Church of Alexandria came out with yet another view which was discussed by the second synod, which concluded that "The Christ had one nature combining both Divinity and humanity."

This view was not universally accepted. Disagreement was rife and another ecclesiastical council met at Khalqidonia in 451 and determined that "The Christ had two natures, not one. Divinity was a nature sacred and different from Humanity. Both met in the Christ." Thus, the second synod of Afsis was totally rejected.

The Egyptians declared that they did not recognise this decision. A bloody conflict erupted between the Egyptian Copts, the Monophysites and the Melkites of Syria whose views became the official ones of the Empire.

This note is sufficient to describe the great variety of deviant concepts about the Divinity of Jesus Christ and the enmity and hatred to which it led between various sects. These divisions and hatred continue even today.

The True Verdict

The final message gives the ultimate ruling on this whole issue, with the final Messenger declaring to the people who received revelations in former times the true nature of the Divine faith: *"Unbelievers indeed are they who say: 'God is the Christ, son of Mary.'"* (Verse 17) *"Unbelievers indeed are those who claim that God is one of a Trinity."* (Verse 73) An effort is made here to persuade them to listen to the voice of reason, upright nature and fact: *"Say: Who could have prevailed with God in any way had it been His will to destroy the Christ, son of Mary, and his mother, and everyone on earth?"* (Verse 17) This represents an absolute and undeniable distinction between God, His nature, will and dominion on the one hand and the nature of Jesus (peace be upon him), his mother and all beings on the other. The difference is clear and total. God is single; nothing is like Him; His will is absolute; His authority is total; no one can do anything to reverse His will should He desire to destroy the Christ, son of Mary, his mother and everyone on earth. He, the most glorious owns and creates everything, while all else are created: *"To God belongs the kingdom of the heavens and the earth and all that is between them. He creates what He wills and God has power over all things."* (Verse 17)

The Islamic faith thus appears to all in its true light: simple, clear, straightforward. Its clarity is even more enhanced in comparison to all erroneous concepts, legends and pagan beliefs which have crept into the faith of a section of those who were given earlier revelations. The first distinctive feature of the Islamic faith becomes prominent as it states without any trace of ambiguity the true nature of Godhead, as well as servitude and submission to God. It separates the two positions most decisively.

Wishful Thinking That Comes to Nothing

The *sūrah* then mentions another claim pressed by the Jews and Christians: *"Both the Jews and the Christians say: 'We are God's children and His loved ones.'"* (Verse 18) They allege that some sort of parenthood belongs to God. If this fatherhood is not a physical one, then it is spiritual. Whatever it is, it throws an element of doubt on the concept of God's oneness and detracts from the decisive separation between the position of God and that of His servants. The fact is that this separation is necessary for the clarity of faith and the proper order of human life. It is essential so that all worship is addressed to God by all His creation. They, thus, have a single legislative authority which sets for them their values, standards, laws and systems, with no confusion of authority resulting from a jumble of qualities and positions. It is not merely a question of deviant beliefs, but a question of their consequences that are bound to corrupt life as a whole.

As a logical consequence of their claim that they are the children of God and His loved ones, the Jews and Christians claimed that He would not punish them for their sins, and that they would not be in Hell for more than a few days, if at all. This means in plain terms that God's justice is not administered properly and that He favours a section of His servants by allowing them to spread corruption on earth without punishing them as He punishes others who would do the same. Can we imagine the sort of corrupt life that may result from such a concept?

At this point, Islam rejects most decisively such deviant beliefs and their practical consequences which corrupt life. It stresses the fact that God's justice is absolute: *"Say: Why then does He punish you for your sins? You are only human beings of His creation. He forgives whom He will and punishes whom He will."* (Verse 18) Their claims of being God's children are, thus, stated to be false. They are no more than other human beings. Forgiveness or punishment is determined by the same rule, based on God's will which has established certain reasons for forgiveness and different ones for punishment. Neither is determined by any special relationship with God.

We then have a reiteration of the fact that everything belongs to God and returns to Him: *"To God belongs the kingdom of the heavens and the earth and all that is between them, and to Him all shall return."* (Verse 18) It goes without saying that the owner is different from what is owned. Limitless as He is in His glory, His will is absolute and to Him will all return.

A renewed address is then made to the people given earlier revelations in order to allow them no excuse whatsoever. They are made to visualise most clearly their eventual destiny: *"People of earlier revelations! Now after an interval during which no messengers have appeared, Our Messenger has come to you to make things plain to you, lest you say: 'No one has come to give us good news or to warn us.' Now there has come to you a bearer of good news and a warner. God has power over all things."* (Verse 19)

With such decisive clarity, all issues are made plain. No longer can the people of earlier revelations claim that the unlettered Messenger has not been sent to them. God tells them: *"People of earlier revelations, Our Messenger has come to make things plain to you."* (Verse 19) No longer can they profess that they have not been warned or given good news for a long period which might have allowed forgetfulness or deviation to creep in. Now someone to warn them and to give them happy news has come to them.

They are reminded that nothing can resist God's power; nothing can defy Him. He can send a Messenger from among the unlettered nation and He can punish the people given revelations earlier for what they may earn: *"God has power over all things."* (Verse 19)

Thus, this round of confrontation with peoples of earlier revelations comes to an end. It has exposed their deviant beliefs which they introduced in the true faith preached by their messengers. It states most clearly the only faith which God accepts from believers and pronounces as false all their excuses which they reiterate in justification of their negative attitude to the unlettered Prophet, Muḥammad (peace be upon him). It calls on them to follow the Divine guidance on the one hand

and weakens the effects of their scheming against the Muslim community on the other. Moreover, the way the Muslim community and all those who seek guidance must follow is clearly marked out.

An Appeal Mixed with Worry

At this point in the *sūrah*, the attitude of the Children of Israel towards God's Messenger sent to them, Moses (peace be upon him), is given. Moses was their saviour who led them out of Egypt towards the holy land God had assigned to them. The *sūrah* also exposes their attitude to the covenant they made with their Lord and how they violated it and were punished for that violation.

And so Moses said to his people: "My people, remember the favours which God has bestowed upon you when He raised up prophets among you, made you kings and granted you what He has not granted to any other community. (Verse 20) My people, enter the holy land which God has assigned to you. Do not turn your back, for then you will be lost." (Verse 21) *"Moses," they answered, "mighty people dwell in that land, and we will surely not enter it unless they depart from it. If they do depart, then we will enter."* (Verse 22) *Thereupon two men who were God-fearing and on whom God had bestowed His grace said: "Go in upon them through the gate. As soon as you enter it, you shall be victorious. In God you should place your trust, if you are true believers."* (Verse 23) *They said, "Moses, we will never go in so long as they are in it. Go forth, then, you and your Lord, and fight, both of you. We shall stay here."* (Verse 24) *"Lord," he said, "I am master of none but myself and my brother. Do, then, draw a dividing line between us and these wrongdoing folk."* (Verse 25) *He replied, "This land shall, then, be forbidden to them for forty years, during which they will wonder aimlessly on earth. Do not grieve for these wrongdoing folk."* (Verse 26)

This is only one episode in the story of the Children of Israel which is related in the Qur'ān in extensive detail to serve several purposes. One purpose relates to the fact that the Children of Israel were the first to confront the Islamic message with wicked designs, plots and open warfare both in Madinah and the whole of Arabia. Their hostile attitude could be traced back to the very early days of the Islamic message. It was they who encouraged and nurtured hypocrisy and the hypocrites in Madinah, providing them with the means to scheme against Islam and the Muslims. They also incited the pagan Arabs to fight the Muslim community and gave them their active support. It was they who started the war of false rumours against the Muslim community raising among them doubts and suspicions about the Muslim leadership and circulating distortions of the Islamic faith before they confronted the Muslim community in open warfare. It was necessary, therefore, to expose them to the Muslim community so that it knew its enemies: their nature, history, methods and means as well as the nature of the battle it had to fight against them.

Another purpose can be seen in the fact that the Israelites were the followers of a Divine faith revealed before the final faith of Islam. They had a long history before Islam, during which distortions crept into their faith and they repeatedly violated their agreement and covenant with God. The practical consequences of these violations and deviations were seen in their lives, their moral values and their traditions. As the Muslim nation is the heir to all Divine messages and the custodian of the monotheistic Divine faith as a whole, it is necessary that it be made fully aware of the history of the Israelites with all its ups and downs. This gave the Muslim community an accurate knowledge of the way it should follow, what slips lay ahead of it and the consequences of such slips, as these are reflected in the history and morality of the Jews. This enabled the Muslim community to add the experience of the Jews to the total sum of its own experience and to benefit by it in future. It could, thus, avoid the slips and deal effectively with deviation right at the start before it had a chance to develop.

Yet another purpose relates to the fact that over their long history the experience of the Jews was highly varied. God is aware that with the passage of time, people may change, and certain generations may deviate from the right path. As the Muslim nation will continue until the end of life, it is bound to go through certain periods which are not dissimilar to what the Jews have gone through. God has, therefore, chosen to make available to the leaders of the Muslim community and its reformers in different generations, clear examples of what could befall nations so that they may be able to diagnose the disease of their particular generation and administer the proper cure. It is a fact of life that those who deviate after having known the truth are the most resistant to calls and appeals to follow right guidance. Those without any prior knowledge of the truth are more responsive because they find something new which appeals to them and helps them shake off the burden of ignorance. They are most impressed by the first call that makes its appeal to them. Winning over those with an earlier experience requires a much more strenuous effort and a great deal of perseverance on the part of advocates of the Divine faith.

There are other purposes for relating the story of the Jews in such detail, but it is sufficient to make only these brief references here and go back to our commentary.

> *And so Moses said to his people: "My people, remember the favours which God has bestowed upon you when He raised up prophets among you, made you kings and granted you what He has not granted to any other community.* (Verse 20) *My people, enter the holy land which God has assigned to you. Do not turn your back, for then you will be lost."* (Verse 21)

Moses' words give us the impression that he may have been worried lest his people disobey. He had tried them before on several occasions. He had led them out of Egypt, liberated them from subjugation with God's help, who parted the sea for them and caused Pharaoh and his soldiers to drown. Nevertheless, when they came by a community engaged in pagan worship, they said to him: *"Moses, set up a deity for us as these people have deities."* (7: 138) On another occasion, he had hardly left them for his appointment with his Lord when the Samaritan used the jewellery stolen from Egyptian women to make them an effigy of the calf which made a lowing sound. They started to worship the calf and claimed that it was the god Moses went to meet.

Another experience which Moses remembered well was when God made springs of water gush out for them in the desert and sent down to them manna and quail, a very wholesome food to eat. Nonetheless, they wanted to have the types of food they were familiar with in Egypt, the land where they were humiliated. They asked Moses to pray to God to bring forth for them herbs, cucumber, garlic, lentils and onions. They would not sacrifice their familiar food for a life of dignity, liberation and the pursuit of a noble goal. He also tested them when he conveyed to them God's order to slaughter a cow but they kept postponing the implementation of this order. When they finally slaughtered it, they did so most reluctantly. When he returned from his appointment with his Lord carrying the tablets which outlined the covenant they should make with God, they refused to make that covenant and fulfil their pledges to their Lord. Despite what God had bestowed on them and the forgiveness of their sins which He granted them, they did not give their pledges until they saw with their own eyes the mountain raised over their heads, and felt that it was about to fall on top of them.

Moses had tested them on several occasions and now they were close to the holy land, their destination. God had promised them they would be the rulers in this land and that He would raise up among them prophets so that they remained in God's care. Moses, however, was worried lest they should disobey. He, therefore, coupled this his last appeal with a reminder of the happiest memories, best incentives and strongest warnings:

> And so Moses said to his people: "My people, remember the favours which God has bestowed upon you when He raised up prophets among you, made you kings and granted you what He has not granted to any other community. (Verse 20) My people, enter the holy land which God has assigned to you. Do not turn your back, for then you will be lost." (Verse 21)

God's promise never fails. He promises here to raise up prophets among them and to make them kings. The fulfilment of this promise brought them what God granted to no other nation until that period in time. The holy land, which they were approaching, was assigned to them by God's promise, which meant that they were certain to have it. They had already known from experience that God always fulfils His promises. Now, they were called upon to meet the conditions for yet another of His promises. To turn back was sure to bring them to ruin. But the Israelites never changed: their instinctive cowardice, argumentativeness and willingness to breach pledges was sure to surface. *"Moses", they answered, "mighty people dwell in that land, and we will surely not enter it unless they depart from it. If they do depart, then we will enter."* (Verse 22)

A Typically Cowardly Attitude

The Israelite nature appears here unmasked, without cosmetics. They were facing danger and, therefore, all attempts to put on a brave face were abandoned. Not even God's promise to them to make this land theirs was sufficient to motivate them. They wanted an easier prize, without having to pay any price. It should come to them from heaven just as manna and quails were sent down for them to eat. *"Mighty people dwell in that land, and we will surely not enter it unless they depart from it. If they do depart, then we will enter."* (Verse 22)

Victory, however, does not come in this manner as the Jews wanted when they were devoid of faith: *"Thereupon two men who were God-fearing and on whom God had bestowed His grace said: 'Go in upon them through the gate. As soon as you enter it, you shall be victorious. In God you should place your trust, if you are true believers.'"* (Verse 23) The value of having faith and of being God-fearing appears very clearly. These were two men who feared God, and being God-fearing made them totally fearless when they confronted mighty people. They had all the courage needed to dispel the imaginary danger. They made this testimony, highlighting the importance of faith and the time of trial and difficulty. They wanted to show what it meant to fear God alone at times when people fear each other. God does not combine the two feelings of fear in any one man's heart: fearing Him and fearing human beings. A person who fears God fears no one else.

"Go in upon them through the gate. As soon as you enter it, you shall be victorious." (Verse 23) This is a basic rule in how to fight the enemy. The Jews are advised here to launch an offensive which takes them right through into the other people's homes. Once they are in, the others will be demoralised while their own morale will be high indeed. Those attacked will suffer a total loss of confidence and the attackers will win.

"In God you should place your trust, if you are true believers." (Verse 23) A believer relies on no one other than God. This is the distinctive mark and the correlative of faith. But who were these two men addressing them with these true words? They were after all addressing the Israelites. True to their nature, the Children of Israel said: *"Moses, we will never go in so long as they are in it. Go forth, then, you and your Lord, and fight, both of you. We shall stay here."* (Verse 24)

Cowardly people are increasingly impudent. They start to kick around like donkeys but they never step forward. Often, cowardice and impudence go hand in hand. A cowardly person is reminded of his duty, but his strength fails him. His neglect of his duty embarrasses him and he abuses this duty as well as the message which imposes on him what he does not want.

"Go forth, then, you and your Lord and fight, both of you. We shall stay here." (Verse 24) A perfect example of rudeness from weak people

who realise that rudeness costs nothing but words. Fulfilment of their duty, on the other hand, requires them to fight in a real war. *"Go forth, then, you and your Lord, both of you."* He is, then, not their Lord if his lordship means that they will have to fight. *"We shall stay here."* We neither desire a kingdom, nor sovereignty, nor even the promised holy land, if it means that we will have to fight these mighty people.

This is now the end for Moses (peace be upon him) after the strenuous efforts he exerted with the Children of Israel and after bearing all impudence and deviation. The result was simply to turn back, to turn away from the holy land when they stood at its doors. This was a clear violation of the covenant they had made with God. But the covenant applied to Moses also. What should he do now? Whose help should he seek?

"Lord", he said, "I am master of none but myself and my brother. Do, then, draw a dividing line between us and these wrongdoing folk." (Verse 25) This is a prayer uttered in pain. It is an appeal to God and one of total submission to Him. It also expresses total determination and a total break with those who disobeyed.

Moses was aware that God knew that he could not account for anyone other than himself and his brother. His are the feelings of weakness experienced by a person who has suffered a major letdown, the faith of a Prophet who spoke to God directly, the determination of an unshakable believer. He could not put his complaint to anyone other than God, to whom he prays to draw a dividing line between him and the evil-doers. Nothing could provide a link with them after they had abandoned their covenant with God. No relationship of family, ancestry, history or previous effort was of any significance. Their only relationship could be one of faith and the pledges they had given to God. As they breached them, then all relations had been severed. As for him, he was determined to fulfil his own promises to God, while they continued to do wrong.

This is the attitude of humble politeness shown by a Prophet and this is the action plan of a firm believer. The tie which could bring believers together was the tie of faith. Nationality, ancestry, race, language, history and all other ties known to mankind are of no significance when the tie of faith is severed.

God answered His Prophet's prayer and pronounced His judgement of the wrongdoers: *"This land shall, then, be forbidden to them for forty years, during which they will wander aimlessly on earth. Do not grieve for these wrongdoing folk."* (Verse 26) As they approached the holy land which God had promised them, He abandoned them to their aimless wandering. He forbade them the land He had assigned to them. The weightier view suggests that the land was forbidden to that particular generation of them, until a new generation came of age, aware of the lessons and strengthened by their upbringing in the desert. The first generation had long been used to subjugation and tyranny in Egypt. As such, it could not shoulder the tough responsibility. Tyranny and humiliation corrupt the nature of individuals as well as communities.

The *sūrah* stops at this point in their history to allow believers to reflect on the lessons learned. The Muslims also learned this tough lesson God relates to them. When they came face to face with difficulty and they were few in number confronting a mightier force of unbelievers in Badr, they said to their Prophet, Muḥammad (peace be upon him): "We will not say to you, Messenger of God, what the Israelites said to their Prophet, *'Go forth, then, you and your Lord, and fight, both of you. We shall stay here.'* But we will say to you: Go forth, then, you and your Lord, and fight; we will fight alongside you."

We see how the Qur'ānic method produces results in educating the Muslim community through relating stories from past generations of believers. We can also see what purpose is served by relating the history of the Children of Israel.

3

The First Murder

Relate to them in all truth the story of the two sons of Adam: how each offered a sacrifice, and it was accepted from one of them while it was not accepted from the other. [The latter] said: "I will surely kill you." [The other] replied: "God accepts only from those who are God-fearing. (27)

Even if you lay your hand on me to kill me, I shall not lay my hand on you to kill you; for I fear God, the Lord of all the worlds. (28)

I would rather you should add your sin against me to your other sins, and thus you will be destined for the Fire; since that is the just retribution of wrongdoers." (29)

His evil soul drove him to kill his brother; and he murdered him, and thus he became one of the lost. (30)

۞ وَٱتْلُ عَلَيْهِمْ نَبَأَ ٱبْنَىْ ءَادَمَ بِٱلْحَقِّ إِذْ قَرَّبَا قُرْبَانًا فَتُقُبِّلَ مِنْ أَحَدِهِمَا وَلَمْ يُتَقَبَّلْ مِنَ ٱلْآخَرِ قَالَ لَأَقْتُلَنَّكَ قَالَ إِنَّمَا يَتَقَبَّلُ ٱللَّهُ مِنَ ٱلْمُتَّقِينَ ۝

لَئِنۢ بَسَطتَ إِلَىَّ يَدَكَ لِتَقْتُلَنِى مَآ أَنَا۠ بِبَاسِطٍ يَدِىَ إِلَيْكَ لِأَقْتُلَكَ إِنِّى أَخَافُ ٱللَّهَ رَبَّ ٱلْعَٰلَمِينَ ۝

إِنِّىٓ أُرِيدُ أَن تَبُوٓأَ بِإِثْمِى وَإِثْمِكَ فَتَكُونَ مِنْ أَصْحَٰبِ ٱلنَّارِ وَذَٰلِكَ جَزَٰٓؤُا۟ ٱلظَّٰلِمِينَ ۝

فَطَوَّعَتْ لَهُۥ نَفْسُهُۥ قَتْلَ أَخِيهِ فَقَتَلَهُۥ فَأَصْبَحَ مِنَ ٱلْخَٰسِرِينَ ۝

God then sent forth a raven which scratched the earth, to show him how he might conceal the nakedness of his brother's body. He cried out: "Woe to me! Am I then too weak to do what this raven has done, and to conceal the nakedness of my brother's body?" He was then overwhelmed by remorse. (31)

فَبَعَثَ ٱللَّهُ غُرَابًا يَبْحَثُ فِى ٱلْأَرْضِ لِيُرِيَهُۥ كَيْفَ يُوَرِى سَوْءَةَ أَخِيهِ قَالَ يَٰوَيْلَتَىٰٓ أَعَجَزْتُ أَنْ أَكُونَ مِثْلَ هَٰذَا ٱلْغُرَابِ فَأُوَٰرِىَ سَوْءَةَ أَخِى فَأَصْبَحَ مِنَ ٱلنَّٰدِمِينَ ﴿٣١﴾

Because of this did We ordain to the Children of Israel that if anyone slays a human being, for anything other than in punishment of murder or for spreading corruption on earth, it shall be as though he had slain all mankind; and that if anyone saves a human life, it shall be as though he had saved all mankind. Our messengers brought them clear evidence of the truth, but despite all this, many of them continue to commit all manner of excesses on earth. (32)

مِنْ أَجْلِ ذَٰلِكَ كَتَبْنَا عَلَىٰ بَنِىٓ إِسْرَٰٓءِيلَ أَنَّهُۥ مَن قَتَلَ نَفْسًۢا بِغَيْرِ نَفْسٍ أَوْ فَسَادٍ فِى ٱلْأَرْضِ فَكَأَنَّمَا قَتَلَ ٱلنَّاسَ جَمِيعًا وَمَنْ أَحْيَاهَا فَكَأَنَّمَآ أَحْيَا ٱلنَّاسَ جَمِيعًا وَلَقَدْ جَآءَتْهُمْ رُسُلُنَا بِٱلْبَيِّنَٰتِ ثُمَّ إِنَّ كَثِيرًا مِّنْهُم بَعْدَ ذَٰلِكَ فِى ٱلْأَرْضِ لَمُسْرِفُونَ ﴿٣٢﴾

It is but a just punishment of those who make war on God and His Messenger, and endeavour to spread corruption on earth, that they should be put to death, or be crucified, or have their hands and feet cut off on alternate sides or that they should be banished from the land. Such is their disgrace in this world, and more grievous suffering awaits them in the life to come; (33)

إِنَّمَا جَزَٰٓؤُاْ ٱلَّذِينَ يُحَارِبُونَ ٱللَّهَ وَرَسُولَهُۥ وَيَسْعَوْنَ فِى ٱلْأَرْضِ فَسَادًا أَن يُقَتَّلُوٓاْ أَوْ يُصَلَّبُوٓاْ أَوْ تُقَطَّعَ أَيْدِيهِمْ وَأَرْجُلُهُم مِّنْ خِلَٰفٍ أَوْ يُنفَوْاْ مِنَ ٱلْأَرْضِ ذَٰلِكَ لَهُمْ خِزْىٌ فِى ٱلدُّنْيَا وَلَهُمْ فِى ٱلْءَاخِرَةِ عَذَابٌ عَظِيمٌ ﴿٣٣﴾

Except those who repent before you overpower them. For you must know that God is Much-Forgiving, Merciful. (34)

إِلَّا ٱلَّذِينَ تَابُواْ مِن قَبْلِ أَن تَقْدِرُواْ عَلَيْهِمْ فَٱعْلَمُواْ أَنَّ ٱللَّهَ غَفُورٌ رَّحِيمٌ ﴿٣٤﴾

Believers, fear God and seek the means to come closer to Him, and strive hard in His cause, so that you may be successful. (35)

يَـٰٓأَيُّهَا ٱلَّذِينَ ءَامَنُواْ ٱتَّقُواْ ٱللَّهَ وَٱبْتَغُوٓاْ إِلَيْهِ ٱلْوَسِيلَةَ وَجَـٰهِدُواْ فِى سَبِيلِهِۦ لَعَلَّكُمْ تُفْلِحُونَ ﴿٣٥﴾

If those who disbelieve had all that is on earth and as much besides to offer as ransom from the suffering of the Day of Resurrection, it would not be accepted from them. Theirs shall be a painful suffering. (36)

إِنَّ ٱلَّذِينَ كَفَرُواْ لَوْ أَنَّ لَهُم مَّا فِى ٱلْأَرْضِ جَمِيعًا وَمِثْلَهُۥ مَعَهُۥ لِيَفْتَدُواْ بِهِۦ مِنْ عَذَابِ يَوْمِ ٱلْقِيَـٰمَةِ مَا تُقُبِّلَ مِنْهُمْ وَلَهُمْ عَذَابٌ أَلِيمٌ ﴿٣٦﴾

They will wish to come out of the Fire, but they shall not come out of it. Theirs shall be a long-lasting suffering. (37)

يُرِيدُونَ أَن يَخْرُجُواْ مِنَ ٱلنَّارِ وَمَا هُم بِخَـٰرِجِينَ مِنْهَا وَلَهُمْ عَذَابٌ مُّقِيمٌ ﴿٣٧﴾

As for the man or the woman who is guilty of stealing, cut off their hands in requital for what they have wrought, as an exemplary punishment ordained by God. God is Almighty, Wise. (38)

وَٱلسَّارِقُ وَٱلسَّارِقَةُ فَٱقْطَعُوٓاْ أَيْدِيَهُمَا جَزَآءًۢ بِمَا كَسَبَا نَكَـٰلًا مِّنَ ٱللَّهِ وَٱللَّهُ عَزِيزٌ حَكِيمٌ ﴿٣٨﴾

But whoever repents after having thus done wrong, and makes amends, shall have his repentance accepted by God. God is Much-Forgiving, Merciful. (39)

فَمَن تَابَ مِنۢ بَعْدِ ظُلْمِهِۦ وَأَصْلَحَ فَإِنَّ ٱللَّهَ يَتُوبُ عَلَيْهِ إِنَّ ٱللَّهَ غَفُورٌ رَّحِيمٌ ﴿٣٩﴾

Do you not know that to God belongs the kingdom of the heavens and the earth? He punishes whom He wills and forgives whom He wills. God has power over all things. (40)

أَلَمْ تَعْلَمْ أَنَّ ٱللَّهَ لَهُۥ مُلْكُ ٱلسَّمَٰوَٰتِ وَٱلْأَرْضِ يُعَذِّبُ مَن يَشَآءُ وَيَغْفِرُ لِمَن يَشَآءُ وَٱللَّهُ عَلَىٰ كُلِّ شَىْءٍ قَدِيرٌ ٤٠

Overview

This passage begins to outline some fundamental legislation concerning human life. Some of these are concerned with life protection in a Muslim community that applies Divine law. Others relate to the protection of the system against any rebellion that may seek to undermine the authority administering Divine law in such a society. All in all, these measures aim to provide proper protection for the Muslim community, as well as wealth and private property in a social set-up based on Divine guidance and ruled by Divine law.

The legislation covering these important aspects of social life take up this whole passage, after an introduction relating the story of Adam's two sons. This story exposes the nature of crime and its motives, and reveals its ugly face, showing the need to stand up to crime and to stamp it out of the life of Islamic society altogether. It stresses the need to punish the criminal and to counter the motives for crime.

The story appears to be firmly welded to the rulings and legislation that are subsequently detailed in this *sūrah*. A reflective reader is bound to feel that the story is given at the right place to fulfil an important function, and present a profound argument that penetrates the reader's consciousness. It thus puts hearts and minds in the right frame to receive the severe penalties Islam legislates for crimes committed against human life, public order, and personal property. These must be put into effect in an Islamic society which implements Divine law.

Islamic society runs all its life affairs, relations and commitments on the basis of the Divine constitution, implementing God's law. Thus, it guarantees for every individual, and for the community as a whole, all elements of justice, stability, reassurance and needful provisions. It protects both the individual and the community against all factors of provocation, oppression, injustice and poverty. Hence, in such a just, balanced society that guarantees mutual solidarity, aggression against personal life, public order, or individual property becomes a horrid crime, without any "extenuating" circumstances. When all factors encouraging a law-abiding life have been provided and motives for crime removed from the life of both individual and society, then a stringent attitude to crime and criminals is totally justified. Nevertheless, Islam ensures for the criminal all that guarantees proper investigation, interrogation and fair judgement, explaining any doubt in his favour, and opening the door to repentance which pardons some crimes in this life and ensures forgiveness of all crimes in the life to come.

We see examples of all this in the present passage and the legislation it puts in place. But before we start our discussion of such legislation we need to say a brief, general word about the environment and social set-up in which such legislation is implemented and the conditions that give its provisions the necessary force.

The legal provisions included in this passage, whether relating to aggression against life, public order or private property have the same status as the rest of Islamic law, prescribing mandatory or discretionary punishments. They are all applicable in Islamic society, in the "land of Islam". In order to understand this, we need to remember that, from the Islamic point of view, the whole world is divided into two parts. The first is the land of Islam, or the land of peace. This includes any area where Islamic law is implemented, whether its population are all Muslims, or they include non-Muslims living under Islamic rule, or they are all non-Muslims but living under an Islamic government implementing Islamic law.[1] It also includes any area which has been occupied by non-Muslims, but its local population, who may all be Muslims or having non-Muslims among them, are able to implement Islamic law in their own life and judge their disputes accordingly. The main criterion in considering an area as a "land of Islam" is whether Islamic law is implemented in it or not.

The second is 'hostile land' which includes any area where Islamic legal provisions and Islamic law in general are not implemented, regardless of what population it may have. Thus, even if its population, or the majority of them describe themselves as Muslims, or followers of other Divine religions, or non-believers, any area that does not

---

1. A non-Muslim is not bound by the entirety of Islamic law. Rather, a non-Muslim is bound to observe such Islamic laws as are not in conflict with his own faith.

implement Islamic law is considered a hostile land to Muslims, both individuals and community.[2]

Islamic society is that which is established in the land of Islam, as defined above. It is such a society which implements Islamic law that deserves to have the full protection of life, property and public order. In such a society it is only appropriate that the punishments outlined by Islamic law should be inflicted on those whose actions threaten its peace and security. It is a noble, free and just society, which ensures work and sufficient provisions for everyone whether they are able or unable to work. It is a society where motives for goodness are plenty and those encouraging evil are few. It is only right that such a society should impose on every one of its subjects the duty of protecting this splendid state of affairs, respecting other people's rights to live in peace and security. It is natural that it should preserve the security of the "land of Islam" in which everyone lives peacefully, with all his rights and privileges guaranteed. Whoever violates the law of such a peaceful society is an evil aggressor who deserves severe punishment, allowing him, however, all the guarantees that ensure fair trial and which interpret doubt in his favour.

The people of a hostile land, as defined above, have no right to enjoy the guarantees provided by Islamic legal provisions and the deterrent they represent. This is because such a land neither implements nor recognises Islamic law. To Muslims who live in the land of Islam, such land is not a land of peace unless it enters into suitable treaties and agreements with the land of Islam. Moreover, Islamic law provides the same guarantees and rights to hostile individuals who come from hostile lands when they enter the land of Islam under a pledge of safety. This applies for the duration of that pledge, and within the area ruled by a Muslim ruler, implementing Islamic law.

Having made this explanation, we may now discuss this passage in detail.

A Murder is Committed

Relate to them in all truth the story of the two sons of Adam: how each offered a sacrifice, and it was accepted from one of them while

---

2. This definition, made by scholars and not used in the Qur'ān or *ḥadīth*, was introduced at a time when the overwhelming majority of Muslims lived under the Islamic state. It has recently been called into question by a number of scholars. – Translator's note.

it was not accepted from the other. [The latter] said: "I will surely kill you." [The other] replied: "God accepts only from those who are God-fearing. (Verse 27) Even if you lay your hand on me to kill me, I shall not lay my hand on you to kill you; for I fear God, the Lord of all the worlds. (Verse 28)

I would rather you should add your sin against me to your other sins, and thus you will be destined for the Fire; since that is the just retribution of wrongdoers." (Verse 29) His evil soul drove him to kill his brother; and he murdered him, and thus he became one of the lost. (Verse 30)

God then sent forth a raven which scratched the earth, to show him how he might conceal the nakedness of his brother's body. He cried out: "Woe to me! Am I then too weak to do what this raven has done, and to conceal the nakedness of my brother's body?" He was then overwhelmed by remorse. (Verse 31)

This story gives us a clear example of the nature of evil and totally unjustified aggression. It also gives us an example showing the nature of goodness and a peaceful attitude towards everyone. The two examples are set in clear contrast. The result is a sordid crime, which makes us feel the need for a legal code to impose just retribution and to stop aggressors even before they commit their crimes. If they, nevertheless, do commit crimes, they are certain to receive a punishment commensurate to their crimes. The legal code will thus be able to protect those who are good and ensure their right to live. It is indeed such people that should feel secure and safe under the protection of the law that deters crime and administers justice.

The Qur'ān does not specify the time or place of the story it relates. Nor does it mention the names of its main characters. Although reports mention the names of Cain and Abel as the two sons involved in the story, and although these reports mention some details about the conflict between them over two of their sisters, we prefer to confine our comments to the story as it is related in the Qur'ān, without adding any details. All reports mentioning details have an element of doubt, in the sense that they are given by people who follow earlier religions. The story is mentioned in the Old Testament with details of names, place and time, as given in these reports. The single *ḥadīth* which refers to the story and has been verified as authentic does not give any details. It is a *ḥadīth* in which 'Abdullāh ibn Mas'ūd quotes the Prophet as saying: "For every soul that is killed unjustly, a share of responsibility is borne by the first son of Adam, who was the first to commit murder." All that we can say about this story is that it took place during humanity's childhood stage. It was the first cold-blooded murder. The perpetrator did not know that dead people should be buried.

Leaving the story in the general terms in which it is given in the Qur'ān ensures that the purpose of relating it is fulfilled and its lessons are understood. Providing more details does not add anything to these basic purposes. Hence, our preference to discuss it as it is given.

> *Relate to them in all truth the story of the two sons of Adam: how each offered a sacrifice, and it was accepted from one of them while it was not accepted from the other. [The latter] said: "I will surely kill you." [The other] replied: "God accepts only from those who are God-fearing." (Verse 27)*

Having related to his followers an account of certain events in the history of the Children of Israel with their Prophet, Moses, the Prophet Muḥammad (peace be upon him) is told by God to relate the story of two people representing two types of human being. The account should be given in all honesty, because it tells of the truth deeply entrenched in human nature. It also emphasises the need for a deterrent legal code to ensure justice.

Adam's two sons were in a situation that gives no rise to any thought of aggression in a good person's mind. The situation is one of obedience to God and offering a sacrifice to draw closer to God: *"How each offered a sacrifice and it was accepted from one of them while it was not accepted from the other."* (Verse 27) We note that the passive mode is used here to indicate that the acceptance or rejection of the offered sacrifice is done by a higher power in a metaphysical way. This mode of expression suggests to us two points: the first is that we should not try to determine how exactly the offering was accepted. We need not discuss reports mentioned in books of commentary on the Qur'ān because these reports are most probably derived from Old Testament fables.

The second point suggests that the one whose offering was accepted had not committed any crime that might cause anyone else to be angry with him to any extent, let alone that that person should plot a murder. He had no say in the acceptance of this offering. The nature of the One who accepted the offering was beyond the perception of either of the two brothers. Hence, thoughts of anger or murder should have been far removed from the minds of both brothers. They were in a situation that is close to worship, since it involves offering a sacrifice for God's sake.

"[The latter] said: 'I will surely kill you.'" (Verse 27) This is a statement of confirmed intention which is met by our disapproval because it is totally unjustified. Indeed, it could only be the result of blind envy which is alien to a good heart. Thus, from the very first moment, we take an attitude of total disapproval of aggression. The *sūrah*, however, greatly enhances the ghastliness of this act of aggression by showing the peaceful, good-natured attitude of the other brother: *"[The other] replied: 'God accepts only from those who are God-fearing.'"* (Verse 27)

This is a simple statement which puts matters in their proper perspective. It indicates that the person saying this is a believer who understands the reason for the acceptance of sacrifices offered to God. Also implied in this statement is a gentle advice to the aggressor to fear God, because this is the way through which he could gain acceptance. It is all done very gently so that his brother might remain responsive and unirritated. Adopting a completely peaceful attitude, the good believer of the two brothers tries further to pacify his brother and quieten him: *"Even if you lay your hand on me to kill me, I shall not lay my hand on you to kill you; for I fear God, the Lord of all the worlds."* (Verse 28)

What we have here is a case of a peaceful man making clear that his attitude is based on fearing God and implementing His commandments. This attitude fills us with enthusiastic support for the victim of aggression, as we admire his calmness, reassurance and the fact that he fears God alone. His gentle words should have been sufficient to quench his brother's rage and reduce his anger. A good response would have been sufficient to re-establish the feelings of brotherhood and the reassurance of faith. To achieve this desirable result, however, the good-natured brother adds a word of warning: *"I would rather you should add your sin against me to your other sins, and thus you will be destined for the Fire; since that is the just retribution of wrongdoers."* (Verse 29)

We may paraphrase this statement by the God-fearing brother as follows: If you were to stretch your hand to me to kill me, it is not in my nature to do the same thing to you. The thought of murder does not occur to me in the first place, not because I cannot do it, but because I fear God, the Lord of all creation. I will leave you to bear the sin of murdering me so as to add it to your other sins which have caused your offering not to be accepted by God. Thus, you end up with a double burden of sin and a double punishment. This is a just reward for a heinous crime.

He, thus, depicted to his brother how loathsome to him was the very thought of committing murder. He did so in the hope that he would help his erring brother to resist all evil thoughts towards him, especially when he, himself, was of a peaceful disposition. He explained to him that the sinful burden of a murder was too heavy and that he would do well to avoid it in order not to end up with a double punishment. The only way to rid himself of it was through fearing God. In his persuasion, he went as far as any man could go. But the example of an evil man cannot be properly depicted until we know what sort of response he made to such persuasion: *"His evil soul drove him to kill his brother; and he murdered him, and thus he became one of the lost."* (Verse 30)

A Lesson Provided by a Raven

After all this admonition and persuasion, in a perfectly peaceful and gentle approach, the evil soul prevailed and the crime was committed. His evil soul was able to override every hindrance and made him less resistant to the thought of killing. Thus, he killed his own brother, only to be doomed: *"Thus he became one of the lost."* (Verse 30) He lost all as he brought himself into ruin, and lost his brother who should have been his friend and support. He also lost his world, since a murderer can never be happy in life. Most certainly, he lost his future life as he added his new sin to his earlier ones.

The ghastliness of his crime was made to appear to him in its most physical shape. The dead corpse of his brother started to rot and its nakedness became intolerable. Murderer as he was, he was soon made to realise his powerlessness, as he did not know how to conceal the nakedness of his brother's corpse. He was weaker than a raven among birds: *"God then sent forth a raven which scratched the earth, to show him how he might conceal the nakedness of his brother's body. He cried out: 'Woe to me! Am I then too weak to do what this raven has done, and to conceal the nakedness of my brother's body?' He was then overwhelmed by remorse."* (Verse 31)

Some reports suggest that there were two ravens and one of them killed the other. Other reports suggest that the raven found a dead raven or brought the dead one with him and started to scratch the earth and buried the dead one. The murderer expressed his feelings in the way reported in the Qur'ān and liked what he saw the raven do. It is clear that the murderer had never seen a dead man being buried. Otherwise, he would automatically have buried his brother. This may have been because the murdered brother was the first of Adam's children to die on earth, or maybe because the killer was still young and had never seen a burial before. Either case is probable. It also appears that his remorse was not one of repentance: otherwise, God would have accepted it from him. It was the sort of remorse which comes with the realisation that one's action is futile and leads to nothing but trouble.

It may be that the burial of the dead raven is something that ravens do, as some people suggest. It may also be a supernatural action God wanted to show to the killer at that particular time. To us, both cases are the same. The Creator who gives every species of His creation its nature and habits can accomplish whatever He wills through anyone of His creatures. His power is similarly indicated by either course.

The Killing of All Humanity

The *sūrah* then makes use of the profundity of relating this story by enhancing a positive response to the legislation enacted to deal with such a crime. The legislation achieves the dual purpose of weakening the motive to commit a murder and establishing the just punishment for such a crime whenever it takes place: *"Because of this did We ordain to the Children of Israel that if anyone slays a human being, for anything other than in punishment of murder or for spreading corruption on earth, it shall be as though he had slain all mankind; and that if anyone saves a human life, it shall be as though he had saved all mankind. Our messengers brought them clear evidence of the truth, but despite all this, many of them continue to commit all manner of excesses on earth."* (Verse 32)

This type of person exists and aggression is committed against peaceful and good-natured people who harbour neither grudges nor ill-feelings towards others. A reminder and a warning may achieve nothing with those who have an evil nature. Adopting a peaceful attitude may not be sufficient to prevent aggression. For all this, the ghastly crime of killing one person is considered so grave and so sordid that it is equated with the crime of killing all mankind. On the other hand, efforts to prevent killing and to spare the life of one person are considered a great action, equal to saving all mankind. The law given to the Children of Israel included this principle which equates the life of any human being with every life. The right to live is applicable to all. Hence, killing one person is an aggression against the right to live in which all people stand equal. Similarly, preventing murder and sparing the life of one person, either through defending the would-be victim or inflicting the death penalty on the killer in order to prevent the murder of another, is to save the basic right of life applicable to all.

It should be clarified here that this rule applies to people in the land of Islam, whether Muslim or not, as long as they are living under the rule and protection of the Islamic authority. As for those who are in a land hostile to Islam, neither their lives nor their properties are protected unless they have concluded a peace treaty with the land of Islam. This legislative rule should be well remembered. We should also remember that the land of Islam is that in which the rule of Islam prevails and Islamic law is implemented. The hostile land is that which does not implement Islamic law.

God has decreed this principle for the Children of Israel, because at that time, they were the recipients of Divine revelation and, as such, they represented the land of Islam as long as they implemented the law of the Torah in its fullness, without any distortion. But the Children of Israel exceeded their limits after God's messengers came to them with clear proof of the truth. Ever since the time of the Prophet Muḥammad (peace be upon him) many of them continue to commit excesses of all sorts. The Qur'ān records against them these excesses as well as the fact that they have no argument to justify their errors: *"Our [i.e. God's] messengers brought them clear evidence of the truth, but despite all this, many of them continue to commit all manner of excesses on earth."* (Verse 32) What excess is greater than distorting or ignoring God's law?

This explained, we need to point out that God has made the perpetration of corruption on earth similar to murder: the perpetrator is put to death because he has forfeited his right to live. The security of the Muslim community in the land of Islam and maintaining law and order within the system which gives the Muslim community the sense of peace and security are essential in the same way as the safety of individuals, if not more. Indeed, the safety of individuals cannot be guaranteed unless the security of the community is achieved. There is also the added reason of protecting this distinguished type of community and providing for it all guarantees of stability and continuity so that its people may carry on with their promotion of a better standard of human life. It is perhaps appropriate to mention here that this community provides to all mankind the guarantees necessary for the promotion of life, helps everything good to flourish and repels all evil. Its prime purpose is prevention, but it also administers the proper remedy for what could not be prevented. It removes every cause tempting human beings to lean towards evil and aggression. When it has done all this, anyone who threatens the security of this community is an evil element and should be removed unless he returns to his senses.

The Just Punishment for Rebellion

The *sūrah* lays down the punishment for the crime that such wicked elements commit. This is known in the Islamic legal code as the punishment for waging war against Islam: *"It is but a just punishment of those who make war on God and His Messenger, and endeavour to spread corruption on earth, that they should be put to death, or be crucified, or have their hands and feet cut off on alternate sides or that they should be banished from the land. Such is their disgrace in this world, and more grievous suffering awaits them in the life to come;* (Verse 33), *except those who repent before you overpower them. For you must know that God is Much-Forgiving, Merciful."* (Verse 34)

The crime to which this legislative statement refers involves rebellion against a Muslim ruler who implements the laws of Islam. The rebels gather in a group renouncing the ruler's authority. They cause fear among the Muslim community living in the Muslim land and they commit aggression against their lives and property. Some scholars also make it a condition that this should take place away from the areas where the ruler's authority is enforced. Others suggest that the very fact that such rebels begin to gather and use force in aggression against the people of the land of Islam, makes this legal provision applicable to them wherever they are. This is probably more practical, because Islam adopts a pragmatic approach.

Such rebels do not merely fight the ruler or the community, but they make war on God and His Messenger, since they fight God's law, wage an assault against the community implementing it and threaten the land where the law is implemented. By doing so, they also spread corruption on earth. There is no worse corruption than the attempt to prevent the implementation of Divine law and to spread fear in a land where Divine law is applied.

It is true that such rebels make war on God and His Messenger, although they surely do not fight God with their swords, and they do not fight His Messenger who has passed away. But by fighting the Muslim ruler and the Muslim community, they actually make war on God as they obstruct His law and prevent its implementation. Phrased in this way, the Qur'ānic statement also signifies that the ruler who is entitled to enforce these punishments against those who rebel against him is the ruler who actually implements God's law in the land of Islam. Without such qualities, no ruler may implement these provisions or enforce these punishments.

We wish to make this statement very clear, because some of those who are happy to be subservient to rulers in all generations try to use this verse for the wrong reasons. They find it easy to encourage the enforcement of such punishments by rulers who neither implement God's law nor promote the establishment of the land of Islam in their countries, even though they may profess to be Muslims. Moreover, they want these punishments to be enforced against people who are not making war against God and His Messenger, but who fight a tyrannical power, disobedient to God and His Messenger. It must be understood that no authority has the backing of God's law in its suppression of its enemies unless it implements God's law. Why should an authority seek endorsement of its actions by God's law anyway, when it rejects its implementation, thus claiming for itself certain qualities of Godhead?

Let us consider a situation where an armed group rebels against the authority of a Muslim ruler who is implementing Islamic law and threatens the lives and properties of Muslims living in the land of Islam. The punishment for those who join such a group is death, or crucifixion, (although some scholars say that they should be crucified after they are put to death, in order to frighten others) or to cut off their right hands and left feet.

Differing Views on Implementation

Scholars have widely different views on whether a Muslim ruler may choose any of these punishments or whether each punishment is implemented in a particular case. According to the Ḥanafī, Shāfiʿī and Ḥanbalī schools of Islam law, these punishments are ordered according to the crime committed. A rebel who kills without taking any property is put to death, while another who has taken property without killing has his limbs cut off. A person who has committed both crimes is put to death and crucified. A rebel who helps spread fear but has neither killed anyone nor taken any property, is banished.

According to Imām Mālik, a rebel who has killed must be killed. The Muslim ruler does not have a choice to enforce the lesser punishments of cutting off his limbs or banishing him. The only choice he has is either to put him to death by a method chosen by the state or to crucify him. If he has taken the property of Muslims but without killing anyone, he cannot be banished. The choices open to the ruler are to kill or crucify him or to cut off his limbs. If he has helped to spread fear, the ruler has all four choices and he may use his discretion. If the culprit is one of the organisers of rebellion, then cutting off his limbs may not be an adequate enough punishment. He should be either killed or crucified. If he is one who helps the rebellion with his physical strength, then cutting off his limbs is the appropriate punishment. If he is of neither type, then the lesser punishment of sending him into exile should be implemented.

We are more inclined to support Imām Mālik's views, especially the latter part which makes the punishment enforceable even in the case of mere rebellion and of spreading fear. This gives a Muslim ruler the right to take pre-emptive action to forestall any rebellion. Those who threaten the security of the Muslim community in the land of Islam, thus, face a stern punishment because the Muslim community is the first to deserve to live in peace and security.

Scholars also differ in their understanding of what is meant by banishing the rebels and whether they should be removed from the land where they committed their crime or from the land where they have their freedom. In the latter sense, they are imprisoned. Or is it that they should be banished from the whole earth, which means that they should be put to death? Our preference is that they should be banished from the land where they committed their crime to a place where they feel lonely and weak. This makes their punishment of the same nature as their crime, which involves spreading fear.

"Such is their disgrace in this world, and more grievous suffering awaits them in the life to come; (Verse 33). This means that their punishment in this life does not waive the punishment of the Hereafter, as it is the case in certain other crimes. This emphasises the gravity of crime and doubles its punishment. The reason being that the Muslim community should live in peace and security in the land of Islam and that the Muslim ruler who implements Islamic rules should be obeyed. Such a social set up and such a just and perfect system deserves to be protected against any design to undermine it.

If the rebels come to realise their mistake and turn to God in repentance when they still have their strength, then their punishment is waived and the Muslim ruler has no way of punishing them. God will forgive them eventually: *"Except those who repent before you overpower them. For you must know that God is Much-Forgiving, Merciful."* (Verse 34)

The wisdom behind discounting the crime and waiving punishment in this case is clear. For one thing, it is an appreciation of their repentance where they still have their power. It is taken as evidence of their good intentions. For another, they are encouraged to repent so that the Muslim nation is spared the need to fight them.

Islam deals with human nature in its entirety. God, who has chosen this religion for us, is the Creator of human nature. He knows what suits man and what does not suit him. *"How could it be that He who has created all should not know all? Indeed, He alone is unfathomable (in His wisdom), all aware."* (67: 14)

Man's Actions Determine His Future

An important feature of the Divine method of moulding human society is that it does not rely solely on legislative action. It certainly arms itself with legal provisions in order to deter those who only fear the force of the law. Indeed, it relies primarily on educative action which smoothes over the rough edges of people's characters. It provides guidance to the human spirit as it establishes a society that helps the seeds of goodness to grow and gives harmful weeds no fertile soil. The previous verses spoke of very stern punishments for serious crimes. However, once the punishments are outlined, so as to ensure their deterrent effect, the *sūrah* addresses people's consciences and spirits, aiming to strengthen faith and consciousness of one's obligations towards God. It urges people to seek proper ways of moving nearer to what pleases God and to strive hard in His cause, so that they may be successful. This is coupled with a warning against disbelief and a vivid description of what awaits disbelievers in the Hereafter.

> *Believers, fear God and seek the means to come closer to Him, and strive hard in His cause, so that you may be successful.* (Verse 35) *If those who disbelieve had all that is on earth and as much besides to offer as ransom from the suffering of the Day of Resurrection, it would not be accepted from them. Theirs shall be a painful suffering.* (Verse 36) *They will wish to come out of the Fire, but they shall not come out of it. Theirs shall be a long-lasting suffering.* (Verse 37)

The Islamic approach makes use of all aspects of human character. It addresses the innermost soul of man and touches on his inner motives as it motivates man to obey God and deters him from disobedience. The prime aim is to keep human nature upright and to prevent it from deviation. Punishment is only one of many methods to be used. It is not the only method, nor is it treated as an aim to be pursued.

This part of the *sūrah* starts with the story of Adam's two sons, which is particularly inspiring. It is followed by an outline of stern punishments calling on people to fear God and to remain conscious of their obligations towards Him: *"Believers, fear God."* It is God alone who should be feared because this is the type of fear which fits in with man's position of honour. To fear the sword and punishment is characteristic of those whose aspirations remain very low. To fear God is much more honourable. In the final resort, it is fear of God and consciousness of Him that work on man's conscience both in public and in private. They are the motives that deter man from committing evil when no other human being sees him and when he is certain that he cannot be brought before the law in this life. Important and necessary as the law is, it cannot replace fear of God, because what escapes the hand of the law is far greater than the number of cases that are brought to justice. No human soul and no society can remain good if it relies only on the law without adding to it the fear of a higher, Divine authority that works on human conscience.

"And seek the means to come closer to Him." (Verse 35) Fear God and seek the proper approaches which bring you nearer to Him. Try always to be in contact with Him. 'Abdullāh ibn 'Abbās, a learned scholar and a Companion of the Prophet, is reported to have said that seeking the means to come to God means to feel in need of Him. When human beings realise that they are in need of God's help and when they pray to Him to answer their needs, they stand in the right position of a servant of God towards his Lord. As such, they are in the best position to bring them success in this life and in the life to come. Both interpretations are correct as they mean that human conscience remains alive and helps man to prosper: *"Believers, fear God and seek the means to come closer to Him, and strive hard in His cause, so that you may be successful."* (Verse 35)

On the other side, the *sūrah* portrays a scene of the unbelievers who neither fear God nor seek the means to come to Him. As such, they will never prosper. It is a very vivid description, because the *sūrah* does not only give a statement outlining a position, but depicts a full scene with movement and interaction. This is, indeed, the Qur'ānic method used in portraying scenes of the Day of Judgement. The Qur'ān uses it for most purposes: *"If those who disbelieve had all that is on earth and as much besides to offer as ransom from the suffering of the Day of Resurrection, it would not be accepted from them. Theirs shall be a painful suffering.* (Verse 36) *They will wish to come out of the Fire, but they shall not come out of it. Theirs shall be a long-lasting suffering."* (Verse 37)

By the longest stretch of imagination, the most that the disbelievers can have is all that is available on the face of the earth. But the *sūrah* goes far beyond that and supposes that they have all that the earth contains twice over, and portrays them trying to pay all that as ransom to spare themselves the suffering of the Day of Resurrection. It also portrays them as they try to get out of the Fire of Hell, but they are unable to do so. They continue to endure their painful, lasting suffering. This is a very vivid scene with actions following one another in quick succession. There they are at first, having everything that is on earth and as much besides. They offer it all to escape punishment. Then we see them disappointed when all their appeals are turned down. They are then forced into the Fire, trying to get out, but having no means of escape. The curtain then falls and they are left to dwell there permanently.

A Severe Punishment for Theft

This is followed by a legislation outlining the punishment for theft: *"As for the man or the woman who is guilty of stealing, cut off their hands in requital for what they have wrought, as an exemplary punishment ordained by God. God is Almighty, Wise. (Verse 38) But whoever repents after having thus done wrong, and makes amends, shall have his repentance accepted by God. God is Much-Forgiving, Merciful. (Verse 39) Do you not know that to God belongs the kingdom of the heavens and the earth? He punishes whom He wills and forgives whom He wills. God has power over all things."* (Verse 40)

Muslim society provides for all inhabitants of the land of Islam, whatever faith they may have, enough to keep any thought of stealing far from any healthy mind. It guarantees good living, proper education and a system of fair distribution. At the same time, it makes private ownership the result of only legitimate means, and assigns to it a beneficial social role. Why, then, should any good person entertain any thought of stealing? When Muslim society has provided all this, it is only fair that it should prescribe a very stern punishment for theft, which represents an aggression on private ownership and the security of the community. This strong approach, however, is qualified by the fact that the enforcement of punishment is blocked when there is doubt as to the crime or its perpetrator. It provides all rights to the accused to prove his innocence so that no one is punished unless proven guilty beyond doubt.

What is left for us to say is that the Islamic system is a fully integrated one. We cannot properly understand the wisdom behind a particular point of detail in its legislation unless we understand the nature of this system, its basic principles and its guarantees. Moreover, details of the Islamic system should not be implemented in isolation of the rest of the system. We cannot simply take one legal provision or one principle of Islam and try to implement it in a non-Muslim social set-up. Such an attempt is useless. Such partial implementation of Islamic law cannot be considered an implementation of Islam, because Islam cannot be implemented piecemeal. Islam has a complete system which affects all aspects of life when implemented. This applies to the legislation regarding theft as well as to all provisions of Islamic law.

To start with, Islam asserts that every individual in the Muslim community and in the land of Islam has the right to live and to have all the safeguards necessary to protect his or her life. Every individual is entitled to have enough to eat and drink, proper clothing and a home providing him with adequate shelter, where he can rest in comfort. The Muslim community represented by the Muslim government must provide every individual with all these essentials, firstly through his own work as long as he is able to work. The community is responsible to teach him how to work and to provide him with the means and the tools to do his work. If he remains unemployed, either because jobs or their tools are unavailable or because he is unable to work, either partially or totally, temporarily or permanently, then he has a claim against the Muslim community. The same applies if his earnings are not sufficient to meet his needs.

This claim gives an individual the right to still have his or her needs satisfied in different ways. There is firstly a maintenance allowance, which could be imposed on those members of his own household who can afford it. Secondly, his maintenance can be imposed on certain people in his locality. Thirdly, he is entitled to be supported by the state, since such a person, man or woman, child or adult, qualifies as a beneficiary of *zakāt*. If *zakāt* funds are insufficient to provide adequate support to all people in need, then the Muslim state, which implements the whole of Islamic law in the land of Islam, can impose an additional tax on those who are well off in order to satisfy the needs of the under-privileged. The condition to be observed in such a situation is that what is so imposed must remain reasonable, fair and adequate. It must not constitute an injustice to those who make their earnings through legitimate means.

Islam is also strict in its view on legitimate earnings. Private ownership can come only through what is permissible. Hence, such ownership does not create a grudge motivating those who are deprived to lay their hands on the property of others, particularly since the system ensures fair distribution and does not neglect anyone's needs.

Moreover, Islam works on people's consciences and strengthens their moral sense. It directs their thinking towards earning through work not through theft. If work is unavailable or insufficient, the community helps them meet their needs. Thus, Islam gives them their right with honour.

Under such a system, why should anyone steal? Theft cannot be committed to satisfy a legitimate need. Its purpose is to get rich without working for it. Wealth cannot be sought through depriving the Muslim community in the land of Islam from the security to which it is legitimately entitled. Those who have earned their money in a fair and legitimate way are entitled to enjoy their earnings in peace.

Similarly, every individual in such a community is entitled to earn money fairly and legitimately. No usury, cheating, monopoly or wrongful exploitation of labour is allowed. Moreover, whoever has money must pay his *zakāt* liability and pay his share of what the community may need. When all this has been fulfilled, it is only right that everyone should have security for their property. If someone steals after having all his needs satisfied, knowing that theft is forbidden and having no reasonable need to lay his hands on the property of others, he commits a crime for which he has no justification. Hence, no mercy should be shown to him once he is proven guilty.

However, when there is doubt as to the circumstances of the crime, then the general Islamic principle of blocking punishment in cases of doubt comes into operation. Hence, when the Muslim state was stricken by famine, 'Umar, the second Caliph, suspended the enforcement of the punishment for theft. He did the same in one particular case, which has been documented. The servants of the son of Ḥāṭib ibn Abī Balta'ah stole a camel which belonged to a man of the tribe of Muzaynah. When they were proven guilty, 'Umar ordered their hands to be cut off. However, on learning that their master kept them hungry, 'Umar stopped the punishment from being enforced. He further punished their master, imposing on him a fine equivalent to the price of two camels. It is within this context that we should understand the punishments imposed by Islam as part of its comprehensive system providing guarantees for all, not for a particular class at the expense of another. It is a system which relies on protection before it imposes punishment. It only punishes wrongdoers who commit totally unjustified crimes.

Having explained this general rule about the Islamic system, let us discuss the particular punishment of theft. Theft is to take surreptitiously the property of others which is kept in a private place. What is taken, therefore, must be a property of a certain value. The minimum limit which, if taken surreptitiously, constitutes theft is agreed by scholars to be equivalent to one quarter of one dinar, which is approximately equal to 25 Egyptian piastres in our present currency.[3] Moreover, what is stolen must be kept in a private place and the thief must take it out of this place. This means that a person who steals property which is given to him for safe custody is not punished by cutting off his hand. Nor does this punishment apply to a servant who is allowed to enter the home of his owner, because what he steals is not kept in a place which is restricted from him. Nor is the punishment enforced against someone who has borrowed a certain property and who then denies having borrowed it, nor in the case of someone who steals fruits or crops until they have been put in a barn or a store. Similarly, the punishment is not enforced in the case of stealing property if it is found lying outside the place where it is normally placed for safekeeping. Moreover, the stolen property must belong entirely to someone else. Therefore, if one partner steals something which belongs to a partnership his hand is not cut off because he has a share in what he has stolen. Nor is a thief punished by cutting his hands off if he has stolen something from the state treasury because he has a partial claim to it. In all such cases, the thief is given a lesser punishment such as flogging, imprisonment or verbal reproach, as the judge may think fit, according to the circumstances of the case.

When a thief is punished, his hand is cut off up to the wrist. If he commits theft again, then his left foot is cut off up to the ankle. In case of a third or fourth theft, scholars have different views as to what is cut off.

Where any doubt exists, enforcement of the punishment is blocked. If it is suspected that the person concerned stole food to eat when he was hungry, or to meet a particular need, or if it is suspected that he had a share in the stolen property, then these are reasons which prevent

---

3. The author wrote this commentary in the early 1960s. Twenty-five piastres then were worth at least 100 times their value at present. Such an estimate should, therefore, be taken as giving a general idea and is not meant to be an exact price. It tells us that there is a minimum limit for theft, below which the punishment is not enforced – Translator's note.

his hands from being cut off. If the theft is proven through personal confession without there being witnesses to give evidence, then withdrawal of the confession is sufficient to prevent enforcement of the punishment. Similarly, if the witnesses recant, punishment is not enforced.

Leading scholars have different views on what constitutes doubt. Imām Abū Ḥanīfah blocks enforcement of the punishment if what is stolen is considered common property in the first place, even though it has been subsequently placed within private ownership. This applies to stealing water from someone's private place or stealing game animals after they have been hunted. Abū Ḥanīfah's view is that since such matters are in the first place common property, there is doubt as to their remaining so after being kept in a private place. Mālik, al-Shāfiʿī and Aḥmad, the founders of the other three schools of Islamic law, are of the view that the punishment of cutting off a thief's hand is enforceable in these cases. Abū Ḥanīfah also blocks enforcement of this punishment in the case of stealing something which may become rotten after a short period of time, as in the case of stealing raw meat or other types of food. The other three schools of law as well as Abū Yūsuf, the second highest ranking scholar of the Ḥanafī school, disagree.

To discuss the different views of scholars in detail is beyond the scope of this commentary. They can be easily referred to in books of *Fiqh*. We have cited these examples to demonstrate how lenient Islam is and how keen it is not to enforce punishment in any case of doubt. God's Messenger (peace be upon him) clearly said: "Block the enforcement of prescribed punishments in any case of doubt." Whilst ʿUmar ibn al-Khaṭṭāb said: "To suspend punishment as a result of doubt is much more preferable to me than to enforce it despite doubt."

A Punishment to Fit the Crime

Having explained the reasons for imposing such a stern punishment for theft in the land where Islamic law is implemented, providing all guarantees of justice and fair distribution as well as the means of protection for all, we need to say a word about the suitability of this punishment to the crime of theft in a Muslim community.

When someone thinks of stealing, he actually thinks of increasing what he owns at the expense of someone else. He feels that what he earns legitimately is too little for him and, therefore, he wishes to add to it in an illegitimate way. The fruits of his own labour do not satisfy his greed and he wants to appear to be wealthy or to get himself in a position where he does not need to work or where he is assured of a comfortable life in future. In short, the motive for stealing is to increase one's income or one's wealth. Islam counters this motive by prescribing the punishment of cutting off the thief's hand or leg, since such a punishment will markedly decrease the thief's ability to work and reduce his income and wealth. When a thief is punished according to Islam, his ability to show off is greatly curtailed and his need to work hard is much greater. Moreover, his worry about his future is infinitely greater.

We see, then, that by prescribing the punishment of cutting off a thief's hand, Islamic law counters the psychological motives of theft with even stronger psychological factors which resist the temptation to steal. If a person, nevertheless, yields to temptation and is guilty of stealing, the severity of the punishment will have lasting effects on him, which will also prevent him from repeating the offence.

This is the basis for the Islamic punishment of theft. It is indeed the best basis for punishing this crime, ever since the creation of mankind.

Most legal codes punish theft with imprisonment, a punishment that has failed miserably in combating crime in general and theft in particular. This failure is due to the fact that imprisonment does not strengthen any psychological influence on a thief to turn him away from stealing. It does not prevent him from work and earning except for the duration of his time of imprisonment, when he has no need to earn since his basic needs are met. When he is discharged, he can go back to his work. Indeed, he has every chance to increase his wealth by both legitimate and illegitimate means. He can easily pretend to be a man of honour and integrity to secure the help of others. If eventually, he achieves his goal, well and good; or that is what he thinks. If not, his loss is minimal.

On the other hand, if a person guilty of stealing has his hand cut off, his punishment drastically reduces his ability to work and earn. This means in practical terms that his chances of increasing his income are almost lost, while a drastic reduction in income is most probable. He will not be able to win people's confidence as his own hand tells of his past crime. The unmistakable result, then, is that a thief will definitely end up in a loss situation if he is punished, while he is more likely to profit if he receives a prison sentence. It is in human nature that people do not hesitate to do what is likely to bring them profit and to refrain from something which makes loss a certainty.

I wonder at those who claim that the Islamic punishment of cutting off the hand of a thief is not suitable to our present society, in view of the great advancement achieved by mankind. Do progress and advancement mean that we should encourage and reward a thief and allow people to live in fear? Or do they mean that we should work hard so that thieves and drop-outs get away with the fruits of our labour? Or do they mean that we ignore the findings of science and human nature as well as the results of human experience and the conclusions of logical thinking in favour of an argument which is supported by new evidence, simply because it receives much propaganda?

If effectiveness in reducing crime is the criterion which makes a certain punishment fitting to an age of progress and advancement, then imprisonment should be abolished as a punishment for theft and replaced by cutting off thieves' hands. This is because the latter is supported by undeniable psychological evidence, human nature and experience as well as logic. While imprisonment as a punishment is supported by none of these.

The basis of this Islamic punishment is a thorough study of human nature and human thinking. It is then, suitable for both the individual and community because it reduces crime and increases security. As such, it is the best and fairest punishment.

Despite all this, some people object to the Islamic punishment for theft, because they find it cruel. Indeed, this is their only argument. But it is indeed a hollow argument, because no punishment is effective if it is felt not to be serious. Indeed, a punishment must be stern if it is to be a true punishment.[4]

God, who is the Most Compassionate of all those who exercise mercy, says as He makes the punishment for theft so severe: *"Cut off their hands in requital for what they have wrought, as an exemplary punishment ordained by God."* (Verse 38) It is, then, a stern punishment meant to be a deterrent. To deter someone from committing a crime is an act of mercy to that person, because he is prevented from becoming a criminal. It is also an act of grace to the whole community, because it ensures peace and security. No one may claim to be more merciful

---

4.   'Abd al-Qādir 'Awdah, *al-Tashrī' al-Jinā'ī al-Islāmī*, Vol. I., pp. 652–4 (Arabic).

to people than God who created them except one with a blind mind and a dull soul. Practical evidence shows that this punishment was not enforced except in a handful of cases during a period approaching a whole century at the beginning of Islam. This is because Islamic society, with its own system and severe punishments and the safeguards it puts in place, did not witness any more crimes.

God then opens the door for anyone who wishes to repent and mend his ways, adding to that a demonstration of positive intent through good action: *"But whoever repents after having thus done wrong, and makes amends, shall have his repentance accepted by God. God is Much-Forgiving, Merciful."* (Verse 39)

Wrongdoing is an active step that produces evil results. Hence, it is not sufficient that a wrongdoer should stop his evil action. He should move further and do some goodly work that produces good results. But the case is more profound in Islamic thinking. A human soul must always be active. If it stops its evil and corrupting work, without moving on to produce something good, it continues to lack fulfilment. This may bring about a setback returning it to evil. When it moves on to active goodness, it is more secure against a return to erring ways. This is, then, the method Islam follows in its work to produce a goodly society. It is a Divine method, meant by God, the Creator of all who knows what suits all, to produce the desired results.

Finally the *sūrah* states the overall principle of punishment in this life and in the Hereafter. God, the Creator and Owner of the universe, can will anything and determine the fate of every creature. It is He who enacts legislation for people to implement in their lives, and it is He who rewards them for their actions both in this life and in the life to come: *"Do you not know that to God belongs the kingdom of the heavens and the earth? He punishes whom He wills and forgives whom He wills. God has power over all things."* (Verse 40) It is then a single authority of dominion which issues legislation in this life and administers reward and retribution in the life to come. There is no division or multiplicity of authority. Indeed, human life can only be set right when the authority to legislate and to reward is united in both this life and the life to come.

4

The Right Basis for Judgement

Messenger, be not grieved by those who plunge headlong into unbelief; such as those who say with their mouths, "We believe", while their hearts do not believe. Among the Jews are some who eagerly listen to falsehood, eagerly listen to other people who have not come to you. They tamper with words out of their context, and say, "If such-and-such [a precept] is given you, accept it; but if you are not given it, then be on your guard." If God wants to put anyone to test, you shall not be able to avail him anything against God. Such are the ones whose hearts God is not willing to purify. They will have disgrace in this world, and awesome suffering in the life to come. (41)

يَٰٓأَيُّهَا ٱلرَّسُولُ لَا يَحْزُنكَ ٱلَّذِينَ يُسَٰرِعُونَ فِي ٱلْكُفْرِ مِنَ ٱلَّذِينَ قَالُوٓاْ ءَامَنَّا بِأَفْوَٰهِهِمْ وَلَمْ تُؤْمِن قُلُوبُهُمْ وَمِنَ ٱلَّذِينَ هَادُواْ سَمَّٰعُونَ لِلْكَذِبِ سَمَّٰعُونَ لِقَوْمٍ ءَاخَرِينَ لَمْ يَأْتُوكَ يُحَرِّفُونَ ٱلْكَلِمَ مِنۢ بَعْدِ مَوَاضِعِهِۦ يَقُولُونَ إِنْ أُوتِيتُمْ هَٰذَا فَخُذُوهُ وَإِن لَّمْ تُؤْتَوْهُ فَٱحْذَرُواْ وَمَن يُرِدِ ٱللَّهُ فِتْنَتَهُۥ فَلَن تَمْلِكَ لَهُۥ مِنَ ٱللَّهِ شَيْئًا أُوْلَٰٓئِكَ ٱلَّذِينَ لَمْ يُرِدِ ٱللَّهُ أَن يُطَهِّرَ قُلُوبَهُمْ لَهُمْ فِي ٱلدُّنْيَا خِزْيٌ وَلَهُمْ فِي ٱلْءَاخِرَةِ عَذَابٌ عَظِيمٌ ۝

103

They eagerly listen to falsehood and greedily devour what is unlawful. Hence, if they come to you (for judgement), you may either judge between them or decline to interfere. If you decline, they cannot harm you in any way. But if you do judge, then judge between them with fairness. God loves those who deal justly. (42)

سَمَّعُونَ لِلْكَذِبِ أَكَّلُونَ لِلسُّحْتِ فَإِن جَآءُوكَ فَٱحْكُم بَيْنَهُمْ أَوْ أَعْرِضْ عَنْهُمْ وَإِن تُعْرِضْ عَنْهُمْ فَلَن يَضُرُّوكَ شَيْـًٔا وَإِنْ حَكَمْتَ فَٱحْكُم بَيْنَهُم بِٱلْقِسْطِ إِنَّ ٱللَّهَ يُحِبُّ ٱلْمُقْسِطِينَ ۝

But how is it that they ask you for judgement when they have the Torah which contains God's judgement, and they still turn away? For certain, they are not true believers. (43)

وَكَيْفَ يُحَكِّمُونَكَ وَعِندَهُمُ ٱلتَّوْرَىٰةُ فِيهَا حُكْمُ ٱللَّهِ ثُمَّ يَتَوَلَّوْنَ مِنْ بَعْدِ ذَٰلِكَ وَمَآ أُو۟لَـٰٓئِكَ بِٱلْمُؤْمِنِينَ ۝

Indeed, it is We who revealed the Torah, containing guidance and light. By it did the prophets, who had surrendered themselves to God, judge among the Jews, and so did the divines and the rabbis: [they gave judgement] in accordance with what had been entrusted to their care of God's Book and to which they themselves were witnesses. So, have no fear of men but fear Me; and do not barter away My revelations for a paltry price. Those who do not judge in accordance with what God has revealed are indeed unbelievers. (44)

إِنَّآ أَنزَلْنَا ٱلتَّوْرَىٰةَ فِيهَا هُدًى وَنُورٌ يَحْكُمُ بِهَا ٱلنَّبِيُّونَ ٱلَّذِينَ أَسْلَمُوا۟ لِلَّذِينَ هَادُوا۟ وَٱلرَّبَّـٰنِيُّونَ وَٱلْأَحْبَارُ بِمَا ٱسْتُحْفِظُوا۟ مِن كِتَـٰبِ ٱللَّهِ وَكَانُوا۟ عَلَيْهِ شُهَدَآءَ فَلَا تَخْشَوُا۟ ٱلنَّاسَ وَٱخْشَوْنِ وَلَا تَشْتَرُوا۟ بِـَٔايَـٰتِى ثَمَنًا قَلِيلًا وَمَن لَّمْ يَحْكُم بِمَآ أَنزَلَ ٱللَّهُ فَأُو۟لَـٰٓئِكَ هُمُ ٱلْكَـٰفِرُونَ ۝

We decreed for them in it: a life for a life, an eye for an eye, a nose for a nose, an ear for an ear, a tooth for a tooth, and a similar retribution for wounds. But for him who forgoes it out of charity, it will atone for some of his sins. Those who do not judge in accordance with what God has revealed are indeed wrongdoers. (45)

وَكَتَبْنَا عَلَيْهِمْ فِيهَآ أَنَّ ٱلنَّفْسَ بِٱلنَّفْسِ وَٱلْعَيْنَ بِٱلْعَيْنِ وَٱلْأَنفَ بِٱلْأَنفِ وَٱلْأُذُنَ بِٱلْأُذُنِ وَٱلسِّنَّ بِٱلسِّنِّ وَٱلْجُرُوحَ قِصَاصٌ فَمَن تَصَدَّقَ بِهِ فَهُوَ كَفَّارَةٌ لَّهُۥ وَمَن لَّمْ يَحْكُم بِمَآ أَنزَلَ ٱللَّهُ فَأُوْلَٰٓئِكَ هُمُ ٱلظَّٰلِمُونَ ﴿٤٥﴾

We caused Jesus, the son of Mary, to follow in the footsteps of those (earlier prophets), confirming what had already been revealed before him in the Torah; and We gave him the Gospel, containing guidance and light, confirming what had already been revealed before it in the Torah and giving guidance and admonition to the God-fearing. (46)

وَقَفَّيْنَا عَلَىٰٓ ءَاثَٰرِهِم بِعِيسَى ٱبْنِ مَرْيَمَ مُصَدِّقًا لِّمَا بَيْنَ يَدَيْهِ مِنَ ٱلتَّوْرَىٰةِ وَءَاتَيْنَٰهُ ٱلْإِنجِيلَ فِيهِ هُدًى وَنُورٌ وَمُصَدِّقًا لِّمَا بَيْنَ يَدَيْهِ مِنَ ٱلتَّوْرَىٰةِ وَهُدًى وَمَوْعِظَةً لِّلْمُتَّقِينَ ﴿٤٦﴾

Let, then, the followers of the Gospel judge in accordance with what God has revealed therein. Those who do not judge in accordance with what God has revealed are indeed transgressors. (47)

وَلْيَحْكُمْ أَهْلُ ٱلْإِنجِيلِ بِمَآ أَنزَلَ ٱللَّهُ فِيهِ وَمَن لَّمْ يَحْكُم بِمَآ أَنزَلَ ٱللَّهُ فَأُوْلَٰٓئِكَ هُمُ ٱلْفَٰسِقُونَ ﴿٤٧﴾

And to you We have revealed the Book, setting forth the truth, confirming the Scriptures which had already been revealed before it and superseding them. Judge, then, between them in accordance with what God has revealed and do not follow their vain desires, forsaking thereby the truth that has come to you. To every one of you We have given a code of law and a way of life. Had God so willed, He could have made you all one community; but (it is His wish) to test you by means of that which He has bestowed on you. Vie, then, with one another in doing good works. To God you shall all return. He will then make you understand all that over which you now differ. (48)

وَأَنزَلْنَآ إِلَيْكَ ٱلْكِتَٰبَ بِٱلْحَقِّ مُصَدِّقًا لِّمَا بَيْنَ يَدَيْهِ مِنَ ٱلْكِتَٰبِ وَمُهَيْمِنًا عَلَيْهِ ۖ فَٱحْكُم بَيْنَهُم بِمَآ أَنزَلَ ٱللَّهُ ۖ وَلَا تَتَّبِعْ أَهْوَآءَهُمْ عَمَّا جَآءَكَ مِنَ ٱلْحَقِّ ۚ لِكُلٍّ جَعَلْنَا مِنكُمْ شِرْعَةً وَمِنْهَاجًا ۚ وَلَوْ شَآءَ ٱللَّهُ لَجَعَلَكُمْ أُمَّةً وَٰحِدَةً وَلَٰكِن لِّيَبْلُوَكُمْ فِى مَآ ءَاتَىٰكُمْ ۖ فَٱسْتَبِقُوا۟ ٱلْخَيْرَٰتِ ۚ إِلَى ٱللَّهِ مَرْجِعُكُمْ جَمِيعًا فَيُنَبِّئُكُم بِمَا كُنتُمْ فِيهِ تَخْتَلِفُونَ ﴿٤٨﴾

Hence, judge between them in accordance with what God has revealed, and do not follow their vain desires and beware of them lest they tempt you away from any part of what God has revealed to you. If they turn away, then know that it is God's will to afflict them for some of their sins. Indeed, a great many people are transgressors. (49)

وَأَنِ ٱحْكُم بَيْنَهُم بِمَآ أَنزَلَ ٱللَّهُ وَلَا تَتَّبِعْ أَهْوَآءَهُمْ وَٱحْذَرْهُمْ أَن يَفْتِنُوكَ عَنۢ بَعْضِ مَآ أَنزَلَ ٱللَّهُ إِلَيْكَ ۖ فَإِن تَوَلَّوْا۟ فَٱعْلَمْ أَنَّمَا يُرِيدُ ٱللَّهُ أَن يُصِيبَهُم بِبَعْضِ ذُنُوبِهِمْ ۗ وَإِنَّ كَثِيرًا مِّنَ ٱلنَّاسِ لَفَٰسِقُونَ ﴿٤٩﴾

Do they desire to be ruled by the law of pagan ignorance? But for those who are firm in their faith, who can be a better law-giver than God? (50)

أَفَحُكْمَ ٱلْجَٰهِلِيَّةِ يَبْغُونَ ۚ وَمَنْ أَحْسَنُ مِنَ ٱللَّهِ حُكْمًا لِّقَوْمٍ يُوقِنُونَ ﴿٥٠﴾

Overview

This ten-verse passage discusses the most important issue of the Islamic faith and its codes of living and justice. The same issue was discussed in the two preceding *sūrahs*, the House of 'Imrān and Women, but in this *sūrah* it involves a more direct and emphatic discussion. The subject is that of government, law and the administration of justice in matters of dispute. This is, indeed, a part of a more comprehensive issue, namely, faith and God's oneness. The whole matter can be summed up in the answer to this question: Are judgement and litigation to be conducted in accordance with covenants made with God, pursuant to His law? The task of implementing this law has been accepted by the followers of all Divine faiths. Moreover, is it a duty God has assigned to His messengers and those who succeed them in positions of authority? Or, will all that be subject to changing views and interests that are not based on a firm and constant foundation? In other words, do Godhead, lordship and authority in human life on earth belong to God, or do they belong, even partially, to any one of His creatures exercising the power to enact laws that are not endorsed by God?

God (limitless is He in His glory) says that He alone is the Godhead and He has no partners. His laws, enacted for His servants, mankind, and which they have pledged to Him to implement, must be the ones to enforce in this world. All disputes must be adjudicated by prophets and rulers on the basis of these laws.

God (glorified be He) says that no argument or concession can be admitted with regard to this principle nor can any deviation, however small, be condoned. Nor can anything approved in a particular generation or by a particular community be accepted if it is in conflict with what God has decreed.

God (limitless is He in His glory) says that this whole issue is one of faith or unfaith, Islam or non-Islam, Divine law or human prejudice. No compromise or reconciliation can be worked out between these two sets of values. Those who judge on the basis of the law God has revealed, enforcing all parts of it and substituting nothing else for it, are the believers. By contrast, those who do not make the law God has revealed the basis of their judgement are unbelievers, wrongdoers and transgressors. Rulers can either implement God's law in total and, thus, they remain within the area of faith, or they may enforce some other law. In this latter case, all three descriptions of unbelief, wrongdoing

107

and transgression apply to them. If people accept God's rule and judgement, administered by rulers and judges, then they are believers. Otherwise, they are not. There is no middle way between the two, nor can any justification or claim of serving legitimate interests be admitted. God, the Lord of mankind, knows what serves people's interests and He has enacted His laws for that very purpose. No law or system of government is superior to His. No servant of God may reject God's law or claim to have better knowledge than God with regard to what serves people's interests. If he makes such a claim, by word or deed, then he pronounces himself an unbeliever.

This highly important and fundamental issue is discussed in this passage in definitive statements. In addition, the passage describes the attitude of the Jews in Madinah and their cooperation with hypocrites in scheming against the Muslim community. God's Messenger is given advice on how to counter such scheming by the Jews, which began with the establishment of the Muslim state in Madinah.

In this passage, the *sūrah* states first that all religions revealed by God agree that His law must be implemented and should govern all human life. It is the acceptance of this condition that makes all the difference between faith and unfaith, Islam and other doctrines, Divine law and human caprice. This is clearly stated in the Torah revealed by God to provide guidance and light for mankind. *"By it did the prophets, who had surrendered themselves to God, judge among the Jews, and so did the divines and the rabbis: [they gave judgement] in accordance with what had been entrusted to their care of God's Book and to which they themselves were witnesses."* (Verse 44) *"They have the Torah which contains God's judgement."* (Verse 43) *"We decreed for them in it: a life for a life, an eye for an eye, a nose for a nose, an ear for an ear, a tooth for a tooth, and a similar retribution for wounds."* (Verse 45)

It is also endorsed by the Gospel God revealed to Jesus, son of Mary, which contains *"guidance and light, confirming what had already been revealed before it in the Torah and giving guidance and admonition to the God-fearing.* (Verse 46) *Let, then, the followers of the Gospel judge in accordance with what God has revealed therein."* (Verse 47)

It is further endorsed by the Qur'ān which God revealed to Muḥammad, His last Messenger, *"setting forth the truth, confirming the Scriptures which had already been revealed before it and superseding them."* (Verse 48) Muḥammad is instructed by God to *"judge between them in accordance with what God has revealed and do not follow their vain desires, forsaking thereby the truth that has come to you."* (Verse 48)

The ultimate verdict is thus pronounced: *"Those who do not judge in accordance with what God has revealed are indeed unbelievers."* (Verse 44) *"Those who do not judge in accordance with what God has revealed are indeed wrongdoers."* (Verse 45) *"Those who do not judge in accordance with what God has revealed are indeed transgressors."* (Verse 47) *"Do they desire to be ruled by the law of pagan ignorance? But for those who are firm in their faith, who can be a better law-giver than God?"* (Verse 50) In this way, the borders of faith and conditions of submission to God are clearly defined for both rulers and ruled. The criterion for rulers is to judge in accordance with what God has revealed, and for people to accept such a judgement and not to prefer anything else to it.

Stated in these terms, the issue is very serious indeed. Let us, therefore, try to identify the reasons for taking matters so seriously either in this particular passage or in the Qur'ān as a whole.

The first consideration is the fact that this whole matter is one of Godhead, Lordship and authority over mankind. These belong to God alone, who has no partners. Hence, it is a question of faith and submission to God or rejection and unfaith. This basic fact is explained throughout the Qur'ān.

God is the Creator of both the universe and man. He has made everything in the heavens and on earth subservient to man. Moreover, He is the only Creator. No one else creates anything in the universe. God is also the owner of the universe. To Him belongs the kingdom of the heavens and the earth and all that is in between. No one else owns anything in the universe. God is also the provider, and no one can provide anything for himself or for others. As He is the Creator, the owner and the provider, God has all authority over the universe and man. He, indeed, has the absolute power to do whatever He wishes.

To be a believer is to acknowledge that all these attributes belong solely and purely to God alone. To believe in Islam is to submit to the practical implications of these attributes. This is submission to God's law, which means, first and foremost, to acknowledge His Godhead, Lordship and authority. Refusal of God's law or the adoption of a different law in any small detail of human life is in effect a rejection of God's Godhead, Lordship and authority. Submission and rejection can be made by word of mouth or by deed. Hence, the whole issue is, as we have already explained, one of faith or unfaith, Islam or ignorance. Hence, the unequivocal statements made in this passage of the *sūrah*: *"Those who do not judge in accordance with what God has revealed are indeed unbelievers ... wrongdoers ... transgressors."* (Verses 44, 45 and 47)

The other consideration in this whole issue is the fact that God's law is inevitably and absolutely better for mankind than any man-made law. It is to this fact that the final verse in this passage refers: *"But for those who are firm in their faith, who can be a better law-giver than God?"* (Verse 50)

This total acknowledgement of the preferability of God's law in all stages and generations is also a part of the whole issue of faith or unfaith. No person can claim that the law enacted by a human being is better or equal to God's law at any stage of human life and claim at the same time that he is a believer or that he belongs to Muslims. By making such a claim, he is indeed claiming that he has better knowledge and superior wisdom than God in understanding mankind and conducting their affairs. Or he claims that certain conditions and needs have come up in human life and God (limitless is He in His glory) was unaware of them when He enacted His law, or was aware of them but did not provide for them in His law. Such a claim cannot be reconciled with that of faith and submission to God, no matter how insistently it is made.

The Superiority of Islamic Legislation

The wisdom and purpose behind Divine legislation may not appear in full to mankind in any particular generation. Furthermore, it is very difficult to give a full discussion of what we ourselves see of this wisdom. Therefore, we will only give brief hints.

God's law represents a complete way of life, which regulates and directs all aspects of human life in whatever stage and shape it finds them. This way of life relies on an infallible and true knowledge of man and his needs, and of the universe in which man lives and the laws that control the universe and human existence. As such, it does not ignore any matter of importance to human life. It does not allow or give rise to any destructive conflict between the different types of human activity or between such activity and natural laws. The reverse is true: it establishes proper balance and fine harmony. These can never result from any man-made system, since man's knowledge is confined to what is within human knowledge at a particular time. Any system which man devises must reflect human ignorance and lead to some conflict between different aspects of human activity. This will inevitably lead to violent shake-ups.

The Islamic system sets absolute justice as its goal. For one thing, it is God alone who knows how and by what means absolute justice can be established. For another, God is the Lord of all and He can establish justice between all. The system He lays down and the law He promulgates are free of prejudice, imbalance, extremism or ignorance. This cannot be said of any system or law which man devises, since man is influenced by his own prejudices, caprice and desire, and his vision is hampered by his imperfect knowledge. This applies to all human laws, whether they are enacted by an individual, a class, a nation or a generation. In no situation can man be free of his prejudices and desires and in none can he have perfect knowledge or a comprehensive, profound and perfect insight, not even in a single case for which a law is required.

Moreover, the Islamic system is in perfect harmony with the laws which govern the universe, because it is devised by the Creator of both the universe and man. When the Creator legislates for man, He treats him as an agent in this universe who has control over certain elements made subservient to him by the will of His Lord, on condition that he follows His guidance and learns the nature of these elements and the laws regulating them. This produces harmony between man and the universe in which he lives. The law which regulates human life acquires, then, a universal aspect to enable man to deal with all living things and objects in the whole universe on the basis of this law. Let us not forget in this context that man cannot break away from this universe. It is inevitable that he will have to deal with it on the basis of a proper and sound system.

Furthermore, the Islamic system is the only one which liberates man from subjugation by others. In all other systems, some people are subservient to others, and some look up to others. Only under the Islamic system do all people share the same position of being servants of God alone.

As we have explained, the most fundamental aspect of Godhead is legislation. When someone enacts legislation for a human community, he claims for himself the position of Godhead. People in that community become his servants instead of being God's servants. By giving the authority to legislate to God alone, Islam declares the liberation of mankind, or indeed, the rebirth of man. For man does not come into real existence unless he is liberated from subservience to another man and unless all human beings stand on an equal footing in front of the Lord of mankind.

This question which is fully discussed in the present passage is the top and most important question of faith. It is the question of Godhood and servitude, justice, freedom, equality and proper existence.

The state of darkness, as used in an Islamic context, does not refer to a particular period of history. Rather, it refers to a particular condition, which may be present in any period of time. In essence, it signifies making law and legislation subject to human desires, not to the Divine system. It is immaterial whether these desires are those of an individual, a class, a nation or a generation. They remain human desires.

An individual may enact laws for a certain community and the result is that the community lives in darkness because his desire or his opinion becomes the law. A class may legislate for the rest of the community and the result is darkness enshrouding its whole life because the interests of that class become law, or let us say, the opinion of the parliamentary majority become law. The representatives of all classes and all sectors in the nation may legislate for themselves, and the result is the same darkness engulfing the whole of life, because the desires of human beings and their imperfect knowledge become law, since people cannot be without prejudices and cannot acquire perfect knowledge. Or it may be the people's view that is the law. And a group of nations may legislate for mankind, but the result is still the same, because the national goals of those nations, or indeed the views of the international community become law. In each one of these situations, the difference is only in words.

But when the Creator of individuals, communities, nations and generations, legislates for all, the result is a Divine law which does not favour an individual, a community, a nation or a generation at the expense of others. God is the Lord of all and He treats them all equally. He knows the nature and the interests of all and He makes His law serve all their interests and meet all their needs in absolute justice. When anyone other than God legislates for mankind, people become subservient, be that person an individual, a class, a nation or the international community. But when God legislates for mankind, they are all free and equal. They bow in front of no one whatsoever and they submit to God alone. This explains how serious this question of legislation in human life and in the life of the universe is. *"Should the truth be subservient to their desires, the heavens and the earth and all those who are in them will become corrupted."* (23: 71) A judgement according to laws other than that revealed by God means evil, corruption and turning away from faith, as the Qur'ān itself says.

Playing Games with Divine Judgement

Messenger, be not grieved by those who plunge headlong into unbelief; such as those who say with their mouths, "We believe", while their hearts do not believe. Among the Jews are some who eagerly listen to falsehood, eagerly listen to other people who have not come to you. They tamper with words out of their context, and say, "If such-and-such [a precept] is given you, accept it; but if you are not given it, then be on your guard." If God wants to put anyone to test, you shall not be able to avail him anything against God. Such are the ones whose hearts God is not willing to purify. They will have disgrace in this world, and awesome suffering in the life to come. (Verse 41) They eagerly listen to falsehood and greedily devour what is unlawful. Hence, if they come to you (for judgement), you may either judge between them or decline to interfere. If you decline, they cannot harm you in any way. But if you do judge, then judge between them with fairness. God loves those who deal justly. (Verse 42) But how is it that they ask you for judgement when they have the Torah which contains God's judgement, and they still turn away? For certain, they are not true believers. (Verse 43)

It is apparently clear that these verses were revealed in the early years after the Prophet's settlement in Madinah where the Jews were part of its community. This means that they were revealed sometime before the attack on Madinah by the confederate tribes, and before severe punishment was inflicted on the Jewish tribe of Qurayẓah, or even much earlier. Most probably they were revealed when the two Jewish tribes of al-Naḍīr and Qaynuqāʿ were still in Madinah. The first of these two tribes were evacuated from Madinah after the Battle of Uḥud in the third year of the Islamic calendar and the Qaynuqāʿ were evacuated even before that. In that early period, the Jews concocted many of their tricks and manoeuvres, and the hypocrites received much support from them. Both groups plunged headlong into disbelief, even though the hypocrites might have claimed by word of mouth that they were believers. Their actions grieved the Prophet and caused him much distress.

God (limitless is He in His glory) consoles His Messenger (peace be upon him) and comforts him. He exposes to the Muslim community the truth about those who plunge headlong into disbelief, as did some of the Jews and the hypocrites. He directs His Messenger to the line of action he should adopt with them when they come to him for arbitration, after explaining to the Prophet what plots they have concocted before coming to him: *"Messenger, be not grieved by those who plunge headlong into unbelief; such as those who say with their mouths, 'We believe', while their hearts do not believe. Among the Jews are some who eagerly listen to falsehood, eagerly listen to other people who have not come to you. They tamper with words out of their context, and say, 'If such-and-such [a precept] is given you, accept it; but if you are not given it, then be on your guard'."* (Verse 41)

Some reports suggest that these verses speak of a group of Jews who committed certain sins including adultery and theft, which carry specific punishments outlined in the Torah. The Jews, however, at least in the first place, had established different punishments, because they did not want to enforce the provisions of the Torah on those of them who were in power. They later wanted to waive these punishments of the Torah in all cases. They replaced them with other punishments, as has been done by those who claim to be Muslims these days. When some of them committed these sins at the time of the Prophet, they thought to seek his judgement. If he judged according to the lesser punishments, which they had legislated, they would enforce them and justify their action to God by saying that they had enforced the verdict of His Messenger. If he judged that they should be punished according to the Torah, they would refuse his judgement. They, thus, sent some of their people to seek his ruling. This, then, explains their statement, *"If such-and-such [a precept] is given you, accept it; but if you are not given it, then be on your guard."* (Verse 41)

They had indeed gone that far in playing games with God's law and in being dishonest in their dealings with God and His Messenger (peace be upon him). This is a stage which can be reached by any people who, having received Divine revelation, have long ignored their duties. In such a situation hearts are hardened and the light of faith is stifled. Evasion of the laws and duties of their faith becomes the goal for which means are sought and rulings and justifications are found. Does this not apply today to those who claim to be Muslims and who *"say with their mouths, 'We believe', while their hearts do not believe."* (Verse 41) Do they not seek rulings to evade their religious duties, rather than carry them out? Do they not occasionally try to pay lip service to religion so that it may approve and endorse their desires? If religion insists on the word of the truth and the ruling of justice, they have no need for it: They say: *"If such-and-such [a precept] is given you, accept it; but if you are not given it, then be on your guard."* (Verse 41) The two situations are identical. Perhaps God has given us such an account of the history of the Children of Israel, so that future generations may be forewarned of the slips that lie along their way.

God (glorified be He) says to His Messenger with regard to those who rush into disbelief and those conspirators who engage in such schemes that he should not be grieved by such people's actions. They seek to create confusion and they will fall victim to it, while he [i.e. God's Messenger] himself has no say in the matter and cannot help them through their test when they have brought confusion upon themselves: *"If God wants to put anyone to test, you shall not be able to avail him anything against God."* (Verse 41) Such people have sunk their hearts into impurity, so God is unwilling to purify them: *"Such are the ones whose hearts God is not willing to purify."* (Verse 41) He will cause them to suffer ignominy in this life and grievous suffering in the Hereafter: *"They will have disgrace in this world, and awesome suffering in the life to come.* (Verse 41) He tells the Prophet not to worry about them, and not to be grieved by their disbelief. Their fate is sealed.

The *sūrah* goes on to give us further details of their situation and how far they have sunk into moral corruption, prior to giving guidance to the Prophet on how to deal with them: *"They eagerly listen to falsehood and greedily devour what is unlawful. Hence, if they come to you (for judgement), you may either judge between them or decline to interfere. If you decline, they cannot harm you in any way. But if you do judge, then judge between them with fairness. God loves those who deal justly."* (Verse 42)

Their listening to falsehood is repeated again, to suggest that this has become an established habit of theirs. They are pleased to listen to falsehood, and they are annoyed when they hear the voice of truth. This applies to all deviant hearts, corrupt souls and communities. To them, falsehood carries much appeal and the truth appears too hard. In these miserable days, falsehood sells like hot cakes, while the word of truth has no buyers.

Those people do not only listen to falsehood, but they greedily devour what is unlawful, prominent among which are usury, bribes and the price of false rulings and false testimony. Again, this evil quality spreads in all communities that deviate from God's law. The term the Qur'ān uses here for "unlawful" also connotes lack of blessings. Indeed, blessings are the first thing to be obliterated in deviant communities, as we see with our own eyes nowadays.

God has given the Prophet the choice whether to judge between them or to turn away from them, if they ask him for judgement. If he chooses not to pay any attention to them, they can harm him in no way. But if he chooses to judge between them then his must be a fair judgement, unaffected by their prejudices or their rushing into disbelief or by their plots and schemes: *"God loves those who deal justly."* (Verse 42)

God's Messenger (peace be upon him), Muslim rulers and judges deal directly with God in such matters and exert their efforts to establish justice in order to serve God because God loves those who deal justly. If people commit injustice or perjury or deviate from the truth, justice continues to carry its superior status. Fair judgement is not passed in order to please people but to please God. This is, indeed, the most effective guarantee provided by Islamic law everywhere and in all times.

A Baffling Attitude Towards God's Judgement

The fact that the Prophet was given this choice with regard to those Jews who came to him for judgement further supports our view that this was in the early period after the Prophet's settlement in Madinah. Later on, judgement according to Islamic law was compulsory, because the land of Islam does not enforce any law other than that of God. All people living there must refer their disputes to this law. This, however, does not contradict the Islamic rule which applies to people of earlier revelations living side by side with the Muslim community in the land of Islam. This principle makes only such laws as are endorsed by their faith or that relate to the general social order applicable to them. Permissible to them is what their religions permit them, such as owning and eating pork, the possession and drinking of intoxicants, but without their selling these to Muslims. But they are forbidden all usurious transactions because these are also forbidden in their religions. The punishments prescribed for adultery and theft are applicable to them, because they are stated in their Scriptures. Also enforceable are the punishments prescribed for rebellion against the legitimate authority, and for spreading corruption in the land. Such enforcement is necessary to guarantee the safety and security of the land of Islam and all its inhabitants, Muslims and non-Muslims alike. Such punishments cannot be waived in respect of anyone of those living in the land of Islam.

During that period in which the Prophet had the choice whether to judge between them or to ignore them, they used to come with some of their disputes to God's Messenger (peace be upon him). An example of this is reported by 'Abdullāh ibn 'Umar: "Some Jews came to God's Messenger (peace be upon him) and told him that a Jewish man and a Jewish woman committed adultery. The Prophet asked them: 'What does the Torah say about stoning adulterers?' They said: 'We publicise their crime and punish them by flogging.' 'Abdullāh ibn Sallām (a Jewish rabbi who had embraced Islam) said, 'This is a lie. The Torah prescribes stoning.' They brought the Torah and opened it up. One of them put his hand over the verse that mentioned stoning and read the preceding and the following verses. 'Abdullāh ibn Sallām told him to lift his hand off. When he did, the relevant verse on the death punishment by stoning was there. They said, 'He (meaning 'Abdullāh ibn Sallām) has told the truth. It specifies death by stoning.' The Prophet gave his orders for the two adulterers to be stoned to death. I saw the man bending over the woman to shelter her from the stones." (Related by al-Bukhārī and Muslim.)

Another example is given in a *hadīth* related by Imām Aḥmad on the authority of 'Abdullāh ibn 'Abbās, the Prophet's learned cousin, who says: "These verses were revealed in connection with two groups of Jews, one of which had triumphed over the others in pre-Islamic days. They later worked out a reconciliation agreement which stated that every victim of the defeated tribe killed by the victorious one would be compensated with blood money equal to fifty measures of agricultural produce, while every victim of the victorious tribe killed by the defeated one would have one hundred measures of agricultural produce as blood money. They operated this system until the Prophet (peace be upon him) migrated to Madinah. It so happened then that the defeated tribe killed a man of the victorious one. The latter sent them a message to prepare the full amount of blood money agreed, which was one hundred measures of agricultural produce. The defeated tribe said: 'How is it that two tribes belonging to the same faith, having the same ancestry and living in the same land, have two tariffs of blood money with one tariff being double the other? We had agreed to this measure of injustice you had imposed on us because we feared you. Now that Muḥammad has arrived in Madinah, we will not give you that.' War was about to flare up between the two tribes, before they agreed to refer the matter to God's Messenger for arbitration. The victorious tribe then reflected on this matter. Some of them said: 'Muḥammad will never give you twice the blood money you are prepared to give them. They indeed have told the truth when they said that they agreed to this as a matter of injustice imposed by us on them. Let us, then, sound out Muḥammad, to determine whether he will give us a favourable judgement. If so, we will refer the matter to him. If not, we will have been forewarned.' They sent to the Prophet some of their hypocrite friends to sound him out. God informed His Messenger of the whole affair and revealed to him the passage starting with *"Messenger, be not grieved by those who plunge headlong into unbelief; such as those who say with their mouths, 'We believe', while their hearts do not believe. Among the Jews are some who eagerly listen to falsehood, eagerly listen to other people who have not come to you. They tamper with words out of their context, and say, 'If such-and-such [a precept] is given you, accept it; but if you are not given it, then be on your guard'."* (Verse 41) (Related by Abū Dāwūd) Another version of this report names the victorious tribe as the al-Naḍīr and the defeated one as the Qurayẓah. This again supports our view that these verses were revealed in the early days of the Madinah period before these Jewish tribes were evacuated.

Indeed, the attitude of the Jews in such matters has always been consistent. Hence, the Qur'ān asks this rhetorical question: *"But how is it that they ask you for judgement when they have the Torah which contains God's judgement, and they still turn away?"* (Verse 43)

It is indeed a very grave and serious matter. They refer something to God's Messenger for arbitration and he judges between them on the basis of God's law. Moreover, they also have the Torah which contains

God's judgement. Both judgements are identical, because the Qur'ān has endorsed Divine judgements contained in the Torah. But they nevertheless, turn their backs on God's judgement, either in their dissatisfaction or by not enforcing it. This rhetorical question is followed by an Islamic rule in such matters: *"For certain, they are not true believers."* (Verse 43)

It is certainly not possible that a true believer will not submit to God's law or would not accept its rulings. Those who claim to themselves or to others that they believe and still refuse to implement God's law in their lives or who are not satisfied when it is enforced on them do indeed make false claims. Their attitude is described in this definitive statement: *"For certain, they are not true believers."* It is not simply a question of rulers not implementing God's law, but also a question of ordinary people not being satisfied with God's law and judgement. Such dissatisfaction takes them out of the ranks of believers, no matter how emphatically they claim to believe.

This Qur'ānic statement confirms a similar one in the preceding *sūrah*, "Women", which states: *"But no, by your Lord! They do not really believe unless they make you judge in all disputes between them, and then find in their hearts no bar to an acceptance of your decisions and give themselves up in total submission."* (4: 65) Both statements speak about the ruled, not the rulers. Both classify as unbelievers those who do not accept God's judgement as outlined by His Messenger and turn away from it.

As we have already said, the point at issue is that of acknowledging God's authority as the only God and His Lordship of mankind and the universe. To accept God's law and to be satisfied by its rules and judgements is the practical demonstration of accepting Him as the Supreme Godhead and the Lord of the universe. Rejecting the law and being dissatisfied with its judgement is a practical demonstration of disbelieving in God as such.

Light and Guidance Shine from the Torah

Such is God's verdict in relation to ordinary people who refuse to accept judgement in accordance with God's law. These have been described as unbelievers. Beginning with this verse, the *sūrah* speaks of rulers who do not judge in accordance with God's revelations. As we are soon to realise such judgements are endorsed by all religions revealed by God. The first reference is to the Torah: *"Indeed, it is We who revealed the Torah, containing guidance and light. By it did the prophets, who had surrendered themselves to God, judge among the Jews, and so did the divines and the rabbis: [they gave judgement] in accordance with what had been entrusted to their care of God's Book and to which they themselves were witnesses. So, have no fear of men but fear Me; and do not barter away My revelations for a paltry price. Those who do not judge in accordance with what God has revealed are indeed unbelievers.* (Verse 44) *We decreed for them in it: a life for a life, an eye for an eye, a nose for a nose, an ear for an ear, a tooth for a tooth, and a similar retribution for wounds. But for him who forgoes it out of charity, it will atone for some of his sins. Those who do not judge in accordance with what God has revealed are indeed wrongdoers."* (Verse 45)

Every religion revealed by God has been meant as a way of life. It has been so devised as to assume the leadership of human life and to organise, direct and protect it. No religion has been revealed by God only to be a set of personal, moral values or a set of rituals that are offered in a temple or a mosque. Necessary as both are for human life, and vital as they are in refining human conscience, they are not sufficient on their own to reorganise, direct and protect human life. They must provide the basis for a complete way of life and a code of law which are implemented and enforced. Any offence against them must be accounted for and punished, if necessary.

Human life cannot be properly organised unless it derives its faith, rituals, way of life and code of law from a single source which can exercise authority over consciences and behaviour alike. It must be able to administer reward and punishment according to its law in this life, and reward people in accordance with its own system of reckoning in the life to come.

Multiplicity of authority and source will only bring about results that are highly undesirable. If God's authority over consciences and rituals is recognised, but not over the law of the land, when reward in the Hereafter is according to God's law, but in this life it is subject to a different authority, then man is torn between two authorities moving in opposite directions. This leads to the total corruption of human life, as clearly and repeatedly mentioned in the Qur'ān: *"Had there been in heaven or on earth any deities other than God, they both would have fallen into ruin."* (21: 22) *"If the truth were to follow their caprice, the heavens and the earth and all those who live in them would have fallen into ruin."* (23: 71) *"We have set you on a way by which the purpose [of faith] may be fulfilled. Follow it, then, and do not follow the vain desires of those who are devoid of knowledge."* (45: 18)

For this reason every religion revealed by God has been designed to serve as a way of life. Whether directed to a single village, or to a particular nation, or for all generations of humanity, every religion brought, in addition to a faith setting out the proper concept of life and a set of worship rituals providing a strong link with God, a code of law to regulate human practices. Certain elements or aspects form the basis of every Divine religion. Human life cannot be set on a proper footing unless it follows Divine faith.

Numerous references in the Qur'ān show that early religions, some of which might have been addressed to small communities, contained all three mutually complementary aspects in a fashion suitable to that particular community's stage of development. At this point, such complementarity in the three major religions, Judaism, Christianity and Islam, is outlined, starting with the Torah: *"Indeed, it is We who revealed the Torah, containing guidance and light."* (Verse 44) As revealed by God, the Torah was the Book providing guidance for the Children of Israel, lighting up the way they should follow in life in order to lead them to God's pleasure. It contained the essence of monotheistic faith, and a variety of worship rituals, as well as a code of law: *"By it did the prophets, who had surrendered themselves to God, judge among the Jews, and so did the divines and the rabbis: [they gave judgement] in accordance with what had been entrusted to their care of God's Book and to which they themselves were witnesses."* (Verse 44)

God revealed the Torah to provide guidance and light not only for hearts and consciences with the faith and rituals it outlined, but also to provide guidance and light generated by the code of law which regulated practical life and protected it in accordance with God's system. The Prophets who had submitted themselves totally to God in absolute and complete dedication and who made no claim whatsoever to any attribute of Divinity, used to judge among the Jews on its basis. It was the law given to that particular community. So did the divines and rabbis, i.e. the Jewish scholars and judges, because they had been assigned the task of making sure that God's law was implemented and they were required to be witnesses to its truth. They would fulfil this task through organising their own lives in accordance with the directives and laws of the Torah and through implementing its laws within their communities.

Before finishing its reference to the Torah, the Qur'ān addresses the Muslim community with regard to judgements in accordance with revelations in general and the opposition people may show to such judgements. It also outlines the duty of everyone entrusted with the implementation of God's law and the punishment incurred by neglecting this duty: *"So, have no fear of men but fear Me; and do not barter away My revelations for a paltry price. Those who do not judge in accordance with what God has revealed are indeed unbelievers."* (Verse 44)

God knows that enforcing His revealed law will be met with opposition in every period of time and in every community. Some people will not easily submit to it. Those who have power, tyrants and despots, and those who claim authority by right of inheritance will put up stiff resistance to it, because they realise that its enforcement will deprive them of the mask of Godhead they wear and acknowledge Godhead as totally belonging to God alone. This is done through depriving them of their claimed authority to legislate and to judge in accordance with their legislation. Resistance will also be put up by those whose material interests can only be served through exploitation and injustice. God's just law will never endorse their unjust interests. Similarly, there will always be opposition to the implementation of God's law by those who pursue their vain desires and wanton caprice. A Divine religion will always require them to purify themselves from such evil, and will eventually punish indulgence in them. Further opposition will be put up by other quarters who dislike to see goodness, righteousness and justice flourish.

As God knows that opposition to His law will come from all these quarters, and that those to whose care His message is entrusted must face up to this opposition and make all the necessary sacrifices for its sake, He addresses them in these words: *"Have no fear of men but fear Me."* (Verse 44) No fear of tyrants, exploiters or deluded masses should deter them from implementing God's law. It is God alone that they should fear, because fearing Him dispels all other fear.

An Eye for an Eye, a Tooth for a Tooth

God also knows that some of those who are charged with the safekeeping and implementation of God's law may find worldly temptations too strong to resist. As they realise that people with power or money and those who seek all types of pleasure oppose God's legislation, they may flatter them in order to gain something of the riches and pleasures of this world. Professional clerics in all generations have yielded to such temptation, as did some Jewish rabbis. God addresses all those, saying to them: *"Do not barter away My revelations for a paltry price."* (Verse 44) That is the price they may get in return for their silence or for their distortion of God's revelations or for issuing doubtful rulings. Indeed, every price offered is paltry, even if it includes all that is in this world. How could it be described otherwise when it is no more than a position, a salary, a title and a petty interest for which faith is bartered away and Hell is purchased?

Nothing is more wicked than treachery by a person who is in a position of trust and nothing is more vile than the distortion of facts by a witness. Those who are given the title "religious men" do commit such treachery and distortion. They remain idle when they are called upon to work for the implementation of God's revelation and they lift words out of their context in order to please those in power at the expense of God's revelation.

In a most decisive and definitive statement, God tells us: *"Those who do not judge in accordance with what God has revealed are indeed unbelievers."* (Verse 44) The generality of this statement makes it absolutely unrestricted to time or place. The ruling is definitive and applicable to everyone who does not judge according to God's revelations, regardless of where and in which period he lives.

The reason is the one we have already explained. A person whose judgement is at variance with God's revelations denies that Godhead belongs to God alone. A basic quality of Godhead is the authority to legislate as also His sovereignty. Whoever observes something other than God's revelations in his judgement not only rejects a particular aspect of Godhead but also claims for himself certain qualities of Godhead. If that is not unbelief, I wonder what is. For what use is a verbal claim of being a believer or submitting to God, when action denies such a claim?

Any argument about this definitive and decisive ruling is no more than an attempt to avoid facing the reality. To try to give this ruling a different interpretation is simply an attempt to lift words out of their context. Such arguments change nothing of God's clear and definitive judgement.

Having explained this basic rule in all Divine faiths, the *sūrah* gives some examples of the law contained in the Torah which God revealed so that on its basis, prophets, divines, and rabbis might judge among the Jews: *"We decreed for them in it: a life for a life, an eye for an eye, a nose for a nose, an ear for an ear, a tooth for a tooth, and a similar retribution for wounds."* (Verse 45)

These provisions outlined in the Torah have been retained as an integral part of Islamic law, since it is meant to be the law of all mankind, till the end of time. It is true that these provisions may not be implemented except in the land of Islam, but this is only for practical reasons. Islamic authority cannot implement these provisions beyond the borders of the land of Islam. Whenever and wherever Muslim rulers can implement these laws, they are required to do so, since Islamic law is a code for all mankind in all generations. One provision has been added to them under Islam. This is the one to which reference is made in the following Qur'ānic statement: *"But for him who foregoes it out of charity, it will atone for some of his sins."* (Verse 45) This was not included in the law of the Torah. Retaliation was inevitable. No one could waive it or forego it. Hence, atonement of sins could not be achieved through such a charitable gesture.

A word on the concept of retaliation in punishment for injuries will not go amiss. The basic principle which is established through this concept is that of the equality of human beings and their equality before the law. No law other than Divine law acknowledges such an equality so as to make the punishment equal to the crime and to remove all considerations of class, position, lineage and race. This principle is amplified by its comprehensive application: *"A life for a life, an eye for an eye, a nose for a nose, an ear for an ear, a tooth for a tooth, and a similar retribution for wounds."* (Verse 45) There is no distinction between one class and another, rulers and ruled. All are equal before God's law, since they all descend from one single soul created by God.

This great principle established by God's law is the true and complete declaration of the birth of man when all human beings are considered equal, subject to the same law which rules on the basis of absolute equality. It is the first declaration of its kind. Human laws lagged behind for tens of centuries before they began to rise to its level, but even then, their aspirations have remained partial and theoretical. As for their practical application, human laws continue to lag behind.

The Jews, in whose Scripture, the Torah, this great principle was established, deviated from it in their relations with other people. They used to say: *"We have no obligation to keep faith with Gentiles."* (3: 75) They also deviated from it in their own internal relations, as we have already explained when two Jewish tribes in Madinah, the Qurayẓah and the al-Naḍīr established a system of blood money which gave the victorious twice as much as it gave the defeated. The Prophet Muḥammad (peace be upon him) brought them back to the implementation of God's law based on equality. He put them all on the same level.

Apart from its being a declaration of the birth of man, retaliation on the basis of equality is a most effective deterrent which makes anyone who contemplates killing another or causing him bodily harm think twice before putting his thoughts into action. He knows that regardless of his position, family connections, class or race, he will be executed for killing and he will suffer the same bodily harm as he causes.

If he cuts off a hand or a leg of another person, he will have his own hand or leg cut off; and if he destroys an eye, an ear, a nose or a tooth, he will be similarly impaired. But if he were only to face a period of imprisonment, long as it may be, for such actions, then he is unlikely to be deterred for long. His own physical agony or handicap is so very different from a period of imprisonment.

Moreover, retaliation on the basis of equality is the sort of punishment which appeals to human nature. It quenches the desire for revenge which may be fuelled by blind fury and it pacifies hearts and heals wounds. Some people may accept blood money while others insist on retaliation.

Under Islam, Divine legislation takes full account of human nature, just as it did in the Torah. Having ensured the satisfactory punishment of retaliation, Islam appeals to the benevolent element in human nature to encourage charitable forbearance: *"But for him who foregoes it out of charity, it will atone for some of his sins."* (Verse 45) It is up to the killed victim's next of kin or to the injured person himself in all cases of wounds and injuries to be charitable and forego retaliation. It is up to either person, out of his own free choice, to forego his right to retaliation and to accept blood money in place of it, or to forego both. If he does, God will forgive him some or all of his sins. It should be added, however, that even if such a person foregoes retaliation for blood money, the Muslim ruler may enforce a lesser punishment, as he deems fit, on the killer.

Guidance and Light Given in the Gospel

Such encouragement to show benevolence to forgive in the hope of being forgiven one's own sins by God may appeal to many a person to whom blood money or retaliation may be poor compensation for past losses. A next of kin may reflect on what benefit he may draw from having the killer executed, or what blood money would be for him. Neither will bring back the person who has been slain. It is true, however, that these punishments are the maximum that can be enforced in order to establish justice and to safeguard the community. But there remain certain feelings which cannot heal unless they look to God for compensation.

Imām Aḥmad relates that "a man from the Quraysh broke the tooth of a man from the Anṣār. The latter complained to Mu'āwiyah, (the overall ruler of the Islamic state). Mu'āwiyah said that he would satisfy him, (i.e. he was offering financial compensation). The Anṣārī man insisted on retaliation. Mu'āwiyah said: You may have your retaliation. Abū al-Dardā', one of the Prophet's Companions who was present said, 'I heard God's Messenger [peace be upon him] say: Any Muslim who suffers a physical injury and forgoes retaliation out of charity will be raised by God to a higher rank or will have some of his sins atoned.' The Anṣārī man said, 'I forgive him.'"

This is a typical case of readiness to forgive in the hope of receiving reward from God. Financial compensation had no similar appeal to the injured man. This gives us an idea of how effective God's law is, since it is based on a perfect knowledge of human nature, what motivates and satisfies people, as well as the type of legislation that gives people a feeling of peace and security.

Having explained this part of the law of the Torah, which has been incorporated into Qur'ānic law, the *sūrah* gives a general rule: *"Those who do not judge in accordance with what God has revealed are indeed wrongdoers."* (Verse 45) This is again a general rule worded in a most general mode. The description used here for those who refuse to judge in line with God's revelations is that they are wrongdoers. This, however, does not mean that this is a different case from the preceding one in which the same people are described as unbelievers. It is only an additional description of anyone who does not judge on the basis of God's revelations. He is first a disbeliever, since he does not acknowledge God's covenant and that He is the only one who has the authority to legislate. Since such a person claims such an authority for himself, he

126

actually claims a property of Godhead. Such a claim makes him an unbeliever. Moreover, he does wrong when he forces people to accept a law different from that laid down by their Lord, which ensures a better life for them. He also wrongs himself by putting himself in a position that incurs the punishment meted out to unbelievers. He wrongs his community by exposing its life to corruption.

The fact that both qualities apply to *"those who do not judge in accordance with what God has revealed"* is necessitated by the fact that the subject in both sentences use the same wording. Hence, both parts in the two statements are applicable.

The *sūrah* goes on to emphasise that this ruling remained in force in the period that followed the revelation of the Torah: *"We caused Jesus, the son of Mary, to follow in the footsteps of those (earlier prophets), confirming what had already been revealed before him in the Torah; and We gave him the Gospel, containing guidance and light, confirming what had already been revealed before it in the Torah and giving guidance and admonition to the God-fearing. (Verse 46) Let, then, the followers of the Gospel judge in accordance with what God has revealed therein. Those who do not judge in accordance with what God has revealed are indeed transgressors."* (Verse 47)

God gave Jesus, son of Mary, the Gospel so that it may serve as a way of life and a code of law. The Gospel did not present new legislation, but rather introduced a few modifications into the law of the Torah. It, thus, confirmed this earlier law by endorsing it with a few modifications. In the Gospel, God gave guidance, light and admonition, but only "to the God-fearing". It is the God-fearing who open their hearts to God's revealed Books and who find in them guidance, light and admonition. Hardened hearts, on the other hand, miss the meaning of the words and the essence of the directives. They neither appreciate the value of its words, benefit by the guidance and light provided, nor do they gain any new knowledge. The light is there, but it needs an open heart to benefit from it; guidance is available, but it only benefits a searching soul; and admonition is given but it is only picked up by a keen intellect.

As we have already said, God has provided in the Gospel guidance, light and admonition to the God-fearing. He made it a way of life and a code of law for its people. It is not, however, a universal message for all mankind. This is the case of the Gospel, the Torah and all books and messages revealed before the final message of the Qur'ān. Whatever provisions of legislation in the Gospel or in the Torah agree with those of the Qur'ān form part of the Qur'ānic law, as explained in connection with the case of retaliation.

The followers of the Gospel were, then, required to apply the legal code of the Torah, which was confirmed and endorsed by the Gospel: *"Let then, the followers of the Gospel judge in accordance with what God has revealed therein."* (Verse 47) The universal rule is to judge in accordance with God's revelations, to the exclusion of all other laws. Neither the Christians nor the Jews can have a sound basis unless they implement the Torah and the Gospel. That, however, is what applied prior to Islam. After the revelation of Islam, they must also implement all that was revealed by their Lord, because all of it forms a single law to which they must subscribe. *"Those who do not judge in accordance with what God has revealed are indeed transgressors."* (Verse 47)

This is again a very general statement which means that the quality of transgressing is added to the two earlier qualities of unbelief and wrongdoing, which were used to describe those who do not judge in accordance with God's revelations. The new description does not refer to any new case or any new group who are separate from those described in the first two verses. All three qualities are applicable to all those who reject God's revealed law, in all generations and in all nations.

They disbelieve when they reject God's law, and thereby reject that Godhead belongs solely to God. They are indeed wrongdoers when they impose on people a law other than that of God and help spread corruption in the land. They transgress when they deviate from the way of life chosen by God. All three descriptions apply to the same person in equal manner and he confirms them all through his actions.

A Book to Supersede All Scriptures

Having spoken about earlier Divine messages and laws, the *sūrah* now speaks of the final message which embodies Islam in its final and complete form. It is the religion revealed for all mankind, giving a law which supersedes all preceding laws and forms the final arbiter in all affairs and disputes. It outlines a way of life which regulates all aspects of all human activities and gives a basis for the formulation of a concept of faith, a social system and a code for personal and social behaviour. None of this is given as an academic exercise. It must be implemented in full. Nothing of it may be substituted by something else. People either accept this and be true Muslims, or refuse it and follow ignorance and vain desires. No one may justify any deviation by claiming that he is uniting people by being flexible in matters of religion. Had God so willed, He would have made all mankind a single community. What He wants of us is to implement His law and let people decide on how they want to conduct their lives.

And to you We have revealed the Book, setting forth the truth, confirming the Scriptures which had already been revealed before it and superseding them. Judge, then, between them in accordance with what God has revealed and do not follow their vain desires, forsaking thereby the truth that has come to you. To every one of you We have given a code of law and a way of life. Had God so willed, He could have made you all one community; but (it is His wish) to test you by means of that which He has bestowed on you. Vie, then, with one another in doing good works. To God you shall all return. He will then make you understand all that over which you now differ. (Verse 48) Hence, judge between them in accordance with what God has revealed, and do not follow their vain desires and beware of them lest they tempt you away from any part of what God has revealed to you. If they turn away, then know that it is God's will to afflict them for some of their sins. Indeed, a great many people are transgressors. (Verse 49) Do they desire to be ruled by the law of pagan ignorance? But for those who are firm in their faith, who can be a better law-giver than God? (Verse 50)

This is a definitive statement, expressed in the clearest of terms. It takes extreme care to forestall any temptation to abandon even a small part of this law, regardless of the circumstances. When one reflects on this, one is bound to wonder how a person who claims to be a Muslim can abandon God's law in its totality, justifying his action by force of circumstance. How can he find it in himself to continue to claim that he is a Muslim after so doing? How can people call themselves Muslims when they have refused to acknowledge God's Godhead, turned their backs on God's law and denied its suitability for all situations!

"And to you, We have revealed the Book, setting forth the truth." (Verse 48) Since it is revealed by God, the only One who has the authority to enact laws, then it certainly sets forth the truth. Everything that it contains of matters of faith, law, directives and stories are true.

Hence, it is the Book of the truth. Moreover, it confirms *"the Scriptures which had already been revealed before it and superseding them."* (Verse 48) It, thus, provides the final version of the Divine faith. It is the final arbiter not only in this regard, but also with regard to the way of life mankind should follow, the legislation that should be implemented and the system that should be established. No modification is admissible. Any disagreement over any of these matters, whether between followers of Divine religions or between Muslims themselves, must be referred to this Book. No opinion advanced by any human being has any value unless it is supported by this final authority.

As this is an undeniable fact, it must have its practical implementation: *"Judge, then, between them in accordance with what God has revealed and do not follow their vain desires, forsaking thereby the truth that has come to you."* (Verse 48) This command is addressed in the first instance to God's Messenger (peace be upon him) with respect to those of the followers of earlier religions who came to him for arbitration. But its import is not confined to this particular aspect. It is a general order, applicable till the end of time since there will never be a new messenger or a new message to modify anything in this final version of God's message to mankind.

This religion has been made complete, and through it God has perfected the grace He has bestowed on Muslims. Moreover, God has been pleased to choose this religion as a way of life for all mankind. As we have repeatedly said, no modification or amendment is possible or admissible. When God chose it for human life, He knew its inherent suitability. As God makes it the final arbiter, He knows that it benefits all mankind and that it can be implemented in all generations till the Day of Judgement. Anyone who seeks to modify it, let alone abandon it altogether, takes himself out of the fold of Islam altogether, even though he reiterates a thousand times his claim to be a Muslim.

Twice in this short passage God warns the Prophet (peace be upon him) against yielding to the desires of those who come to him for arbitration trying to tempt him away from any part of his revelations. At times, the thought may occur to some people that under certain circumstances, a certain provision of God's law may be modified or set aside. One such motivation could be the desire to establish a measure of unity among all sects and faiths living in the same country. Some people, however, may advocate a conciliatory attitude in matters which may not appear to be so fundamental.

Some reports suggest that the Jews in Madinah made an offer to the Prophet (peace be upon him) that they would follow him, if he agreed to waive certain provisions of the law including that of stoning adulterers. These reports suggest that the warning contained in these verses relate to that particular offer. It is perfectly clear, however, that the order given here has general application. The followers of this Divine faith may face similar temptations and similar offers. God chooses to give His final word in such matters and to leave no room for a compromise. He tells His Messenger that had He so willed, He would have made all mankind a single community. But He has chosen to give each community a code of law and a way of life in order to test them according to what He has given them. Each community will follow its own way but they will all return to God when He will hold them accountable for their actions and the method they had chosen to implement. He will tell them the truth over which they differ. As such, no compromise can be pursued in order to unite those who differ in method and way of life. Such a unification is out of the question: *"To every one of you We have given a code of law and a way of life. Had God so willed, He could have made you all one community; but (it is His wish) to test you by means of that which He has bestowed on you. Vie, then, with one another in doing good works. To God you shall all return. He will then make you understand all that over which you now differ."* (Verse 48)

As we clearly see, God has left no loophole. Even when a compromise may promise good results, such as national unity, it is inadmissible. God's law is too precious for any part of it to be sacrificed in return for something which God knows will never happen. People have been created with varying susceptibilities and different methods and ways. God has created them so for a particular purpose of His. He has offered them His guidance and called on them to vie with one another in doing good works. When they return to Him, He rewards them according to their deeds.

The Temptation to Abandon God's Law

It is a false notion to try to unite people at the expense of God's law. Moreover, the attempt is bound to fail. The price asked is too high, since any modification of God's law will lead to corruption on earth, injustice and the subservience of some people to others. This is, indeed,

131

a great evil. If no compromise of God's law is admissible for pursuing the noble purpose of uniting people, how can it be justified for something which is more petty. Some of those who claim to be Muslims argue that God's law should not be implemented so that we do not lose the tourist trade! Absurdity knows no limit!

> *Hence, judge between them in accordance with what God has revealed, and do not follow their vain desires and beware of them lest they tempt you away from any part of what God has revealed to you. If they turn away, then know that it is God's will to afflict them for some of their sins. Indeed, a great many people are transgressors.* (Verse 49) *Do they desire to be ruled by the law of pagan ignorance? But for those who are firm in their faith, who can be a better law-giver than God?* (Verse 50)

Again, this principle is stated with greater clarity. In the first statement, the Prophet is instructed in these words: *"Judge, then, between them in accordance with what God has revealed, and do not follow their vain desires, forsaking thereby the truth that has come to you."* (Verse 48) This statement may be construed as meaning abandoning God's law in total and following their vain desires in preference to it. In the second part, the Prophet is warned against compromising even a portion of what has been revealed to him: *"Judge between them in accordance with what God has revealed, and do not follow their vain desires and beware of them lest they tempt you away from any part of what God has revealed to you."* (Verse 49) The warning here is more precise, stricter and stronger. It also states the matter in its true nature. It is a temptation which must be resisted. The choice is either to implement God's law in full, or to follow vain desires.

At that time, they had the choice whether to refer their disputes to God's law, a choice which was later abrogated in the land of Islam. God's law has to be implemented except in those areas where the followers of other religions have specific provisions. These they are allowed to implement. As this was the case, the Prophet is told not to worry about them if they do not like his commitment to every detail of God's law or if they turn away from Islam: *"If they turn away, then know that it is God's will to afflict them for some of their sins. Indeed, a great many people are transgressors."* (Verse 49) Do not worry about them if they turn away. Do not let their attitude weaken your resolve to implement God's law in full. It is they who will suffer as a result of their turning away because God will then afflict them with their sins. Neither the Prophet, nor the Muslim community, nor indeed God's law will come to any harm as a result of their turning away. Moreover, it is in human nature that many people will transgress. The Prophet is told that he has no say in this state of affairs. Nor is it the fault of God's law. It is they who will not follow the right path.

Having made it absolutely clear to all believers that nothing of the provisions of God's law will be compromised for any purpose and under any circumstances, the *sūrah* then contrasts the choices available. It is either God's law or man-made law, based on inadequate knowledge and vain desire. There can be no meeting ground between the two. *"Do they desire to be ruled by the law of pagan ignorance? But for those who are firm in their faith, who can be a better law-giver than God?"* (Verse 50)

This statement defines the meaning of *jāhiliyyah*, rendered here as "pagan ignorance", as the term is used in the Qur'ān. *Jāhiliyyah* means that people are ruled by people, because this signifies that they submit to one another. They refuse to submit to God alone and reject His Godhead, acknowledging instead that some human beings have qualities of Godhead and hence they submit to their authority. As such, the term pagan ignorance, or *jāhiliyyah*, does not refer to a particular period of time, but to a certain situation which may come into existence at any time. Whenever it exists, it must be described as *jāhiliyyah* which is in contrast to Islam.

In all ages and places, people may implement God's law, yielding no part of it for any reason, submitting to it willingly. As such, they follow the religion chosen for them by God. Alternatively, they may acknowledge and implement a man-made law in any shape or form. As such they follow ignorance. In this latter situation, they submit to the one who gives them the law and they cannot be described as following God's religion. Anyone who does not wish to be ruled by God's law actually desires to be ruled by the law of pagan ignorance. It is at this point that the two ways part and people are left to their choices.

The final sentence is a rhetorical question which decries their pursuit of the law of *jāhiliyyah* and emphasises the superiority of God's law: *"For those who are firm in their faith, who can be a better law-giver than God?"* (Verse 50) Indeed, who can be? Who can claim that he can give people a better law than that of God? What argument can be given to prove this hollow claim? Can anyone say that he knows mankind's nature better than their Creator? Can he say that he is more compassionate and sympathetic to mankind than God? Can he say that he knows their interests better than the God of mankind? Or can he say that when God promulgated the final version of His law and sent His last Messenger to all mankind, giving him the final and complete version of the Divine message, He might have been unaware of future circumstances and needs and as a result did not take them into account in His legislation?

What can anyone say in justification of setting God's law aside and substituting for it a law of *jāhiliyyah*, placing in the process his own desires, or those of a particular community or generation, above God's law? What can he say if, in spite of this, he still claims to be a Muslim? What is his justification: circumstances, events, people's unwillingness, or fear of the enemy? Were all these not known to God when He commanded Muslims to implement His law and follow His way of life and never be tempted away from any part of His revelations? Or does he justify his attitude by claiming that God's law does not cater for new needs and new situations? Were these needs and situations not known to God when He made this very stern warning? A non-Muslim may say anything he wants, but what can those who claim to be Muslims say of any of this and imagine that they continue to be within the fold of Islam? As we have said: this is the point where the ways part. It is either Islam or *jāhiliyyah*, faith or unfaith, the rule of God or the rule of pagan ignorance. Those who choose not to judge in accordance with what God has revealed are unbelievers, wrongdoers and transgressors. People who do not accept God's law are not believers.

This question must be absolutely clear in every Muslim's mind. Unless it be so, a Muslim will not be able to differentiate between truth and falsehood and will not be able to take one step in the right direction. If it is still not that clear to some people, it cannot remain so in the minds of those who want to claim for themselves the most honourable title of being Muslim.

5

Delineation of an Essential Relationship

Believers, do not take the Jews and the Christians for your allies. They are allies of one another. Whoever of you allies himself with them is indeed one of them. God does not bestow His guidance on the wrongdoers. (51)

۞ يَـٰٓأَيُّهَا ٱلَّذِينَ ءَامَنُوا۟ لَا تَتَّخِذُوا۟ ٱلْيَهُودَ وَٱلنَّصَـٰرَىٰٓ أَوْلِيَآءَ بَعْضُهُمْ أَوْلِيَآءُ بَعْضٍ وَمَن يَتَوَلَّهُم مِّنكُمْ فَإِنَّهُۥ مِنْهُمْ إِنَّ ٱللَّهَ لَا يَهْدِى ٱلْقَوْمَ ٱلظَّـٰلِمِينَ ﴿٥١﴾

Yet you see those who are sick at heart rush to their defence, saying, "We fear lest a change of fortune should befall us." God may well bring about victory (for believers) or some other event of His own making, and those (waverers) will terribly regret the thought they had secretly harboured within themselves. (52)

فَتَرَى ٱلَّذِينَ فِى قُلُوبِهِم مَّرَضٌ يُسَـٰرِعُونَ فِيهِمْ يَقُولُونَ نَخْشَىٰٓ أَن تُصِيبَنَا دَآئِرَةٌ فَعَسَى ٱللَّهُ أَن يَأْتِىَ بِٱلْفَتْحِ أَوْ أَمْرٍ مِّنْ عِندِهِۦ فَيُصْبِحُوا۟ عَلَىٰ مَآ أَسَرُّوا۟ فِىٓ أَنفُسِهِمْ نَـٰدِمِينَ ﴿٥٢﴾

The believers will say: "Are these the self-same people who swore by God their most solemn oaths that they were with you?" All their works are in vain and they will lose all. (53)

وَيَقُولُ ٱلَّذِينَ ءَامَنُوٓا۟ أَهَـٰٓؤُلَآءِ ٱلَّذِينَ أَقْسَمُوا۟ بِٱللَّهِ جَهْدَ أَيْمَـٰنِهِمْ إِنَّهُمْ لَمَعَكُمْ حَبِطَتْ أَعْمَـٰلُهُمْ فَأَصْبَحُوا۟ خَـٰسِرِينَ ﴿٥٣﴾

Believers, if you renounce your faith, God will bring forth (in your stead) people whom He loves and who love Him, humble towards the believers, proud towards the unbelievers. They will strive hard for God's cause and will not fear to be censured by any critic. Such is God's favour which He grants to whom He wills. God encompasses all and knows all. (54)

يَـٰٓأَيُّهَا ٱلَّذِينَ ءَامَنُواْ مَن يَرْتَدَّ مِنكُمْ عَن دِينِهِ فَسَوْفَ يَأْتِى ٱللَّهُ بِقَوْمٍ يُحِبُّهُمْ وَيُحِبُّونَهُۥٓ أَذِلَّةٍ عَلَى ٱلْمُؤْمِنِينَ أَعِزَّةٍ عَلَى ٱلْكَـٰفِرِينَ يُجَـٰهِدُونَ فِى سَبِيلِ ٱللَّهِ وَلَا يَخَافُونَ لَوْمَةَ لَآئِمٍ ذَٰلِكَ فَضْلُ ٱللَّهِ يُؤْتِيهِ مَن يَشَآءُ وَٱللَّهُ وَٰسِعٌ عَلِيمٌ ٥٤

Your patron is only God, and His Messenger and those who believe – those who attend to their prayers, pay their *zakāt* (i.e. purifying alms) and bow down in worship. (55)

إِنَّمَا وَلِيُّكُمُ ٱللَّهُ وَرَسُولُهُۥ وَٱلَّذِينَ ءَامَنُواْ ٱلَّذِينَ يُقِيمُونَ ٱلصَّلَوٰةَ وَيُؤْتُونَ ٱلزَّكَوٰةَ وَهُمْ رَٰكِعُونَ ٥٥

Those who ally themselves with God and His Messenger and the believers (will find that) the party of God will be victorious. (56)

وَمَن يَتَوَلَّ ٱللَّهَ وَرَسُولَهُۥ وَٱلَّذِينَ ءَامَنُواْ فَإِنَّ حِزْبَ ٱللَّهِ هُمُ ٱلْغَـٰلِبُونَ ٥٦

Believers, do not take for your friends those among the people of earlier revelations who mock at your faith and make a jest of it or those who are unbelievers. Fear God, if you are truly believers. (57)

يَـٰٓأَيُّهَا ٱلَّذِينَ ءَامَنُواْ لَا تَتَّخِذُواْ ٱلَّذِينَ ٱتَّخَذُواْ دِينَكُمْ هُزُوًا وَلَعِبًا مِّنَ ٱلَّذِينَ أُوتُواْ ٱلْكِتَـٰبَ مِن قَبْلِكُمْ وَٱلْكُفَّارَ أَوْلِيَآءَ وَٱتَّقُواْ ٱللَّهَ إِن كُنتُم مُّؤْمِنِينَ ٥٧

For, when you call to prayer, they mock at it and make a jest of it. They do this because they are people who do not use their reason. (58)

وَإِذَا نَادَيْتُمْ إِلَى ٱلصَّلَوٰةِ ٱتَّخَذُوهَا هُزُوًا وَلَعِبًا ذَٰلِكَ بِأَنَّهُمْ قَوْمٌ لَّا يَعْقِلُونَ ۝

Say: People of earlier revelations! Do you find fault with us for any reason other than that we believe in God [alone], and in that which has been revealed to us as well as that which has been revealed previously, while most of you are transgressors? (59)

قُلْ يَـٰٓأَهْلَ ٱلْكِتَٰبِ هَلْ تَنقِمُونَ مِنَّآ إِلَّآ أَنْ ءَامَنَّا بِٱللَّهِ وَمَآ أُنزِلَ إِلَيْنَا وَمَآ أُنزِلَ مِن قَبْلُ وَأَنَّ أَكْثَرَكُمْ فَٰسِقُونَ ۝

Say: Shall I tell you who, in God's sight, deserves an even worse retribution than these? They whom God has rejected and who have incurred His anger, and whom He has turned into apes and pigs, and who worship false gods. These are yet worse in station and they have gone farther astray from the right path. (60)

قُلْ هَلْ أُنَبِّئُكُم بِشَرٍّ مِّن ذَٰلِكَ مَثُوبَةً عِندَ ٱللَّهِ مَن لَّعَنَهُ ٱللَّهُ وَغَضِبَ عَلَيْهِ وَجَعَلَ مِنْهُمُ ٱلْقِرَدَةَ وَٱلْخَنَازِيرَ وَعَبَدَ ٱلطَّٰغُوتَ أُوْلَٰٓئِكَ شَرٌّ مَّكَانًا وَأَضَلُّ عَن سَوَآءِ ٱلسَّبِيلِ ۝

When they come to you, they say: "We believe", whereas, in fact, they come unbelievers and depart unbelievers. God is fully aware of all that they would conceal. (61)

وَإِذَا جَآءُوكُمْ قَالُوٓا ءَامَنَّا وَقَد دَّخَلُواْ بِٱلْكُفْرِ وَهُمْ قَدْ خَرَجُواْ بِهِۦ وَٱللَّهُ أَعْلَمُ بِمَا كَانُواْ يَكْتُمُونَ ۝

You see many of them rushing into sin and transgression and in devouring the fruits of unlawful gain. Evil indeed is that which they do. (62)

وَتَرَىٰ كَثِيرًا مِّنْهُمْ يُسَٰرِعُونَ فِى ٱلْإِثْمِ وَٱلْعُدْوَٰنِ وَأَكْلِهِمُ ٱلسُّحْتَ لَبِئْسَ مَا كَانُواْ يَعْمَلُونَ ۝

Why do not their divines and their rabbis forbid them to make sinful assertions and to devour the fruits of unlawful gain? Evil indeed is that which they contrive. (63)

لَوۡلَا يَنۡهَىٰهُمُ ٱلرَّبَّـٰنِيُّونَ وَٱلۡأَحۡبَارُ عَن قَوۡلِهِمُ ٱلۡإِثۡمَ وَأَكۡلِهِمُ ٱلسُّحۡتَ لَبِئۡسَ مَا كَانُواْ يَصۡنَعُونَ ﴿٦٣﴾

The Jews say: "God's hand is shackled!" It is their own hands that are shackled. Rejected [by God] are they for what they say. Indeed, both His hands are outstretched. He bestows [His bounty] as He wills. But that which has been revealed to you by your Lord is bound to make many of them more stubborn in their overweening arrogance and unbelief. We have cast enmity and hatred among them, [to last] until the Day of Resurrection. Every time they light a fire for war, God puts it out. They labour hard to spread corruption on earth; and God does not love those who spread corruption. (64)

وَقَالَتِ ٱلۡيَهُودُ يَدُ ٱللَّهِ مَغۡلُولَةٌ غُلَّتۡ أَيۡدِيهِمۡ وَلُعِنُواْ بِمَا قَالُواْ بَلۡ يَدَاهُ مَبۡسُوطَتَانِ يُنفِقُ كَيۡفَ يَشَآءُ وَلَيَزِيدَنَّ كَثِيرًا مِّنۡهُم مَّآ أُنزِلَ إِلَيۡكَ مِن رَّبِّكَ طُغۡيَٰنًا وَكُفۡرًا وَأَلۡقَيۡنَا بَيۡنَهُمُ ٱلۡعَدَٰوَةَ وَٱلۡبَغۡضَآءَ إِلَىٰ يَوۡمِ ٱلۡقِيَٰمَةِ كُلَّمَآ أَوۡقَدُواْ نَارًا لِّلۡحَرۡبِ أَطۡفَأَهَا ٱللَّهُ وَيَسۡعَوۡنَ فِي ٱلۡأَرۡضِ فَسَادًا وَٱللَّهُ لَا يُحِبُّ ٱلۡمُفۡسِدِينَ ﴿٦٤﴾

If only the people of earlier revelations would believe and be God-fearing, We should indeed efface their [past] bad deeds, and bring them into gardens of bliss. (65)

وَلَوۡ أَنَّ أَهۡلَ ٱلۡكِتَٰبِ ءَامَنُواْ وَٱتَّقَوۡاْ لَكَفَّرۡنَا عَنۡهُمۡ سَيِّـَٔاتِهِمۡ وَلَأَدۡخَلۡنَٰهُمۡ جَنَّٰتِ ٱلنَّعِيمِ ﴿٦٥﴾

If they would observe the Torah and the Gospel and all that has been revealed to them by their Lord, they would indeed be given abundance from above and from beneath. Some of them do pursue a right course, but many of them are of evil conduct. (66)

وَلَوْ أَنَّهُمْ أَقَامُوا ٱلتَّوْرَىٰةَ وَٱلْإِنجِيلَ وَمَآ أُنزِلَ إِلَيْهِم مِّن رَّبِّهِمْ لَأَكَلُوا مِن فَوْقِهِمْ وَمِن تَحْتِ أَرْجُلِهِم مِّنْهُمْ أُمَّةٌ مُّقْتَصِدَةٌ وَكَثِيرٌ مِّنْهُمْ سَآءَ مَا يَعْمَلُونَ ﴿٦٦﴾

Overview

This passage confirms that not all the verses of this *surah* were revealed after *Sūrah* 48, The Conquest, or *al-Fath,* which was revealed after the peace agreement signed at al-Hudaibiyah between the Muslims and the unbelievers of the Quraysh in the sixth year of the Islamic calendar. Indeed, several passages in this *surah* were, most probably, revealed well before that, perhaps before the evacuation from Madinah of the Jewish tribe of the Qurayẓah in the fourth year, if not even earlier, i.e. before the evacuation of the al-Naḍīr and Qaynuqā' Jews. A number of verses in this *surah* refer to events and situations that took place within the Muslim community in Madinah as also the circumstances and attitudes adopted by the Jews and hypocrites. These could not have taken place after the power of the Jews was finally broken with the evacuation of the Qurayẓah.

We have, for example, a clear warning against taking the Jews and the Christians as allies. The warning states that whoever establishes an alliance with them actually belongs to them. There is another reference to the fact that those who were sick at heart maintained an alliance with them protesting that they feared a change of fortune. The Muslims are warned against maintaining an alliance with those who mock their faith. There is a clear reference to the fact that the Madinah Jews did mock the Muslims' prayer, making a jest of it. None of this could have happened unless the Jews enjoyed a degree of power and influence in

Madinah. Otherwise, there would have been no call for such a clear warning and a threat. Nor would there be any need for exposing the true nature of the Jews, condemning them and denouncing their scheming in such a manner which uses a variety of styles and expressions.

Some reports suggest that certain verses in this passage directly relate to specific events. Some refering to the confrontation with the Jewish Qaynuqā' tribe which followed the Battle of Badr. At that time, 'Abdullāh ibn Ubayy was keen to demonstrate his special relationship with the Jews, and declared, "I am a man who fears a change of fortune, and, therefore, I will not disown my alliances." Even without these reports, an objective study of these statements in relation to the events that took place in Madinah at the time of the Prophet is sufficient to support our view concerning its time of revelation.

Verses in this passage provide a few glimpses of the Qur'ānic method in educating the Muslim community and preparing it to assume the role God assigned to it. They also explain some of the constituent elements in this method as well as a few principles Islam likes to see established in the minds of individual Muslims as well as in the Muslim community. These elements and principles are constant and apply to all generations, since they influence the very making of the Muslim individual and the Muslim community.

The cornerstone of the Qur'ānic method of moulding a true Muslim is to instil in him that his allegiance must be given, pure and total, to his Lord, God's Messenger, his faith, and the Islamic community. This is coupled with the need to instil in one's consciousness the complete distinction between the Islamic camp and any camp that does not raise God's banner, follow God's Messenger or belong to God's party. The Muslim is also to be made to feel that he is chosen by God to be a means of accomplishing His will in human life and history. Such a choice, with all its attending duties, is a demonstration of God's limitless bounty which He bestows on whom He wills. To be in alliance with a community other than that of the Muslims is to turn away from God's faith and reject His choice and bounty. This message is clearly given in several places in the forthcoming passage, such as verses 51 and 54–6.

The Qur'ān also cultivates a Muslim's understanding of the true nature of his enemies and the war they wage against him. It is a battle of faith since faith is the permanent issue between a Muslim and all his enemies. They take a hostile attitude towards him primarily on account of his faith and because they have deviated from Divine faith. Hence, they hate everyone who follows it with diligence and a clear conscience: *"Say: People of earlier revelations! Do you find fault with us for any reason other than that we believe in God [alone], and in that which has been revealed to us as well as that which has been revealed previously, while most of you are transgressors?"* (Verse 59) This is, indeed, the crux of the matter.

This method and its essential directives are of great importance. To be totally dedicated to God and His Messenger, to faith and the Muslim community and to know the true nature of the battle and the enemies are conditions of vital importance in the fulfilment of the conditions of true faith. They are also a prerequisite in the moulding of a true Muslim and the organisation of the Muslim community. Those who claim to be advocates of this faith do not truly believe in it and are not able to accomplish anything of value on earth unless they come to feel that they are a community apart. They are different from all other communities and camps except for those who raise the same Islamic banner, dedicate their total allegiance to God and His Messenger and have a leadership who shares their belief in God and His Messenger. They will also have to know the true nature of their enemies and their motives, and the nature of the battle they have to fight against them. They also need to know that all their enemies are in actual alliance against them and that they patronise one another in fighting the Muslim community and the Islamic faith.

In this passage, we are not only told of the true motives of the Muslim community's enemies. Instead, the very nature of those enemies and the extent of their transgression are also exposed so that every Muslim is aware of whom he fights and is reassured as to the justice and the inevitability of this fight. Verses 51, 57, 58, 61 and 64 describe these enemies very clearly, highlighting their main characteristics. Those who take such an attitude towards the Muslim community, mock at its faith and prayer and make a jest of them, must be repelled by every Muslim.

This passage also defines the outcome of this battle and points out the value of faith in the destiny of communities in this life as well as in the life to come: *"Those who ally themselves with God and His Messenger and the believers (will find that) the party of God will be victorious."* (Verse 56) *"If only the people of earlier revelations would believe and be God-fearing, We should indeed efface their [past] bad deeds, and bring them into gardens of bliss. If they would observe the Torah and the Gospel and all that has been revealed to them by their Lord, they would indeed be given abundance from above and from beneath."* (Verses 65–6)

The passage also tells us of the qualities that must be present in a Muslim whom God chooses to be an advocate of His faith, bestowing on him by such choice a favour that is great indeed: *"Believers, if you renounce your faith, God will bring forth (in your stead) people whom He loves and who love Him, humble towards the believers, proud towards the unbelievers. They will strive hard for God's cause and will not fear to be censured by any critic. Such is God's favour which He grants to whom He wills. God encompasses all and knows all."* (Verse 54)

All these statements represent aspects of the Qur'ānic method of moulding the Muslim individual and the Muslim community. It is a method that lays down the best of foundations.

Alliances That Cannot Survive

Believers, do not take the Jews and the Christians for your allies. They are allies of one another. Whoever of you allies himself with them is indeed one of them. God does not bestow His guidance on the wrongdoers. Yet you see those who are sick at heart rush to their defence, saying, "We fear lest a change of fortune should befall us." God may well bring about victory (for believers) or some other event of His own making, and those (waverers) will terribly regret the thought they had secretly harboured within themselves. The believers will say: "Are these the self-same people who swore by God their most solemn oaths that they were with you?" All their works are in vain and they will lose all. (Verses 51–3)

It is most important to begin by defining the meaning of the alliance the believers are forbidden by God to maintain with the Jews and Christians. It is to establish a relationship of mutual support so as to forge one block with them. It has nothing to do with following their faith. It is extremely unlikely that we find among Muslims anyone who may be inclined to follow the Jewish or Christian faith. It is rather the type of alliance involving mutual help that was unclear to some Muslims who initially thought it permissible. It was a fact of life that there were mutual ties and interests between the Arabs in Madinah and groups of Jews. These developed into alliances between the two prior to Islam and continued in the early days after most Arabs in Madinah adopted Islam. Later, God ordered the Muslims not to enter into such alliances with the Jews of Madinah.

The term "alliance", or its Arabic equivalent *walā'*, is well known and has a precise meaning in Islamic terminology. It occurs in the context of the relationship that the Muslims in Madinah were required to have with Muslims who did not migrate to the land of Islam. God says in the Qur'ān: *"You have no alliance with them until they have emigrated."* (8: 72) It is obvious that what is meant here is not support in faith, because every Muslim is a supporter in faith to every other Muslim in all situations. The reference here is to the sort of alliance and patronage that requires mutual cooperation and military assistance. This latter relationship does not exist between Muslims in the land of Islam and those who do not join them in their land. It is this very sort of relationship which these verses block between believers and Jews and Christians in any situation, although it used to exist between them and the Jews in the early days of Islam in Madinah.

Islam insists that its followers maintain an attitude of maximum tolerance towards the people of earlier revelations. To take them as allies and patrons, however, is a different matter altogether. The two may be confused by those who have not formulated a clear concept of the essence of the Islamic faith and its role as a practical and methodical movement aiming to establish a particular order in life according to the unique Islamic concept. As such, Islam clashes with other concepts and situations as it conflicts with people's desires, and hence their deviation and transgression. Thus, it inevitably finds itself engaged in a necessary struggle to establish the new situation.

Those who are thus confused lack a clear vision of the true nature of this faith and a proper understanding of the nature of the battle and the attitude adopted by the people of other religions concerning it. They overlook the clear Qur'ānic directives relating to it. In their minds, the emphasis Islam places on extending a tolerant attitude towards the people of earlier revelations and the need to treat them with kindness in the Muslim community in which they live, enjoying all their rights, is, thus, confused with the alliance that is owed by every Muslim to God, His Messenger and the Muslim community. They forget what the Qur'ān asserts of the people of earlier revelations, of their being allied one with another in fighting the Muslim community. This is their constant attitude. They are hostile to the Muslims because of their faith. They will not be happy with a Muslim unless he abandons his religion and follows theirs. Hence, they persist with their fight with Islam and the Muslim community. Hostility may be clear in what they may say, but what their hearts conceal is much worse.

A Muslim is required to show tolerance in dealing with the people of earlier revelations, but he is forbidden to have a relationship of alliance or patronage with them. His path to establish his religion and implement his unique system cannot join with theirs. No matter how kind he is to them, they will never be happy to implement his faith and establish his system. Nor will it stop them from entering other alliances to scheme against and fight the Muslims. It is too naïve to think that we and they can ever join forces to support religion in general against unbelievers and atheists. For whenever the fight is against Muslims, they join forces with the unbelievers and atheists.

The naïve among us tend to overlook this truth when we think that we can establish an alliance with the people of earlier revelations, i.e. the Christians and Jews, in order to check the advance of materialism and atheism, since we are all people of faith. We forget the teachings of the Qur'ān and the lessons of history. Those very people of earlier revelations used to say to the pagan Arabs that they were *"better guided than the believers"*. (4: 51) It is they who stirred the unbelievers and mobilised them into launching a determined attack against the Muslim community in Madinah. Those people of earlier revelations were the ones who launched the Crusades against the land of Islam, which extended over a period of 200 years. It is they who organised the Spanish Inquisition. In recent history, they turned the Muslim Arabs of Palestine out of their land in order to give it to the Jews. In doing so, they were in alliance with atheism and materialism. The same people of earlier revelations persecuted the Muslims in Abyssinia, Somalia, Eritrea, and Algeria. They further collaborated with atheism, materialism and polytheism in the persecution of Muslims in Yugoslavia, China, Turkistan, India and in many other places.

Nevertheless, totally oblivious to such definitive Qur'ānic statements, some of us may entertain thoughts that we can establish a relationship of alliance or patronage with these people of earlier revelations in order to repel the attacks of atheist materialism on religion. Such people do not read the Qur'ān. If they do, they confuse Islam's attitude of tolerance with the forging of an alliance with such people. It is against this that Islam warns the Muslims. Such people do not actually live

Islam as the only faith acceptable to God or as an active movement seeking to establish a new order on earth. This new order will inevitably stand up to the hostility of today's people of earlier revelations, just as it repelled it in the past. This positive attitude cannot change since it is the only natural one. We, therefore, leave such people in their confusion to reflect on this clear Qur'ānic directive: *"Believers, do not take the Jews and the Christians for your allies. They are allies of one another. Whoever of you allies himself with them is indeed one of them. God does not bestow His guidance on the wrongdoers."* (Verse 51)

Distinctive Values of the Muslim Community

In the first instance, this verse is an address to the Muslim community in Madinah. It is at the same time directed to every Muslim community which comes into existence in any part of the world at any point in time. Its message is meant for every group that may be described as "believers". The particular occasion which necessitated this address was the need for the Muslims in Madinah to have a clearer view of the ties of allegiance which would mould them into a distinct community, totally separate from the people of earlier revelations, especially the Jews. There were ties of alliance, financial dealings, neighbourliness, friendship, etc. All this was natural in the light of the historical, economical, and social conditions which prevailed in Madinah prior to the advent of Islam. This situation, however, allowed the Jews to engage in their scheming against Islam and its followers, as exposed in many Qur'ānic statements, some of which we discussed in the three earlier volumes of this work. The present passage though provides an opportunity to discuss other aspects of this scenario.

As Muslims engage in a fight to establish their new system as a living reality, the Qur'ān provides them with the necessary concept to create, in their subconscious, a sense of distinction between them and all those who do not belong to their community. This distinction does not preclude tolerance and kind treatment; for these come naturally to a Muslim. It only precludes a relationship of alliance, of the sort a Muslim owes only to God, His Messenger and the community of believers. All Muslims, in all generations, have this awareness and feel this distinction: *"Believers, do not take the Jews and the Christians for your allies. They are allies of one another."* (Verse 51)

The fact that they are allies of one another has nothing to do with any particular period of time because it is rooted in the nature of things. They have never been allies with the Muslim community in any land or in any period of history. One generation succeeded another, confirming the truth of this accurate statement. Ever since their collaboration in fighting the Prophet Muḥammad (peace be upon him) and the Muslim community in Madinah, they have maintained their own alliance in all parts of the world at all times. Never was there any exception to this rule. Never did this planet witness anything other than that stated in the Qur'ān as a universal fact. In the original Arabic text the mode of expression selected is the one which is normally used to state permanent facts.

As this is a permanent fact, its consequences are clearly stated. Since the Jews and the Christians are allies of one another, they can only be patronised by someone of their own kind. If someone from the Islamic camp establishes an alliance with them, he actually removes himself from the Muslim camp, abandons the basic quality of Islam and joins the other camp. For this is the natural and practical result: *"Whoever of you allies himself with them is indeed one of them."* (Verse 51) He, thus, wrongs himself and wrongs the Divine faith of the Muslim community. Because of his wrongdoing, God puts him in the same group with the Jews and Christians to whom he has pledged his support and made himself an ally. God neither guides him to the truth nor returns him to the Muslim ranks: *"God does not bestow His guidance on the wrongdoers."* (Verse 51)

This statement represents a very stern warning to the Muslim community in Madinah. Stern it certainly is, but not exaggerated. It simply describes the reality as it is. It is not possible for a Muslim to ally himself with the Jews and Christians and still retain his faith as someone who truly submits himself to God. He simply cannot keep his membership of the Muslim community which acknowledges alliances only with God and His Messenger, and with those who believe.

It is not possible for a Muslim to adopt a "wet" attitude towards the concept of complete distinction between himself and the Muslim community on the one side, and those who follow a system or raise a banner other than that of Islam on the other. If a Muslim does so then he is no longer able to make any contribution or be of any value to the overall Islamic movement, whose first and most essential goal is the establishment of a unique system based on a truly unique concept.

A Muslim believes, with an absolute certainty which admits no hesitation or wavering, that since the Prophet Muḥammad (peace be upon him) has conveyed his message to mankind, his faith is the only one acceptable to God. He believes that the system God required him to adopt as the basis of life is a unique system and cannot be replaced or substituted by another. It is the only one that can realise the full potential of human life. The only way for a Muslim to earn God's forgiveness and acceptance is to exert his maximum effort in establishing both the ideological and social aspects of this system, changing no part of it, however small, and mixing it with no other system, be it religious, social or legal. The only exception is made in the case of what God has chosen to retain of earlier legislation and revelation, incorporating them as He did into the Islamic system.

When a Muslim believes in all this with absolute certainty, he actually has the right motivation to work for the establishment of the system God has chosen for human life, knowing what that involves of hard struggle and pain that often goes beyond what man can normally bear. He also knows that he has to encounter difficult impediments, determined resistance and unending plots. Otherwise, what need is there to go to such trouble if ignorant systems, whether polytheistic, atheistic or based on deviant doctrines, can be made suitable substitutes? Why do we need to trouble ourselves in establishing the Islamic system if the differences between it and the systems of people of earlier revelations or other people are minor, cosmetic or easily ironed out?

Those who try to advocate a less decisive distinction in the name of tolerance and establishing a meeting ground between the followers of Divine faiths are actually mistaken in their concept of faith and their concept of tolerance. The true faith acceptable to God is the final version of His message to mankind. Tolerance remains in the field of personal relations and has nothing to do with ideological concepts or with the social system. These people try to weaken a Muslim's conviction that God does not accept any faith other than that of Islam, which is based on total submission to God alone. They also try to weaken his belief that it is his responsibility to establish the Divine system of Islam and to accept no substitute or amendment to it, however minor. Such a firm conviction is established in a Muslim's mind by Qur'ānic statements such as these: *"The only true faith acceptable to God is [man's] self-surrender to Him."* (3: 19) *"He who seeks a religion other than self-surrender to God, it will not be accepted from him."* (3: 85) *"Beware of them lest they tempt you away from any part of what God has revealed to you."* (Verse 49) *"Believers, do not take the Jews and the Christians for your allies. They are allies of one another. Whoever of you allies himself with them is indeed one of them."* (Verse 51) It is the Qur'ān which has the final say. A Muslim should pay no heed to the attempts of those who try to weaken his resolve or water down his firm beliefs.

The Best Insurance for the Future

The Qur'ān describes the conditions which prevailed in Madinah, and against which it warns the Muslims: *"Yet you see those who are sick at heart rush to their defence, saying, We fear lest a change of fortune should befall us."* (Verse 52)

A report by 'Aṭiyah ibn Sa'd mentions that 'Ubādah ibn al-Ṣamit, a leading figure of the Anṣār from the tribe of the Khazraj, came to the Prophet and said: "Messenger of God. I have a large number of Jewish allies and I disown all alliances with the Jews seeking only the patronage of God and His Messenger." 'Abdullāh ibn Ubayy (the chief hypocrite in Madinah) said: "I am a man who fears changes of fortune. I do not disown my alliances." God's Messenger [peace be upon him] said to 'Abdullāh ibn Ubayy: "Abū al-Ḥubāb, the alliance with the Jews which you seem to value more highly than 'Ubādah ibn al-Ṣamit is left up to you, but not up to him." He said, "I accept." In this respect, then, God revealed the Qur'ānic verse: *"Believers, do not take the Jews and the Christians for your allies."* (Verse 51)

Another report by al-Zuhrī mentions that after the Battle of Badr in which the Muslims achieved a resounding victory, the Muslims said to their Jewish allies: "You had better embrace Islam before God punishes you with a defeat like the one that befell the idolaters in Badr." A Jew called Mālik ibn al-Ṣayf said: "Do not be deluded by the fact that you could defeat a group of the Quraysh who have no knowledge of warfare. If we resolve to collaborate against you, you will have no power to stand up to us." 'Ubādah ibn al-Ṣamit said: "Messenger of God, my Jewish allies have been numerous, well-armed, and very mighty. Nevertheless, I disown all alliances with the Jews to pledge allegiance only to God and His Messenger." 'Abdullāh ibn Ubayy said:

"But I do not disown my alliance with the Jews. I am a man who needs them." God's Messenger, [peace be upon him] said to him: "Abū al-Ḥubāb, your Jewish alliance which you value much more highly than 'Ubādah ibn al-Ṣāmit is given to you as a privilege, but not to him." He said: "I accept."

Muḥammad ibn Isḥāq reports: The first Jewish tribe to violate their treaty with God's Messenger were the Banū Qaynuqā'. It is reported that God's Messenger lay siege to them until they submitted themselves to his rule. 'Abdullāh ibn Ubayy went to him then and said: "Muḥammad, be kind to my allies." The Prophet did not answer him immediately, so he said again: "Muḥammad, be kind to my allies." The Prophet turned away from him, and so he put his hand inside the Prophet's body armour, but the Prophet told him to let go. The Prophet was angry and it appeared in his face. He said to 'Abdullāh: "What are you doing? Let me go!" 'Abdullāh ibn Ubayy said: "By God I will not let you go until you are kind to my allies." There are four hundred unarmoured and three hundred with armour, and they have protected me from all people and you want to get them all in one morning? I am a man who fears changes of fortunes." The Prophet said to him: "They are yours."

Muḥammad ibn Isḥāq also reports: When the Jewish tribe of Qaynuqā' fought against God's Messenger, 'Abdullāh ibn Ubayy took their case and defended them. On the other hand, 'Ubādah ibn al-Ṣāmit, who had the same alliance with them as that of 'Abdullāh ibn Ubayy, went to the Prophet and disowned them. He said: "Messenger of God, I release myself from their alliance and pledge allegiance only to God, His Messenger and the believers. I have no need for an alliance with unbelievers." It is concerning him and 'Abdullāh ibn Ubayy that verses 51–6 of *Sūrah* 5, The Repast, were revealed.

Imām Aḥmad reports on the authority of Usāmah ibn Zayd, a young Companion of the Prophet: "I went with God's Messenger [peace be upon him] to visit 'Abdullāh ibn Ubayy, who was ill. The Prophet said to him (during the conversation): "I used to counsel you against loving the Jews." 'Abdullāh said: "As'ad ibn Zurārah [one of the earliest people from Madinah to embrace Islam] used to hate them and he died."

Taken together, these reports give us a clear idea of the situation in the Muslim community of Madinah, the relations inherited from pre-Islamic days and the concepts that were totally clarified about the sort of ties which may and may not exist between the Muslim community and the Jews. It is noteworthy that all these reports speak of the Jews and none of them mention the Christians. Nevertheless, the Qur'ānic verse speaks of both Jews and Christians because it seeks to establish a permanent concept about the ties and situations which could prevail between the Muslim community and other communities, whether they followed earlier revelations or were non-believers, as will be mentioned later in this passage.

The Qur'ān also refers later in this *surah* to the differences between the attitudes of the Jews and Christians towards the Muslim community at the time of the Prophet: *"You will find that of all people, the most hostile to the believers are the Jews and those who associate partners with God, and the closest friends are those who say: We are Christians."* (Verse 82) Nevertheless, despite the differentiation, the Qur'ān equates the Jews and the Christians at this point and equates both groups with the non-believers in a later verse with regard to the question of alliance and patronage. This is due to the fact that this question relates to a permanent principle which states that a Muslim may not have an alliance except with another Muslim. The only patrons for the Muslim are God, His Messenger and the Muslim community. Beyond these, all sects and groups are the same, although they may adopt different attitudes towards the Muslims in different situations.

When God laid down this uncompromising and decisive principle for the Muslim community, He confirmed it on the basis of His own knowledge which encompassed all time, not only that particular period during the lifetime of His Messenger and its special circumstances. Later events of history have revealed that the hostility of the Christians to this religion and to the Muslim community in most parts of the world has not been less than the hostility of the Jews. If we single out the attitude of the Arab Christians and the Christians of Egypt in extending a warm welcome to Islam, we find that, ever since it came into contact with Islam, the wider Christian area in the West has always harboured grudges and hatred and waged a determined war against it. These cannot be described as different from what the Jews harbour against Islam and the war they have waged against it throughout history. Even Abyssinia, whose ruler had received well the Muslims who emigrated to his land at the time of the Prophet, is now as hostile to Islam and Muslims as the Jews.

Since God knew all this in advance, He laid down this general principle, regardless of the particular circumstances pertaining at the time of the Qur'ānic revelations or any other particular circumstances which may exist at any time in history.

Islam and those who claim to be its followers, highly questionable as their claim may be, continue to be at the receiving end of an unabating war launched against them and their faith by Jews and Christians all over the globe. This is the practical confirmation of what God says: *"They are allies of one another."* (Verse 51) Any Muslim who respects his intelligence, should pay heed to His Lord's advice, or indeed His clear command, implementing His final decision to establish a complete distinction between those who are in alliance with God and His Messenger and those who raise a different banner.

Islam requires every Muslim to establish his ties with all people on the basis of faith. To a Muslim, alliance or hostility can only be in relation to faith. Hence, alliance and patronage cannot exist between a Muslim and a non-Muslim, since they cannot be allies in faith. Not even against atheism can such an alliance be forged, as imagined by some of us who either do not read the Qur'ān or who are too naïve in outlook. How can a Muslim and a non-Muslim be allies when there is no common ground between them?

When Hypocrisy is Laid Bare

Some of those who do not read the Qur'ān properly and do not know the true nature of Islam, and some who are deceived may think that all religions are the same while all denial of faith is the same. They imagine that all those who "respect religion" can stand together in one camp against atheism because atheism opposes all religions and stands against the very idea of being religious. This is, however, unacceptable to Islamic thinking. Nor does it sound right to a person who appreciates Islam as it should be appreciated: as an ideology giving rise to a movement seeking to implement the Islamic system.

In Islamic thinking and to a true Muslim's understanding, matters are clear and simple. Submission to God is the essence of faith. Islam, which means submission, does not recognise any religion which is not based on submission to God, because God says this in the Qur'ān: *"The only true faith acceptable to God is [man's] self-surrender to Him."* (3: 19) He also says: *"He who seeks a religion other than self-surrender to God, it will not be accepted from him."* (3: 85) After the Prophet's message was delivered there is no longer any religion acceptable to

God except this religion of Islam in the form preached by the Prophet Muḥammad (peace be upon him). What used to be accepted from Christians before the Prophet Muḥammad's mission is no longer acceptable, in the same way as what used to be accepted from the Jews before Jesus was no longer acceptable after he was given his message.

The fact that there have lived, after the mission of the Prophet Muḥammad, Jewish and Christian people does not mean that God will accept from them what they do or recognise what they follow as a Divine religion. That was the case before God's last Messenger was sent. Now that he has conveyed his message, there is no longer any acceptable faith other than Islam. The Qur'ān makes a statement of this fact which admits no other interpretation.

Islam does not force anyone to abandon his faith in order to embrace Islam because the Islamic principle is clear: *"There shall be no compulsion in religion."* (2: 256) This, however, does not mean that Islam acknowledges that they have a faith of their own, in the Islamic sense of the word. Hence, there can be no "religious front", as it were, which Islam may join in opposition to atheism. From the Islamic point of view, there is a religious faith, which is Islam, and a non-religion which includes everything other than Islam. "Non-religion" may take many forms including a faith of Divine origin, if distortion has crept into it, or a pagan faith, or an absolute denial of faith altogether. These doctrines may have their disagreements, but they are all in conflict with Islam and there can be no alliance between them and Islam.

As has already been explained, every Muslim is required to deal fairly and kindly with the people of earlier revelations, unless they persecute him on account of his religion. He is permitted to marry from among their chaste women although scholars have different views on whether a Muslim is permitted to marry a Christian who believes in the divinity of Jesus Christ, or claims that he was son of God, or one who believes in the Trinity. Even when we accept the permissibility of marrying a Christian woman, fair treatment and inter-marriages do not mean that a relationship of alliance and patronage may be forged. Such concessions cannot be construed as acknowledgement that, after the message of the Prophet Muḥammad, the religions of the people of earlier revelations remain acceptable to God. They are not. Nor can Islam be lined up in one front with other religions in opposition to atheism.

Islam was revealed in order to correct the beliefs of the people of earlier revelations in the same way as it corrects the beliefs of pagans and idolaters. It calls on them all to accept Islam because it is alone the faith of self-surrender which is acceptable to God. When the Jews claimed that they were not called upon to accept Islam, and felt that it was beneath them to be so called, the Qur'ān confronted them with a clear statement to the effect that if they turned away from Islam, they would be considered unbelievers.

Every Muslim is required to call on the people of earlier revelations, atheists and pagans to submit themselves to God. He is not allowed to compel any of them to accept Islam, because faith cannot be accepted through compulsion. Compulsion is not only forbidden; it is futile. Such a requirement is only logical. If a Muslim were to acknowledge that the beliefs of the people of the Scriptures remained acceptable to God after the mission of the Prophet Muḥammad, he would only be contradicting himself if he were to call on them to believe in Islam. Such a call can have only one basis, namely, that he does not recognise their faith as acceptable to God. Therefore, he calls them to the proper faith. Once this premise is accepted, it follows that a Muslim cannot be consistent if he joins those who do not submit themselves to God in an alliance which aims to establish the faith based on the principle of self-submission.

From the Islamic point of view, this is a question of faith and one of strategy. Perhaps the faith aspect is clear by now and it can be made clearer by reference to Qur'ānic statements which leave us in no doubt that it is not possible to establish an alliance between Muslims and people of the Scriptures. The strategy aspect is also clear. Every effort made by a believer must have as its aim the establishment of the Islamic way of life as outlined in the message of Islam preached by the Prophet Muḥammad. This is a complete system that encompasses all human activities. How, then, can a Muslim cooperate in such an effort with one who does not believe in Islam as a faith, a way of life and a legal system? Such a person directs his efforts towards objectives which are, to say the least, inconsistent with those of Islam, if they are not directly opposed to them. Islam does not recognise any objective or effort which is not based on faith, although it may appear to serve a good purpose: *"As for unbelievers, their works are like burnt ashes which the wind blows about fiercely on a stormy day."* (14: 18)

Islam requires a Muslim to dedicate all his efforts to the cause of Islam. Only a person who does not understand the nature of Islam and its method can imagine that any human activity, however secondary, may be separated from Islam or that there are aspects of life which lie outside the Islamic way of life. Such ignorance of the nature of Islam may cause people to imagine that a true Muslim may cooperate with those who are hostile to Islam or those who will not accept anything from a Muslim unless he abandons his faith, as God states of the Jews and Christians in His revealed Book. Such cooperation is impossible from both a faith and strategy point of view.

'Abdullāh ibn Ubayy, who was one of those described in the Qur'ān as having "disease in their hearts", justified his support of the Jews and his determination to maintain his alliance with them by saying that he feared changes of fortune. His argument was indicative of his lack of faith. It is God's patronage and support that should be sought. To seek the support of others is both futile and erroneous. 'Abdullāh ibn Ubayy's argument is the same as that of everyone like him; hypocrite, sick at heart, ignorant of the true nature of faith. At the other end we find 'Ubādah ibn al-Ṣāmit who disclaimed all alliance with the Jews once he realised their true feelings. The two positions are at variance, since they rely on diametrically opposed concepts and feelings. The same difference exists at all times between a faithful heart and one which is devoid of faith.

The Qur'ān threatens those who seek the support of the enemies of their religion, the hypocrites, by bringing about victory for the believers or by revealing the truth about the hypocrites: *"God may well bring about victory (for believers) or some other event of His own making, and those (waverers) will terribly regret the thought they had secretly harboured within themselves."* (Verse 52) At this point of victory, whether it is here a reference to the conquest of Makkah, or to passing judgement over unclear issues, or to the accomplishment of God's will, those who have disease in their hearts will experience terrible regret over their past attitudes. The believers will wonder at the state of affairs which befalls the hypocrites: *"The believers will say: 'Are these the self-same people who swore by God their most solemn oaths that they were with you?' All their works are in vain and they will lose all."* (Verse 53)

God brought about victory in the past, and true intentions were laid bare, efforts came to nothing and certain groups of people turned out to be the losers. We have here the same promise from God that victory will be brought about every time we hold fast to our ties with God and we dedicate ourselves to Him alone. To do this, we have to understand the Divine way of life and make it the basis of our life. We have to fight our battle in accordance with God's guidance and seek alliance with no one but God, His Messenger and other believers.

The Qualities of God's Beloved People

This passage now completes its first address to the believers, requiring them not to seek an alliance with the Jews and Christians and warning them against such relationships because they may lead them to an unintentional renunciation of the faith of Islam. The second address made in this passage goes on to add a new warning to anyone who renounces his faith, either through making such an alliance or otherwise. Such a person has no position with God, even though he cannot get away from God, and he cannot cause harm to His faith. This faith has its own supporters who are well known to God. If the present group turn away from God's faith, He will bring forth others who will take their place. The *sūrah* describes the main features of this selected group of supporters in pleasant and reassuring terms. It points out the only way to which a Muslim directs his allegiance and it concludes with stating the inevitable outcome of the battle between God's party and other parties.

> *Believers, if you renounce your faith, God will bring forth (in your stead) people whom He loves and who love Him, humble towards the believers, proud towards the unbelievers. They will strive hard for God's cause and will not fear to be censured by any critic. Such is God's favour which He grants to whom He wills. God encompasses all and knows all. Your patron is only God, and His Messenger and those who believe — those who attend to their prayers, pay their zakāt (i.e. purifying alms) and bow down in worship. Those who ally themselves with God and His Messenger and the believers (will find that) the party of God will be victorious. (Verses 54–6)*

This warning, coming in this fashion at this particular point to those who turn away from faith, is taken to refer, in the first instance, to an equation which places on one side the maintenance of an alliance with the Jews and Christians, and, on the other, turning away from Islam altogether. This is highlighted by what has been said earlier of classifying anyone who seeks to be in alliance with them as one of them, having broken away from the Muslim community: *"Whoever of you allies himself with them is indeed one of them."* (Verse 51) In this light, this second address serves to emphasise the first one. This is further supported by another address which follows later in this *sūrah*. This third address forbids alliances with the people of earlier revelations and unbelievers, classifying them all in one group. This means that seeking an alliance with the Christians and Jews is the same as seeking it with unbelievers. Where Islam provides for extending different treatment to the people of earlier revelations from that extended to unbelievers does not relate to having an alliance with them. Rather, it concerns different matters altogether.

> *Believers, if you renounce your faith, God will bring forth (in your stead) people whom He loves and who love Him, humble towards the believers, proud towards the unbelievers. They will strive hard for God's cause and will not fear to be censured by any critic. Such is God's favour which He grants to whom He wills. God encompasses all and knows all.* (Verse 54)

God has chosen the community of believers to be the tool of His will to establish the Divine faith on earth, enforce His rule in human life, and to implement His law in people's affairs and disputes. Thus, they will mould human life on the basis of propriety, goodness and progress. The fact that He has chosen the Muslim community for this purpose is a manifestation of His grace. Whoever rejects this grace and deprives himself of this blessing does so at his own peril. God is in no need of him or anyone else. God chooses from among His servants those whom He knows to deserve this limitless grace.

The chosen people are here given a clear profile, described amidst a bright, evocative picture: *"God will bring forth people whom He loves and who love Him."* (Verse 54) Mutual love is the relationship between them and their Lord. It is a love that gives an air of compassion, which is pleasant, gentle, bright, and friendly. It provides the basis of their relationship with their compassionate Lord.

No one can appreciate the value of God's love to any one of his servants except a person who knows God with all His attributes as He has described Himself and one who feels the effect of these attributes within himself. No one can appreciate the value of this bounty except one who truly knows God, the Giver who has created this vast universe and created man. Man, small creature as he is, sums up the creation of the whole universe. To appreciate the value of God's love requires that one recognises God's greatness, ability and oneness as the only Lord of the universe. How great is the difference between God and man to whom He grants His love. It is He – limitless is He in His glory – who has made man, while He remains Majestic, Eternal, the First and the Last, the Lord of the Universe.

For a servant of God to love his Lord is also a great bounty bestowed on that servant himself. This is something that can be appreciated by those who have experienced it. If God's love to any of His servants is something great and a clear manifestation of endless grace, then, for God to guide one of His servants to love Him and appreciate that unparalleled kind of love is also something great and a clear manifestation of His endless grace.

God's love to any of His servants remains beyond description. At the same time, a human being's love of His Lord is something that is very rarely described adequately except, perhaps, in the occasional touch of excellence manifested in a true lover's description. In this respect, a very small number from among a great multitude of Sufis have demonstrated their truthfulness and have been able to excel in describing their love of God. A few lines of poetry by Rābi'ah al-'Adawiyah give us a sense of her appreciation of this unique type of love. Addressing her Lord, she says:

How tenderly I wish to feel that You are sweet when life is bitter!

How dearly I wish to feel that You are pleased when everyone else is angry.

When the relationship between You and me is sound, I do not care if my relationship with all the worlds is left in ruin.

If You truly grant me Your love, everything else is of no consequence. All those who are on earth are nothing but dust.

God's love, Majestic as He is in His glory, for one of His servants and the love of God, who bestows all grace, by one of His servants spread in this wide universe puts its mark on every living creature and on every object. It imparts an air of love to the whole universe and to human existence. This does not refer to something that occurs once only or to a passing moment. It speaks of an essential truth and a basic Islamic concept: *"God will certainly bestow love on those who believe and do righteous deeds."* (19: 96) *"My Lord is Merciful, Loving."* (11:

90) *"He is the Forgiving, the Loving."* (85: 14) *"When My servants ask you about Me, well, I am near; I answer the prayer of the supplicant when he calls to Me."* (2: 186) *"True believers love God more than all else."* (2: 165) *"Say: If you love God, follow me; God will love you and forgive you your sins."* (3: 31) Many other verses speak in the same vein.

It is a great wonder that people may read all this and claim that Islamic philosophy is stringent and violent. They claim that it visualises the relationship between God and man as one of compulsion, punishment, suffering and neglect. They compare it with the philosophy that makes of Jesus Christ a son of God and a manifestation of Him. Thus, they establish an arbitrary link of duality between God and human beings.

The clarity of Islamic philosophy, as it separates between the nature of Godhead and that of servitude, detracts in no way from the pleasant relationship that exists between God and His servants. This is a relationship based on compassion, justice, love and purity. It is a complete concept which includes all the needs of human existence in man's relationship with the Lord of all the worlds.

To Love God and Be Loved by Him

The description of the chosen community of believers is remarkable: *"Whom He loves and who love Him."* (Verse 54) This mutual love is indeed remarkable, generating as it does a feeling of strength the believer needs to fulfil his difficult task. He feels that it is a great honour to have been chosen for this task through which he earns his position of favour, close to God, the Beneficent, the Almighty.

The *sūrah* gives further details of this community which is dedicated to the service of God's cause: *"Humble towards the believers."* (Verse 54) This humility means that they are affable, gentle, and tolerant. When they deal with other believers, they do not adopt a difficult attitude or show any stubbornness. They are approachable, responsive, friendly. To adopt such an attitude towards believers does not mean any self-humiliation. Indeed, it is an aspect of brotherhood which removes barriers and formalities. One does not feel that one has anything to withhold from one's fellow brothers. It is self-consciousness that makes someone difficult and unamenable. On the other hand, when he feels himself belonging to the group of believers, he has nothing to withhold or begrudge. What can he retain for himself when they have all been united by faith, loving God and being loved by Him, and feeling this sublime love spreading over them?

"Proud towards the unbelievers." (Verse 54) When they have to deal with unbelievers, they show their dignity and high status. This is the attitude to adopt in such a situation. There is no trace of arrogance or conceit. It is being proud of the faith they have chosen and being honoured to fight unbelievers under the banner of faith. It is their unshakable trust in what they have, which is goodness itself, and their knowledge that their role is to make others submit to this goodness. It is not a personal submission by one group of people to another. It is rather a matter of complete trust that the Divine faith, God's party, will eventually triumph over all creeds based on personal prejudice and also over ignorance. It is they who will eventually triumph though they may be defeated in certain battles along the way.

"They will strive hard for God's cause and will not fear to be censured by any critic." (Verse 54) To strive hard in order to establish the Divine system and implement it in human life so as to achieve all that is good for mankind is a distinctive characteristic of the community of believers chosen by God to accomplish His will on earth. They strive hard for God's cause not to serve their own interests, nor the interests of their people, country or race, but rather to establish God's authority through the implementation of His law and to achieve all that is good for mankind. Personally, they gain nothing for themselves from such hard striving. It is all for God's sake.

They strive in this way, fearing no criticism. Why should they worry about being blamed by people when they have been guaranteed that the Lord of all people loves them? Why should they bother about people's values and traditions when they follow God's own method and call on people to adopt the Divine way of life? It is the person who derives his values and judgement from others' views and who seeks their support that fears to be blamed by them. The one who defers to God's values and standards and tries to make them govern people's values and inclinations, and who derives his power from God's power, cares nothing for what people may say or do, regardless of their position, importance or standard of advancement and civilisation.

We pay so much attention to what people may say, do, or accept, and to their values and standards, because we overlook the standard to which we should refer in evaluating matters. That standard is God's law and system. It is only God's law that is right and everything that is contrary to it is wrong, even though it may be accepted by millions and millions of people and endorsed by successive generations and centuries. The merit of any situation, tradition, or value does not derive from the fact that it exists or that millions of people believe in it or implement it in their lives. Such reasoning is unacceptable to Islam. No situation, custom or tradition has any value unless it is sanctioned by the system revealed by God.

It is for these reasons that the community of believers strives hard for God's cause without fearing to be criticised or censured by anyone. This is the mark of the chosen believers. Moreover, that those believers are chosen by God, that there is mutual love between Him and them, that they have their own distinctive characteristic and the reassurance they have to conduct their affairs on the basis of Divine guidance are all favours bestowed on them by God: *"Such is God's favour which He grants to whom He wills. God encompasses all and knows all."* (Verse 54) He gives in abundance and He chooses the ones to whom He grants His favours on the basis of perfect knowledge. His grace is abundant, limitless.

God defines for the believers the only group with whom they may have a relationship of patronage and the ones to patronise: *"Your patron is only God and His Messenger and those who believe – those who attend to their prayers, pay their zakāt (i.e. purifying alms), and bow down in worship."* (Verse 55) The definition is made here in a way which leaves no way for liberal interpretation or confusion. Matters have to be so clearly defined because the central issue here is that of faith and its implementation through a movement. Hence, submission to God must be complete, trust in Him must be absolute, and self-surrender is the only religion. The question is, then, one of a complete distinction between the Muslim camp and all other camps which do not adopt submission to God as a faith and Islamic law as a way of life. The Islamic movement must be serious in its organisation so that it admits no allegiance except to its own leadership. Thus, loyalty and support can exist only between members of the community of believers, because such loyalty and support are based on faith.

The Party Assured of Triumph

Islam is not a mere title, slogan or verbal claim nor is it a hereditary relationship or a description of people who live in a certain area. The *sūrah* mentions here some essential characteristics of believers: *"Those who attend to their prayers, pay their* zakāt *and bow down in worship."* (Verse 55)

The first characteristic is that of attending to prayers, not merely offering them. This means paying full attention to them so that prayers produce their effects as explained by God when He says: *"Prayer restrains man from loathsome deeds and from all that is bad."* (29: 45) Those who pray but are not prevented by their prayer from such indulgence have not attended to it properly.

Another characteristic is that they pay *zakāt*, which means that they fulfil their financial obligation willingly, without hesitation and in obedience to God. *Zakāt* is not a simple tax; it is an act of worship which may be described as financial worship. This is indicative of the Islamic system which achieves several objectives through the same duty. This distinguishes it from man-made systems which may achieve one goal and remain short of achieving the rest.

It is not possible for social welfare to be achieved through the mere imposition of civil taxes, or that financial contributions be levied from the rich for the benefit of the poor in the name of the state or the people or any other worldly authority. In such a pattern, only one goal is achieved, namely, the payment of money to the needy.

Zakāt, on the other hand, has a specific significance which is indicated by its very name, which means "purifying alms". First and foremost, *zakāt* is purification and growth. It purifies man's conscience because it is an act of worship and it is paid willingly with a feeling of love towards those who need it, because as a worship its payer expects to be well rewarded for it in the life to come and hopes that his wealth in this life will increase through the implementation of the blessed economic system of Islam. There is also a healthy feeling generated by it among the poor who receive it because they feel that it is part of God's grace that He has determined its payment to them by the rich. They entertain no grudge against the rich. (It is useful to remind ourselves here that under the Islamic system, the rich earn their money through legitimate means and do not usurp the right of anyone as they earn their income.) Needless to say, *zakāt* also achieves the objective of financial taxes in a healthy and satisfactory atmosphere characterised by purity and growth.

The payment of *zakāt* is a characteristic of the believers confirming that they implement God's law in their lives. Its very payment is an acknowledgement that God has the authority over all their affairs. This is exactly what is meant by Islam, which is based on total submission to God.

"And bow down in worship." (Verse 55) The way this phrase is expressed in the Arabic original indicates that bowing down in worship is their normal and essential condition. The Qur'ānic verse has already stated that they attend to their prayer, but this second description is even more comprehensive because it makes it appear as if worship is the most prominent characteristic by which they are known. In such contexts, Qur'ānic expressions are very powerful indeed.

In return for having complete trust in Him, and seeking only His support and maintaining a tie of patronage with Him only and, in consequence, with His Messenger and the believers, and in return for a complete split between them and all other camps that do not submit to Him, God promises the believers victory: *"Those who ally themselves with God and His Messenger and the believers (will find that) the party of God will be victorious."* (Verse 56)

This promise of victory comes only after the basic principle has been outlined. It is to be in alliance only with God, His Messenger and the believers. This follows a clear warning against having an alliance with the Jews or Christians since it is tantamount to leaving the Muslim camp and belonging to the Jews and Christians. In other words, it is a complete rejection of faith.

What we have here is a consistant Qur'ānic point. God wants people to be Muslims because Islam is good, not because they will triumph or gain power in this world. These are fruits which come only at their appropriate time, and only as a means to accomplish God's will, manifested in the practical implementation of His faith. They are never offered as a temptation to encourage people to accept Islam. Moreover, when Muslims triumph, they gain nothing out of their victory for themselves. They are simply the means through which God accomplishes His will. He grants them victory not as something they add to their personal credit, but to the advantage of their faith. As such, they earn the reward for having striven hard to achieve this victory and enjoy the results of the implementation of the Divine faith. Similarly, God may promise Muslims victory in order to strengthen them and free them from the shackles of the present, which may be overwhelming at times. When they are assured that the ultimate result will be in their favour, they are more determined to overcome the present impediment. In other words, they entertain hopes that God will fulfil His promise to the Muslim nation through their own efforts.

The fact that this statement occurs here tells us something about the Muslim community's situation at that time and its need for such reassurance by reiterating the rule that God's party will eventually triumph. This again confirms our view with regard to the timing of the revelation of this passage.

This rule, however, remains true regardless of time or place. We realise that it is one of God's laws which never fail. If the community of believers experiences some reversals and loses some battles, the constant rule, which will always remain true, is that God's party will remain victorious. Such a clear promise by God is more true than what may appear to be the case at any particular juncture. To maintain a relationship of patronage with God, His Messenger and the believers is the only way to eventually ensure the fulfilment of God's promise.

When Faith and Prayers Are Mocked

The approach utilised in this *sūrah* adopts several ways to impress on the believers the prohibition of taking as allies those who follow a faith different to their own, be they followers of earlier revelations or unbelievers associating partners with God. The aim of using such different methods is to make this rule of faith well established in their minds and consciences. This, in turn, indicates how important this rule is in the overall Islamic concept and the methods adopted by the Islamic movement.

In the first address, as we have seen, a straightforward prohibition has been emphasised, coupled with a warning that God may well bring about victory for the believers or bring about some other event of His own making, and thus the reality which the hypocrites try hard to cover up will be laid bare. In the second address, a warning is given against the renunciation of faith through the establishment of an alliance with the enemies of God, His Messenger and the believers. This is coupled with raising the far better prospect of belonging to the selected group who love God and are loved by Him, with the additional promise of victory to God's party.

Now this passage adds a third address to the believers, appealing to them to defend their faith, worship and prayers which are mocked at and made a jest of by their enemies. Alliances with the people of earlier revelations or with unbelievers is forbidden in the same way. This prohibition is made directly relevant to fearing God. Belonging to the community of believers is made conditional on compliance with it. The actions of the unbelievers and the people of earlier revelations are shown in their true light and they are described as having no reason: *"Believers, do not take for your friends those among the people of earlier revelations who mock at your faith and make a jest of it or those who are unbelievers. Fear God, if you are truly believers. For, when you call to prayer, they mock at it and make a jest of it. They do this because they are people who do not use their reason."* (Verses 57–8)

This is the sort of action which is bound to infuriate any believer who feels that he himself is treated in total disrespect, when an insult is directed against his faith and worship, and when his position as he stands to offer his worship is ridiculed. How, then, can any alliance or patronage be forged between the believers and anyone who shares in such a disgraceful action, simply because his mind is impaired? No man of sound mind would ever ridicule the Divine faith or the worship of believers, because a sound mind recognises the pointers to faith in everything around it. It is only when the mind is impaired or when it deviates from the truth that such pointers are not recognised? This because such a person's attitude towards the whole universe around him is unsound. Everything in existence gives the same message that it has a Creator who deserves to be worshipped and glorified. A sound mind appreciates the beauty of worshipping the Creator of the universe. Hence, it does not make fun of something so beautiful and dignified.

Such mockery and ridicule used to be the work of unbelievers. In particular, it used to be the action of the Jews when the Qur'ān was being revealed to God's Messenger, (peace be upon him), so that he would convey it to the Muslim community. We have no mention in the history of the period of any single incidence of this type by the Christians. However, God is stating for the Muslim community a basic principle of faith, as well as the Islamic concept and way of life. God has always been aware of what will take place in all future generations and the attitudes of other people towards Muslims.

We have seen that the enemies of this faith and the Muslim community, in all generations, from among those who claim to be Christians, have been much greater in number than the Jews and unbelievers who have fought against Islam. All those groups have taken a hostile attitude against Islam, schemed and fought an unabating war against it ever since the Muslim community clashed with the Byzantine Empire at the time of Abū Bakr and 'Umar, the first two Caliphs. This continued right down to the Crusades and then to the "Oriental Question" which witnessed the grouping of Christian powers throughout the world in an alliance aimed at destroying the Muslim state altogether. This was followed by imperialism, which embodied the spirit of the Crusades. Such spirit continued to indicate itself in slips of the tongue made by imperialist leaders. Missionary work was initiated to further prepare the ground for imperialism and to give it support. This was followed by an unabating war against the pioneers of Islamic revival the world over. In all such campaigns and efforts, Jews, Christians and unbelievers of all sorts have taken part and joined forces.

The Qur'ān has been revealed so that it remains the constitution of the Muslim community until the Day of Judgement. It gives this community its methodological concept of faith, and lays down for it its social order and its method of operation. Hence, it teaches the Muslim community that it must never share patronage with anyone other than God, His Messenger and the believers. Alliances with Jews, Christians or unbelievers are forbidden outright, and their prohibition is repeatedly emphasised.

This religion of ours impresses on its followers the need for tolerance and that they must extend kind treatment to the people of earlier revelations, particularly those among them who claim to be Christians. It forbids them, however, to have a relationship of alliance and patronage with them. Tolerance and kind treatment is a question of behaviour and good manners.

Alliances, on the other hand, are a matter of faith and organisational groupings. Patronage and alliance mean mutual support between two camps and groups. This cannot take place between Muslims and the people of earlier revelations or with unbelievers, because to a Muslim such support is only a support for the cause of faith and for striving to establish its methods and system in practical life. How can such help and support operate between Muslims and non-Muslims over such a matter? This question is clear cut and allows no wavering. Indeed, God does not accept any attitude over this issue other than that of complete seriousness, which is the only attitude a Muslim may have towards his religion.

Finding Fault with Dedicated Believers

When all these addresses to the believers have been completed, the *sūrah* instructs the Prophet to put a direct question to the people of the Scriptures: What fault do they find with the Muslim community? Do they take anything against it other than the fact that Muslims believe in God and in His past revelations, as well as His revelations to the Prophet of Islam? In other words, the only fault they find with the Muslims is that the Muslims are believers, while they, i.e. the people of earlier revelations, are mostly transgressors. It is a confrontation that is embarrassing and decisive at the same time, because it points out the true cause of hostility.

> *Say: People of earlier revelations! Do you find fault with us for any reason other than that we believe in God [alone], and in that which has been revealed to us as well as that which has been revealed previously, while most of you are transgressors? Say: Shall I tell you who, in God's sight, deserves an even worse retribution than these? They whom God has rejected and who have incurred His anger, and whom He has turned into apes and pigs, and who worship false gods. These are yet worse in station and they have gone farther astray from the right path.* (Verses 59–60)

God directs His Messenger to put this question to the people of earlier revelations in order to emphasise the actual fact about their motives which shape their attitude towards the Muslim community and its faith. It is at the same time a question which rebukes them for their attitudes and their motives. Moreover, it seeks to enlighten the Muslims so that the idea of binding themselves in an alliance with such people becomes repugnant to them.

The people of earlier revelations never found fault with the Muslim community at the time of the Prophet, and they do not find fault today with the advocates of Islamic revivalism, except for the fact that Muslims in all ages believe in God and what He has revealed to them in the Qur'ān as well as what the Qur'ān endorses of the revelations sent down to earlier Prophets. They are hostile to Muslims simply because they are Muslims; that is to say, because Muslims do not follow Judaism or Christianity. The other reason is that they themselves are transgressors who have deviated from what God has revealed to them. The most damning proof of their transgression and deviation is the

fact that they do not believe in the final message which endorses what God has revealed to them, except that which they have invented or distorted. Moreover, they do not believe in the final Messenger who has come to confirm earlier messages and honour all previous Messengers.

God states this fact absolutely clearly when He says to His Messenger in another *sūrah*: *"The Jews and the Christians will never be pleased with you unless you follow their faith."* (2: 120) In this *sūrah*, God tells him that it is time to confront the people of earlier revelations with the truth which shapes their motives and provides the logic behind their attitude: *"Say: People of earlier revelations! Do you find fault with us for any reason other than that we believe in God [alone], and in that which has been revealed to us as well as that which has been revealed previously, while most of you are transgressors?"* (Verse 59)

This fact is stated by God in several places. Nevertheless, it is this act which many among the people of earlier revelations and among those who call themselves Muslims try to dilute or present in a confused way. By so doing, they seek to justify what they term as the cooperation of "religious" people against materialism and atheism.

The people of earlier revelations wish to dilute this fact and to cover it up altogether, because they want to cheat the people of the Islamic world, or, more correctly, the world which claims to be Islamic. They try to distort the penetrative vision Islam gives to its followers as they implement its system. Equipped with such a sound vision and profound awareness, Muslims were able to tower over the imperialism of the Crusaders. Having failed in their direct campaigns, and in their open missionary warfare, those Crusaders felt that the only option left to them was that of deception. They have tried, therefore, to promote among latter day Muslims that the whole episode of religious warfare is over and that it belongs to the dark ages. Now that the world has become more "enlightened" and more "advanced", it is unacceptable for people to be involved in religious conflict. Hence, conflicts of today are over wealth, resources, markets, and investments. Therefore, Muslims, or more correctly their heirs, must remove all thoughts of religion and religious conflict from their minds.

When the people of earlier revelations who colonise Muslim countries are reassured that Muslims have been so hypnotised and that the whole question has been confused in their minds, then they are reassured that they will not have to face the Muslims' fury when their faith is assaulted.

They realise from their history that they can never stand up to such fury when it is so motivated. Now that the senses of the Muslims have been benumbed, the people of earlier revelations not only win the war over religion, but they also win with it the materialistic war, enjoying their loot in the shape of investments and resources.

We also find within the Muslim world, agents for the people of earlier revelations repeating the same words. These people claim that the Crusades were not truly crusades and they describe the Muslims who fought against the Crusaders under the banner of faith as "nationalists", not Muslims.

There is a third group who are deluded. They listen to the descendants of the Crusaders of the imperialist West making a call to them: let us meet together to defend religion against the schemes of the "atheists". Naïve and well intentioned, this deluded group respond favourably, oblivious of the fact that these very descendants of the Crusaders have always joined forces with the atheists whenever the confrontation was with Muslims. They have not changed in any way. They are not concerned about fighting atheist materialism as much as they are concerned about fighting Islam. They realise that atheist materialism is a temporary phenomenon, but Islam is, to them, the eternal enemy. This deceptive call aims only to undermine the Islamic revival and to make use of those deluded people to fight the atheists, the political enemies of imperialism. Both are the same, hostile to Islam and Muslims. In this war, a Muslim's only reliable weapon is the penetrating vision imparted to him by the Divine system.

Those who allow themselves to be deceived and think that the people of earlier revelations are serious about joining forces with Muslims in fighting atheism are oblivious to what history has shown throughout 14 centuries, which have seen no exception to this rule. They are also oblivious to what their Lord has told them most clearly and most emphatically on this particular point. When these people read or write, they quote only those Qur'ānic verses and pronouncements of the Prophet which order the Muslims to treat the people of earlier revelations with kindness and to show them maximum tolerance. They, however, prefer to overlook the clear and decisive warnings against entering into a relationship of patronage and alliance with them. They also ignore the penetrating statement about their motives. They shut their minds to the unequivocal instructions relating to the organisation and practical movement of Islam prohibiting the establishment of such alliances with non-Muslims. To a Muslim such an alliance can only be concerned with the establishment of the Islamic system in practical life. There is simply no common ground between Muslims and the people of earlier revelations with regard to Islam, despite the fact that these religions enjoyed the same origins as Islam before they were distorted. After all the people of earlier revelations do not find fault with Muslims except for that they believe in their faith. They are not satisfied unless Muslims abandon their faith, as the Lord of mankind clearly states.

Such deluded people treat the Qur'ān in an ambivalent way, taking only those parts of it which endorse their naïve call, assuming that it is innocent, and abandon what is in conflict with it. As for us, we prefer to listen to God's words in this whole question. His word is clear, unequivocal, decisive.

God, however, gives another reason for their grudge against the Muslims, namely, that the majority of the people of earlier revelations are indeed transgressors. Transgression motivates the transgressor to try to find fault with those who are keen to follow Divine instructions and not to violate God's orders. This is a psychological and practical rule confirmed by this remarkable Qur'ānic verse. Indeed, those who transgress cannot stand those who follow Divine guidance, because their very presence presents them with the ugly sight of their own deviation and transgression. Hence, they begrudge them their obedience of God's orders and try hard to make them follow their own deviation, or to smash them if they prove to be difficult to control.

This is a constant rule, which is not limited to the attitude of the people of earlier revelations towards the first Muslim community in Madinah. Indeed, it describes their attitude in general towards the Muslims as a whole, and includes the attitude of every deviant transgressor towards every group of believers who seriously observe Divine orders. It tells us the cause of the unabating war launched against the good, the honest and the obedient in any society where the evil, the transgressor, and the deviant have the upper hand. Such a war is only natural in view of this rule, stated in this remarkable verse.

God, limitless He is in His glory, knows that goodness and right will always be viewed with hostility by wickedness and evil, and that obedience to Him will always provoke the anger of transgressors. He also knows that goodness, right and obedience will need to defend themselves and fight the war launched against them by wickedness, evil and transgression. It is an inevitable battle, which right must fight and goodness cannot avoid because wickedness and evil will inevitably try to eliminate them. If the advocates of right, goodness and obedience to God imagine that they can steer away from this war, or that wickedness, evil or transgression can be persuaded to leave them alone to observe some sort of peace or truce between them, then they are infinitely naïve. The people of goodness and right must be prepared for fighting the inevitable battle, or else they will be vanquished.

Those in the Worst Position of All

The *sūrah* then refers to some events pertaining to the history of the people of earlier revelations, their past attitude towards their Lord and the painful punishment awaiting them: *"Say: Shall I tell you who, in God's sight, deserves an even worse retribution than these? They whom God has rejected and who have incurred His anger, and whom He has turned into apes and pigs, and who worship false gods. These are yet worse in station and they have gone farther astray from the right path."* (Verse 60)

Here we are face to face with the Jews and their history. It is they whom God has rejected and who have incurred His anger, and whom He has turned into apes and pigs for worshipping false gods. The first three points to which reference is made here are mentioned elsewhere in the Qur'ān. Their worship of false gods needs to be explained here because it has particular significance in the context of this *sūrah*.

The expression "false gods" refers in the Qur'ānic context to every authority that is not derived from God's own authority, every system of government that does not have God's law as its basis, and to every aggression exceeding the boundaries of what is right. The worst type of aggression which the Arabic term *ṭāghūt*, rendered here as "false gods", relates is that made against God's authority, and His Godhead. The people of earlier revelations did not worship rabbis and monks, but they followed their rule in preference to that of God's. Therefore, God describes them as their worshippers and terms them polytheists. It is to this fine point that reference is made here. They worshipped false gods in the sense that they obeyed tyrannical authorities in so far as they exceeded their rightful limits. They worshipped them not in the sense of bowing and prostrating themselves before them, but by simply obeying and following them. This is, indeed, a type of worship which removes its perpetrator from the ranks of God's worshippers who follow His faith.

God directs His Messenger to confront the people of earlier revelations with this history and the punishment they have incurred, as if they are one generation, since they all share the same deviant nature. The Prophet is directed to tell them that the result of such an attitude is much worse: *"Say: Shall I tell you who, in God's sight, deserves an even worse retribution than these?"* (Verse 60) This means that they incur something much worse than those people of earlier revelations who preceded them. Incomparable indeed is God's anger and His retribution. Here, we have His verdict that those people of earlier revelations have turned away from the right path: *"They whom God has rejected and who have incurred His anger, and whom He has turned into apes and pigs, and who worship false gods. These are yet worse in station and they have gone farther astray from the right path."* (Verse 60)

The Exposure of a Horrid Nature

The *sūrah* continues to warn the Muslims against fraternising with them, by exposing their qualities and features, after having referred briefly to their history and punishment. Their schemes are exposed in order that the Muslims be warned against them. The Jews feature prominently here because the *sūrah* speaks of actual events, most of which were perpetrated by them:

When they come to you, they say: "We believe," whereas, in fact, they come unbelievers and depart unbelievers. God is fully aware of all that they would conceal. You see many of them rushing into sin and transgression and in devouring the fruits of unlawful gain. Evil indeed is that which they do. Why do not their divines and their rabbis forbid them to make sinful assertions and to devour the fruits of unlawful gain? Evil indeed is that which they contrive. The Jews say: "God's hand is shackled!" It is their own hands that are shackled. Rejected [by God] are they for what they say. Indeed, both His hands are outstretched. He bestows [His bounty] as He wills. But that which has been revealed to you by your Lord is bound to make many of them more stubborn in their overweening arrogance and unbelief. We have cast enmity and hatred among them, [to last] until the

Day of Resurrection. Every time they light a fire for war, God puts it out. They labour hard to spread corruption on earth; and God does not love those who spread corruption. (Verses 61–4)

With these words, the *sūrah* draws moving pictures and living scenes in front of our eyes. Despite the passage of centuries, the reader of these verses visualises the Jewish people to whom the Qur'ān most probably refers. Although the context applies to the Jews, it is possible, however, that it also refers to some of the hypocrites in Madinah. Those hypocrites would go to the Muslims claiming to be believers. Nevertheless, they held on to their disbelief in all situations, whether coming or going, yet all the while their tongues stated something altogether different.

It was most probably the Jews who were trying to create confusion among the Muslim community, as they said to one another: let us believe in this Qur'ān at the beginning of the day and disbelieve in it at the end of the day, so that those who now believe in it may return to their old unbelief. In other words, they hoped that the confusion and doubt they raised would cause the Muslims to abandon their faith.

"God is fully aware of all that they would conceal." (Verse 61) God makes this statement of truth in order to reassure the believers that their Lord will look after them and will not abandon them to the schemes of their enemies. He is fully aware of their scheming. Hence, He warns its perpetrators, calling on them to abandon their nefarious ways.

A Confirmed Attitude of Unbelief

The *sūrah* moves on to draw a vivid picture of what these people do, as if we see their movements and actions through the words. *"You see many of them rushing into sin and transgression and in devouring the fruits of unlawful gain. Evil indeed is that which they do."* (Verse 62) They are depicted as if they are racing at full speed towards sin and aggression, devouring all that is unlawful. Although this picture is drawn here to denounce those people and to show how ugly they appear, it depicts a certain condition of individuals and communities when they become infested with corruption, lose their values, and give in to evil. When we look at communities that have so degenerated, it appears to us as if all these people race towards evil, plunge into sin and aggression. The strong and the weak among them are alike in such actions. In corrupt societies, sin and aggression are not the monopoly of the powerful. Even the weak move with the tide of sin. It is true that they cannot assault the strong, but some of them can assault others and violate what God has sanctified. In corrupt societies, what God has restricted has become subject to violation, because neither the ruler nor the ruled are ready to honour God's action. When a society becomes corrupt, sin and aggression feature high among its characteristics.

Such was the Jewish community in those days, and such was their devouring of what was unlawful. Indeed, devouring what is forbidden is characteristic of the Jews at all times. *"Evil indeed is that which they do."* (Verse 62)

The *sūrah* points out another characteristic of corrupt societies, as it denounces the silence adopted by divines and rabbis, supposedly those scholars who guard the implementation of Divine law. Instead, they remain silent when they see their people plunging into sin and aggression and devouring what is unlawful, when they should be condemning such practices: *"Why do not their divines and their rabbis forbid them to make sinful assertions and to devour the fruits of unlawful gain? Evil indeed is that which they contrive."* (Verse 63) This is, indeed, a feature of societies that are on the verge of collapse, after becoming corrupt. As described in the Qur'ān, the Children of Israel used not to counsel each other against committing evil.

A main feature of a good, virtuous and strong society is the high esteem given to enjoining what is right and forbidding what is wrong. Such a society is rich with people who undertake this task and with ones who are ready to listen to them. Its traditions are such that those who deviate from their path do not turn their back on this quality or abuse those who speak out, encouraging what is right and forbidding what is wrong. Hence, God's description of the Muslim community: *"You are the best community that has ever been raised for mankind: you enjoin the doing of what is right and forbid what is wrong and you believe in God."* (3: 110) He describes the Children of Israel as people who *"would never restrain one another from wrongdoing."* (Verse 79) This is the criterion by which the two communities are separated.

The divines and rabbis, however, do not speak out against sin, aggression or devouring what is forbidden. Nor do they fulfil the covenant by which God's revelations were entrusted to them. Hence, they are strongly denounced. This denunciation serves as a warning to the people of every religion. For a society to be good depends on the fulfilment by its divines and scholars of their duties to enjoin what is right and forbid what is wrong. As we have said on more than one occasion in this commentary, this requires the presence of an "authority" which commands and forbids. This is different from advocacy, which is mainly concerned with explaining the message and conveying it to people, for it requires power and authority. Therefore, those who enjoin what is right and forbid what is wrong should be equipped with the power that makes their task effective, and not confined to verbal statements.

As an example of their most ghastly and sinful assertions, the Qur'ān tells us of the following statement made by the Jews: *"The Jews say: 'God's hand is shackled!' It is their own hands that are shackled. Rejected [by God] are they for what they say. Indeed, both His hands are outstretched. He bestows [His bounty] as He wills."* (Verse 64) Such a statement is the outcome of the Jews' wrong concept of God, limitless is He in His glory. The Qur'ān has given us many examples of the results of this wrong concept. When they were told to give money in charity they said: God is poor and we are rich. Here they say that God's hand is shackled in order to justify their miserliness. They claim that God does not give people enough, and that He gives them very little. How, then, could they be required to give money in charity?

They are too insensitive and too hard-hearted to use the straight-forward description of the meaning they had in mind, namely, miserliness. False as that is, they went further choosing an even more aggressive and blasphemous expression. They claimed that God's hand is shackled!

The answer to them asserts that they are the ones to be described in such terms, and furthermore that they are cursed and deprived of God's mercy: *"It is their own hands that are shackled. Rejected [by God] are they for what they say."* (Verse 64) This is indeed an apt description, for they are the most stingy and miserly people on earth. Then, God is described by His most appropriate attribute, whereby He bestows His limitless bounty on His servants: *"Indeed, both His hands are outstretched. He bestows [His bounty] as He wills."* (Verse 64) His inexhaustible bounty is apparent to everyone. It gives irrefutable proof of His limitless grace, giving testimony to His outstretched hands. It speaks in every language, but the Jews do not hear it, because they are preoccupied with gathering as much gain as they can, using obscene language even when they speak of God Himself.

God tells His Messenger (peace be upon him) about what those people will do and what will happen to them because of the grudge they harbour against him. He further describes the hostility they show the Prophet because God has chosen him to be His Messenger and because his message exposes their attitude, both past and present: *"But that which has been revealed to you by your Lord is bound to make many of them more stubborn in their overweening arrogance and unbelief."* (Verse 64) Having refused to accept the faith, it was inevitable that they should go to the other extreme and remain entrenched in their arrogance and disbelief. Hence, God's Messenger will bring mercy to believers and Divine punishment to unbelievers.

God then tells His Messenger of the inevitability of His will to cause enmity and hatred among them, and to render their schemes futile even when they are at their strongest. Hence, their war against the Muslim community will end in defeat: *"We have cast enmity and hatred among them, [to last] until the Day of Resurrection. Every time they light a fire for war, God puts it out."* (Verse 64)

Jewish groups continue to be hostile to one another, even though world Jewry may appear to be united at this period of time and capable of launching wars against Muslim countries and winning them. We must not, however, look at only a short period of time or cast only a partial view. Over 13 centuries, indeed since pre-Islamic days, the Jews have been hostile to one another, humiliated, and dispersed all over the globe. They will inevitably share the same fate, despite all the support they are receiving. The key to the whole matter is the existence of a true Islamic community, to whom God fulfils His promise. Where do we find today such a community which receives God's promise and becomes the means by which God accomplishes His purpose?

When the Muslim nation returns to Islam, truly believes in it and conducts its whole life in accordance with Islamic law and constitution, God's warning to His most evil creatures will come true. The Jews know this and they use all their power and wicked scheming against the advocates of Islamic revival throughout the world. They level at them, through their puppets and stooges, brutal blows in total disregard of all laws and values. God, will, however, accomplish His will. His promise will certainly come true: *"We have cast enmity and hatred among them, [to last] until the Day of Resurrection. Every time they light a fire for war, God puts it out."* (Verse 64)

The evil and corruption which the Jews represent will inevitably be smashed by God's will. For God does not like corruption to spread on earth. What God does not like will certainly be removed and uprooted by some of His servants, whom He entrusts with this task: *"They labour hard to spread corruption on earth; and God does not love those who spread corruption."* (Verse 64)

Advance Results of Implementing Divine Law

The passage is concluded with a statement of a basic rule that people's implementation of faith in their lives ensures the achievement of goodness and prosperity in the life of believers in this world as well as the next. Faith provides a single code of living which looks after the material and the spiritual aspects of life. This rule is stated in connection with the discussion of the deviation of the people of earlier revelations from proper Divine faith, to their devouring unlawful gains, and their distortion of God's words in order to achieve immediate gain. Had they followed the Divine faith, they would have benefited in this world as well as in the world to come.

> *If only the people of earlier revelations would believe and be God-fearing, We should indeed efface their [past] bad deeds, and bring them into gardens of bliss. If they would observe the Torah and the Gospel and all that has been revealed to them by their Lord, they would indeed be given abundance from above and from beneath. Some of them do pursue a right course, but many of them are of evil conduct.* (Verses 65–6)

This is a major concept in Islamic philosophy. Hence, the two verses that state this reflect a great truth of human life. In view of the great confusion which engulfs the human mind, human standards and situations, and the numerous doctrines that compete to influence man's thinking, the need to explain this concept properly and lucidly has never been greater.

God says to the people of earlier revelations – and His words apply to every community that has received Divine revelations – that if they would believe and be God-fearing, He would forgive them their sins and admit them into gardens of bliss. This is the reward of the Hereafter. Had they implemented in their lives God's law embodied in the Torah and the Gospel and what He had revealed to them, without distortion, they would have enjoyed a good life as well as one of prosperity and affluence. But they neither believe nor implement God's law and are not God-fearing. Apart from a small group of them, who have pursued a right course in their long history, the majority of them are of evil conduct.

These two verses then tell us that to believe and to be God-fearing, to implement God's law in human life ensures more than the reward of the Hereafter, which is certainly the better and longer-lasting reward. To take such a course also ensures a healthy type of life and a good reward in this present world in the shape of prosperity and affluence. This is described in a tangible form, bringing the meaning of affluence before our eyes: *"They would indeed be given abundance from above and from beneath."* (Verse 66) This shows that ensuring a good reward in the Hereafter does not have a special way, separate or independent from that which ensures a good, prosperous life in this world. It is the same way, giving the best results in both this life and the life to come. If it is abandoned, then life in this world becomes corrupt and the life to come is lost. This single way is that of faith, being God-fearing and implementing Divine law.

This approach is not merely a spiritual one, concerned only with beliefs. It is also a code for practical human life, the implementation of which, together with a strong faith and fear of God, ensure a good, prosperous and affluent life. All people will enjoy this abundance and its fair distribution. The code of living that is formulated by faith does not make religion a substitute for this world. Nor does it make happiness in the Hereafter a substitute for happiness in this life. Nor does it set one way for heaven and one for earth. It is sad that this principle has been clouded in people's minds and thoughts.

In most people's minds and in their practical lives, the way leading to Heaven is different from that which brings about the benefits of this life. Ordinary people, and indeed the general human outlook, visualise no meeting place between the two. Hence, people tend to choose this world and abandon the Hereafter, or choose the road that ensures a good life in the Hereafter and, in consequence, abandon everything to do with this world. This is because everything in people's lives at this point in time tends to support this view.

It is true that all situations in this ignorant way of life, which is totally removed from God and the code He has revealed for human life, tend to widen the gulf between working for the benefits of this world and working for those of the Hereafter. It is inevitable that those who wish to achieve prominence in their communities and good worldly gains sacrifice their moral values and religious teachings as also their clean behaviour which religion encourages. It is also inevitable that those who wish to achieve a good life in the Hereafter steer away from the main current of this life and its dirty and corrupt situations.

But is this truly inevitable? Is there no meeting ground between the road to doing well in this life and the road to Heaven? No, there is nothing inevitable in this. The conflict between this life and the life to come, or between the material and spiritual is not the ultimate, unchangeable truth. Indeed, it is not part of the nature of this life at all. It is an accidental situation which is the consequence of temporary deviation. It is inherent in the nature of human life that the roads to prosperity in this life and to success in the next should meet and be united. This means that good productivity, affluence and hard work in this world, will be the very things which ensure prosperity in this life and reward in the Hereafter. Similarly, faith, fearing God, and good actions are the means to build human life on earth and guarantee God's reward in the Hereafter. This is what is inherent in the nature of human life but it does not demonstrate itself in reality unless human beings conduct their lives on the basis of the code God has chosen for mankind. This code makes work and action a part of worship. It also makes the building of a human civilisation on the basis of the Divine method man's duty. It is this which ensures prosperity and abundance for all human beings.

Development and Faith Go Hand in Hand

According to Islamic concepts, man's role on earth is to be in charge of it, by God's will and permission and according to the conditions God has set. Hence, productive work and ensuring prosperity through the utilisation of all potentials and resources on earth, as well as universal resources, is the proper way for fulfilling man's duty. Such fulfilment, on the basis of the Divine code, is a demonstration of obedience to God, to be rewarded in the Hereafter. At the same time, it ensures enjoyment of all the riches of this world, or the enjoyment of abundance *"from above and from beneath"*, as the Qur'ān puts it in its inimitable style.

According to Islamic principles, a man who does not tap the resources of the earth and the universe is a disobedient servant of God; he does not work for the purpose for which he has been created. This purpose is defined in God's statement to the angels: *"I am appointing a vicegerent on earth."* (2: 30) We should also mention here God's statement, as He addresses mankind: *"He has made all that is in heaven and on earth subservient to you, as a bounty from Him."* (45: 13) Such a man wastes God's bounty, which has been gifted to mankind. As such, he is an absolute loser both in this life and in the life to come.

As such, the Islamic way of life combines, in absolute coherence, work for this world and work for the Hereafter. Hence, man does not need to waste his life on earth in order to win a better life in the world to come, nor does he waste the latter in order to fulfil the former. Reaping the best of the two is by no way contradictory.

This applies to mankind in general and to Muslim communities, wherever they exist on earth, and as long as they want to implement the Divine method. As for individuals, matters are not different. According to Islam, the goals of the individual and the community are not in conflict. The Islamic method makes it incumbent on the individual to use all his physical and mental abilities in his work to ensure maximum productivity and to make his purpose in all that the earning of God's pleasure. Hence, he neither commits injustice, cheating or betrayal, nor does he allow himself to take unlawful gain or to retain something he owns when it is needed by his brother in the community.

Islam fully recognises, however, the right of the individual to own what his work produces and the right of the community to have a share of what its individuals own, in accordance with what God has legislated. The Islamic method also considers an individual's work within these limits and according to these considerations, a sort of worship for which he is rewarded with blessings in this life and with Heaven in the Hereafter. An individual's link with his Lord is enhanced with obligatory worship. This requires man to remind himself of his link with His Lord five times every day through prayers and for 30 days every year during fasting, and on a special occasion which is obligatory at least once in his lifetime, namely, pilgrimage, and in every season or year when he pays his *zakāt*.

This explains to us the importance of obligatory Islamic worship. Such worship, in all its different aspects, serves as a renewal of man's pledge to God to implement the way of life He has chosen for man. Islamic worship is, at the same time, a set of actions drawing man closer to God as he resorts to fulfil all his obligations under this complete system for life. Through them, man feels afresh that God helps him fulfil his obligations and overcome his desires, as also people's opposition and their deviant practices which stand in his way.

These obligatory acts of worship are not separate from ordinary matters such as work, productivity, fair distribution, government, justice, and striving to implement the Divine method to establish God's authority in human life (i.e. *jihād*). To have faith, to be God-fearing, and to discharge obligatory worship are all one part of the system which enables man to fulfil the other part. In this way, to be a believer, to be God-fearing, and to work for the establishment of the Divine law in human life, means to achieve abundance just as God promises in these two verses. In Islamic philosophy, and the Islamic systems based on it, the world to come is not offered as a substitute for this life, nor is the latter to be preferred to the former. Both can be achieved in the same effort. The two cannot co-exist in human life, however, unless man follows only the Divine way of life without introducing into it amendments that are borrowed from man-made situations or formulated according to man's own thoughts.

Islamic principles and the Islamic way of life do not offer belief, worship and a high standard of piety and morality as a substitute for work, productivity, and development in man's material world. It is not a method which promises people a latter-day paradise and shows them the way to it, while leaving them to make their own way towards a worldly paradise, as some naïve people tend to think. Work, productivity and development represent, according to Islamic principles, man's way to fulfil his task as vicegerent on earth. Faith, worship and fearing God represent, on the other hand, the constraints, motives and incentives to implement the Divine way of life. The two together lead to the achievement of paradise in this life and in the life to come. The same way leads to both and there is no schism between the spiritual and the material sides of human life, as it is the case in all non-Islamic situations we see today.

This depressing split between what relates to this world and what relates to the Hereafter, between spiritual worship and material creativity, between success in this life and success in the life to come is not inevitable. It is simply a depressing tax man has imposed on himself as he abandoned God's constitution in order to adopt a variety of constitutions that are in conflict with what God has chosen for man. It is a tax people pay with their blood and their whole constitution.

What they pay for it in the life to come is much worse. In this world, it manifests itself in worry, misery and confusion because they lack the reassurance and peacefulness of faith. This is the result of abandoning their religion as a whole, alleging that such an abandonment is the only way to increase their productivity, knowledge and experience and to achieve individual and communal success. The net outcome of this state of affairs is that they put themselves in conflict with their own nature and try to suppress their natural hunger to have a faith that brings self-fulfilment into their lives. No social, philosophical or artistic doctrine can satisfy such hunger, because it is a hunger to know the Divine Being.

People's worry, misery and confusion cannot be dispelled if they try to maintain their faith in God and at the same time be part of the international community which adopts a system, concepts, methods of work and standards of success that are in conflict with faith and with the moral standards and practices acceptable to faith. Humanity will continue to suffer this misery if it adopts materialistic creeds, be they atheistic or ones that try to retain religion as a faith, provided it has nothing to do with practical life. The enemies of man try to depict a deceptive picture showing that religion is a matter between man and God while human life belongs to man alone. They claim that religion is faith, feeling, worship and morals while life is a system, legal code, work, and productivity.

Humanity has to pay this hefty tax of worry, misery, confusion, and emptiness because it cannot see the benefit of implementing God's method. It is a method that does not separate this life from the life to come, but rather combines them both. It does not see affluence in this world to be contradictory with success in the second world, rather it sees them both as mutually complementary.

We must not be deluded by false appearances when we see that nations which do not believe or implement the Divine method are enjoying abundance and affluence. It is all a temporary prosperity which lasts until the natural laws have produced their effects, allowing the consequences of the miserable split between material excellence and spiritual fulfilment to appear in full. We see some of these consequences surface in a variety of ways.

We see first maldistribution within these nations, which allows hatred, grudges, misery and fear of the unexpected to take root. This is, indeed, an ominous state of affairs, despite prosperity. We also see suppression and fear dominant in those nations which have tried to ensure at least a partially fair distribution. To achieve this, they have resorted to destruction, suppression, and terror in order to enforce their measures of redistribution. In this terrible state of affairs, man is always in fear, never reassured.

We also see the weakening of moral values which leads, sooner or later, to the destruction of material prosperity. Work, productivity and fair distribution need to be guaranteed by high moral standards. Man-made laws cannot on their own provide such guarantees, as human experience has shown throughout the world.

We also see all types of worry spreading throughout the world, particularly in the most affluent of societies. This inevitably makes people less intelligent and reduces their tolerance. It then leads to lowering standards of work and productivity and eventually helps destroy material prosperity. Very clear indications of this impending development can easily be recognised at the present time.

We see the fear, which engulfs all humanity, of the total ruin which threatens the whole world at any moment, as risks of all-out war continue to be in the air. Such fear places great strain on people's minds, whether they realise it or not. It leads to a whole range of nervous disorders. Is it not significant that death through heart failure, mental disease and suicide are at their highest rate in affluent societies?

The clearest example today is the French. But their case is only an example of the ultimate effect of a continuous split between the material and spiritual aspects of human existence, a split between this life and the life to come, religion and human life. Or, to put it another way, by treating the method given by God as the one to ensure success in the Hereafter while success in this life comes through the following of a different, man-made method.

Worship Gives a New Face to Human Life

Before we conclude our comment on this very important truth, we would like to emphasise that it is most important to achieve harmony between faith, piety and implementation of the Divine method in practical life on the one hand and work, productivity and the fulfilment of man's mission on earth on the other. It is this harmony which ensures the fulfilment of God's promise to the people of earlier revelations, and indeed to all communities, that they will have abundance from above and from beneath, and that they will be forgiven their sins and admitted into gardens of bliss in the Hereafter. Thus, they have paradise on earth and paradise in Heaven. We must not forget, however, that the fundamental principle and the mainstay of the whole system is faith, piety and the implementation of the Divine way of life. This indeed implies hard work, better productivity and development. Moreover, when man maintains a constant link with God, all aspects of life will bring about better enjoyment, to enhance man's values and correct his standards. This is the starting point from which everything else follows.

We should also mention that faith, piety, worship and the establishment of God's law in human life yield all their fruits in human life and give their benefits to man himself. God is in no need of anyone. It is true that Islam lays strong emphasis on these fundamental principles and makes them the basis of all actions and activities. Any action which is not based on them is rejected. The reason for this is not that God gains anything from people's worship and piety; He does not. But He knows that their life and their affairs cannot be established on the right footing unless His method is followed. It is in this light that we should read the sacred *ḥadīth* in which the Prophet relates God's own words:

> My servants, I have forbidden oppression for Myself and have made it forbidden among you, so do not oppress one another. My servants, all of you are astray except for those I have guided, so seek guidance from Me and I shall guide you. My servants, all of you are hungry except for those I have fed, so seek food from Me and I shall feed you. My servants, all of you are naked, except for those I have clothed, so seek clothing from Me and I shall clothe you. My servants, you sin by night and by day and I forgive all sins, so seek forgiveness from Me and I shall forgive you. My servants, you will never be able to harm Me and you will never be able to bring Me benefit. My servants, were the first of you and the last of you, the human of you and the *jinn* of you to be as pious as the most pious heart of any one of you, that would not

increase My kingdom in any thing. My servants, were the first of you and the last of you, the human of you and the *jinn* of you to be as wicked as the most wicked heart of any one of you, that would not decrease My kingdom in anything. My servants, were the first of you and the last of you, the human of you and the *jinn* of you to rise up in one place and make a request of Me, and were I to give everyone what he requested, that would not decrease what I have, anymore than a needle decreases the sea if put into it. My servants, it is but your deeds that I reckon up for you and then recompense you for. So let him who finds good praise God and let him who finds other than that blame no one but himself.

(Related by Muslim.)

It is on this basis that we should understand the purpose of having a strong faith, being pious and devoted and working for the implementation of the code of living God has revealed. All these qualities work in our favour, in this life and in the life to come. They are essential for the welfare of humanity.

Needless to say, this condition made by God to the people of earlier revelations is not exclusive to them. It is even more applicable to those who have been favoured with the revelation of the Qur'ān; those who claim to be Muslims. It is these whose faith requires them to believe in what has been revealed to them and what has been revealed earlier and to implement all that has been sent down to them, as well as those parts of the laws of earlier nations which God has retained in their faith. After all, theirs is the only religion that is acceptable to God. All religions have been incorporated into it. Hence, they are the ones to have God's pledge with all its terms and conditions. It goes without saying that they should accept what God has given them and enjoy what He has promised them of forgiveness of their sins and admission into Heaven, and having abundance from above and from beneath. This is much more preferable to hunger, disease, fear and poverty which they suffer throughout the Muslim world, or more accurately, throughout the world which was Islamic. God's pledge with its conditions is still operative. The way to enjoy its benefits is still there, if only we would follow it.

6

Who Follows Divine Faith?

Messenger, proclaim what has been revealed to you by your Lord. For, unless you do it fully, you will not have delivered His message. God will protect you from all men. God does not guide those who reject faith. (67)

۞ يَـٰٓأَيُّهَا ٱلرَّسُولُ بَلِّغْ مَآ أُنزِلَ إِلَيْكَ مِن رَّبِّكَ ۖ وَإِن لَّمْ تَفْعَلْ فَمَا بَلَّغْتَ رِسَالَتَهُۥ ۚ وَٱللَّهُ يَعْصِمُكَ مِنَ ٱلنَّاسِ ۗ إِنَّ ٱللَّهَ لَا يَهْدِى ٱلْقَوْمَ ٱلْكَـٰفِرِينَ ﴿٦٧﴾

Say: People of earlier revelations! You have no ground to stand upon unless you observe the Torah and the Gospel and that which has been revealed to you by your Lord. That which is revealed to you by your Lord is bound to make many of them even more stubborn in their arrogance and disbelief. But do not grieve for unbelieving folk. (68)

قُلْ يَـٰٓأَهْلَ ٱلْكِتَـٰبِ لَسْتُمْ عَلَىٰ شَىْءٍ حَتَّىٰ تُقِيمُوا۟ ٱلتَّوْرَىٰةَ وَٱلْإِنجِيلَ وَمَآ أُنزِلَ إِلَيْكُم مِّن رَّبِّكُمْ ۗ وَلَيَزِيدَنَّ كَثِيرًا مِّنْهُم مَّآ أُنزِلَ إِلَيْكَ مِن رَّبِّكَ طُغْيَـٰنًا وَكُفْرًا ۖ فَلَا تَأْسَ عَلَى ٱلْقَوْمِ ٱلْكَـٰفِرِينَ ﴿٦٨﴾

Those who believe, and those who are Jews, and the Sabians, and the Christians – anyone who believes in God and the Last Day and does what is right shall have no fear, nor shall they grieve. (69)

إِنَّ ٱلَّذِينَ ءَامَنُوا۟ وَٱلَّذِينَ هَادُوا۟ وَٱلصَّـٰبِـُٔونَ وَٱلنَّصَـٰرَىٰ مَنْ ءَامَنَ بِٱللَّهِ وَٱلْيَوْمِ ٱلْأَخِرِ وَعَمِلَ صَـٰلِحًا فَلَا خَوْفٌ عَلَيْهِمْ وَلَا هُمْ يَحْزَنُونَ ﴿٦٩﴾

Surely, We accepted a solemn pledge from the Children of Israel, and We sent to them messengers. But every time a messenger came to them with something that was not to their liking, [they rebelled:] some they denounced as liars and some they put to death. (70)

لَقَدۡ أَخَذۡنَا مِيثَٰقَ بَنِىٓ إِسۡرَٰٓءِيلَ وَأَرۡسَلۡنَآ إِلَيۡهِمۡ رُسُلٗاۖ كُلَّمَا جَآءَهُمۡ رَسُولُۢ بِمَا لَا تَهۡوَىٰٓ أَنفُسُهُمۡ فَرِيقٗا كَذَّبُواْ وَفَرِيقٗا يَقۡتُلُونَ ۝٧٠

They reckoned no harm would come to them, so they were wilfully blind and deaf [to the truth]. Thereafter, God accepted their repentance: still many of them acted blind and deaf. But God sees all that they do. (71)

وَحَسِبُوٓاْ أَلَّا تَكُونَ فِتۡنَةٞ فَعَمُواْ وَصَمُّواْ ثُمَّ تَابَ ٱللَّهُ عَلَيۡهِمۡ ثُمَّ عَمُواْ وَصَمُّواْ كَثِيرٞ مِّنۡهُمۡۚ وَٱللَّهُ بَصِيرُۢ بِمَا يَعۡمَلُونَ ۝٧١

Unbelievers indeed are those who say: "God is the Christ, son of Mary." The Christ himself said: Children of Israel, worship God, my Lord and your Lord. Whoever associates partners with God, God shall forbid him entrance into Paradise and his abode will be the Fire. Wrongdoers will have no helpers. (72)

لَقَدۡ كَفَرَ ٱلَّذِينَ قَالُوٓاْ إِنَّ ٱللَّهَ هُوَ ٱلۡمَسِيحُ ٱبۡنُ مَرۡيَمَۖ وَقَالَ ٱلۡمَسِيحُ يَٰبَنِىٓ إِسۡرَٰٓءِيلَ ٱعۡبُدُواْ ٱللَّهَ رَبِّى وَرَبَّكُمۡۖ إِنَّهُۥ مَن يُشۡرِكۡ بِٱللَّهِ فَقَدۡ حَرَّمَ ٱللَّهُ عَلَيۡهِ ٱلۡجَنَّةَ وَمَأۡوَىٰهُ ٱلنَّارُۖ وَمَا لِلظَّٰلِمِينَ مِنۡ أَنصَارٖ ۝٧٢

Unbelievers indeed are those who say: "God is the third of a trinity." Of certain, there is no god save the One God. Unless they desist from so saying, grievous suffering will surely befall those of them who are unbelievers. (73)

لَّقَدۡ كَفَرَ ٱلَّذِينَ قَالُوٓاْ إِنَّ ٱللَّهَ ثَالِثُ ثَلَٰثَةٖۘ وَمَا مِنۡ إِلَٰهٍ إِلَّآ إِلَٰهٞ وَٰحِدٞۚ وَإِن لَّمۡ يَنتَهُواْ عَمَّا يَقُولُونَ لَيَمَسَّنَّ ٱلَّذِينَ كَفَرُواْ مِنۡهُمۡ عَذَابٌ أَلِيمٌ ۝٧٣

Will they not, then, turn to God in repentance and seek His forgiveness? God is Much-Forgiving, Merciful. (74)

أَفَلَا يَتُوبُونَ إِلَى ٱللَّهِ وَيَسْتَغْفِرُونَهُۥ وَٱللَّهُ غَفُورٌ رَّحِيمٌ ﴿٧٤﴾

The Christ, son of Mary, was but a Messenger: other messengers have passed away before him. His mother was a saintly woman. They both ate food [like other human beings]. Behold how clear We make [Our] revelations to them and behold how perverted they are. (75)

مَّا ٱلْمَسِيحُ ٱبْنُ مَرْيَمَ إِلَّا رَسُولٌ قَدْ خَلَتْ مِن قَبْلِهِ ٱلرُّسُلُ وَأُمُّهُۥ صِدِّيقَةٌ كَانَا يَأْكُلَانِ ٱلطَّعَامَ ٱنظُرْ كَيْفَ نُبَيِّنُ لَهُمُ ٱلْءَايَٰتِ ثُمَّ ٱنظُرْ أَنَّىٰ يُؤْفَكُونَ ﴿٧٥﴾

Say: Would you worship in place of God anything that has no power to harm or to benefit you? It is God alone who hears all and knows all. (76)

قُلْ أَتَعْبُدُونَ مِن دُونِ ٱللَّهِ مَا لَا يَمْلِكُ لَكُمْ ضَرًّا وَلَا نَفْعًا وَٱللَّهُ هُوَ ٱلسَّمِيعُ ٱلْعَلِيمُ ﴿٧٦﴾

Say: People of earlier revelations! Do not overstep the bounds of truth in your religious beliefs, and do not follow the vain desires of those who have gone astray in the past, and have led many others astray and are still straying from the right path. (77)

قُلْ يَٰٓأَهْلَ ٱلْكِتَٰبِ لَا تَغْلُوا۟ فِى دِينِكُمْ غَيْرَ ٱلْحَقِّ وَلَا تَتَّبِعُوٓا۟ أَهْوَآءَ قَوْمٍ قَدْ ضَلُّوا۟ مِن قَبْلُ وَأَضَلُّوا۟ كَثِيرًا وَضَلُّوا۟ عَن سَوَآءِ ٱلسَّبِيلِ ﴿٧٧﴾

Those of the Children of Israel who disbelieved were cursed by David and Jesus, son of Mary. That was because they rebelled and persisted in their trans-gression. (78)

لُعِنَ ٱلَّذِينَ كَفَرُوا۟ مِنۢ بَنِىٓ إِسْرَٰٓءِيلَ عَلَىٰ لِسَانِ دَاوُۥدَ وَعِيسَى ٱبْنِ مَرْيَمَ ذَٰلِكَ بِمَا عَصَوا۟ وَّكَانُوا۟ يَعْتَدُونَ ﴿٧٨﴾

They would never restrain one another from wrongdoing. Vile indeed were the things they did. (79)

كَانُوا۟ لَا يَتَنَاهَوْنَ عَن مُّنكَرٍ فَعَلُوهُ لَبِئْسَ مَا كَانُوا۟ يَفْعَلُونَ ۝

Now you can see many of them allying themselves with un-believers. So evil is that which their souls make them do. They have incurred God's wrath and in suffering they shall abide. (80)

تَرَىٰ كَثِيرًا مِّنْهُمْ يَتَوَلَّوْنَ ٱلَّذِينَ كَفَرُوا۟ لَبِئْسَ مَا قَدَّمَتْ لَهُمْ أَنفُسُهُمْ أَن سَخِطَ ٱللَّهُ عَلَيْهِمْ وَفِى ٱلْعَذَابِ هُمْ خَٰلِدُونَ ۝

Had they truly believed in God and the Prophet and all that which was revealed to them, they would not have taken them for allies, but many of them are evildoers. (81)

وَلَوْ كَانُوا۟ يُؤْمِنُونَ بِٱللَّهِ وَٱلنَّبِىِّ وَمَآ أُنزِلَ إِلَيْهِ مَا ٱتَّخَذُوهُمْ أَوْلِيَآءَ وَلَٰكِنَّ كَثِيرًا مِّنْهُمْ فَٰسِقُونَ ۝

Overview

These verses begin a passage which further exposes the reality of the people of earlier Scriptures, particularly the Jews and Christians. It highlights their deviant beliefs and evil deeds and establishes the basis of the relationship that may exist between them and the Prophet and the Muslim community, outlining the duties of the Prophet and the Muslims in dealing with them. The passage also states a number of basic principles of faith and of the actions the Muslim community should take against deviant beliefs.

God addresses the Prophet giving him the task of conveying everything that has been revealed to him by His Lord, keeping nothing for himself and delaying nothing for any particular reason or circumstance. If he does not act on His instructions, even though he may be motivated by the desire to avoid conflict, he would not be delivering His message. Part of what the Prophet has been commanded to convey, was to tell the people of earlier revelations that they had nothing to stand on unless they implemented the Torah, the Gospel, and what had been revealed to them by their Lord. He was to make this statement in the clearest and most decisive of terms.

Moreover, the Prophet was also to declare that by going back on their covenant with God and by killing prophets, the Jews had rejected the faith and become unbelievers. The Christians did likewise, by claiming that Jesus Christ, son of Mary, was God Himself, and by stating that God was one of a trinity. The Prophet was also to declare that Jesus, (peace be upon him), warned the Children of Israel against associating partners with God. Moreover, God has denied access to Heaven to all those who ascribe partners to Him. He was further to declare that the Children of Israel have been cursed by both David and Jesus, because of their transgression.

The passage ends with an exposé of the people of earlier revelations' attitude when they supported the idolaters against the Muslims. It declares that this came about as a result of their lack of belief in God and the Prophet. They are called upon to believe in what has been revealed to Muḥammad, (peace be upon him). Otherwise, they will be unbelievers. We will now look at the verses in this passage in detail.

A Vital Proclamation to Deliver God's Message

Messenger, proclaim what has been revealed to you by your Lord. For, unless you do it fully, you will not have delivered His message. God will protect you from all men. God does not guide those who reject faith. Say: People of earlier revelations! You have no ground to stand upon unless you observe the Torah and the Gospel and that which has been revealed to you by your Lord. That which is revealed to you by your Lord is bound to make many of them even more stubborn in their arrogance and disbelief. But do not grieve for unbelieving folk. Those who believe, and those who are Jews, and the Sabians, and the Christians – anyone who believes in God and the Last Day and does what is right shall have no fear, nor shall they grieve. (Verses 67–9)

The Prophet is given clear instructions to convey all that has been revealed to him by His Lord, allowing no room for any reservations as he declares the truth. Otherwise, he would not be fulfilling his duty as a Messenger entrusted with conveying God's message. It is God who will protect him against all mankind. Whoever enjoys God's protection has nothing to fear from other humans, powerless as they are.

In matters of faith, the word of truth must always be clear and decisive, and must be stated in full. Let anyone who opposes it say what he may, and let its enemies do what they can; the true word of faith will never make concessions for people's desires. It must be stated clearly so that it penetrates into people's hearts with power. It is a fact of life that when the word of truth is stated clearly, it is immediately well received by people willing to accept the faith. When it is surrounded with equivocation, it cannot win those reluctant hearts which are the very target of the advocates of faith. Hence, clarity is essential in faith advocacy.

"God does not guide those who reject faith." (Verse 67) If so, let the word of truth be clear, decisive, and final. The truth is accepted by a heart which is open, responsive. It is not accepted as a result of patting the shoulders of those who do not possess such qualities.

A powerful and decisive approach to the statement of truth does not have to be harsh or overbearing. God has commanded His Messenger (peace be upon him) to call all mankind to the path of his Lord using wisdom and goodly exhortation and advice. There is no contradiction between Qur'ānic directives. Wisdom, goodly advice and exhortation are not contrary to clarity and decisiveness in stating the truth. The method of conveying something, however, is different from what is being conveyed. The requirement here is not to resort to equivocation in stating the full truth about faith and not to seek a middle way with people who do not accept it. There can be no compromise when it comes to the essence of faith.

Right from the very early days of his Islamic call, the Prophet employed wisdom and kindly advice in conveying his message, but he made it clear that there could be no compromise in faith. He was commanded to say: *"Unbelievers, I shall not worship what you worship."* (109: 1–2) He never suggested to anyone that he was simply after minor amendments to their beliefs. Instead, he told them that their beliefs were totally false and that his faith was the whole truth. He proclaimed the truth in its fullness, using a kindly and gentle approach.

In this *sūrah*, his duty is stated clearly: *"Messenger, proclaim what has been revealed to you by your Lord. For, unless you do it fully, you will not have delivered His message. God will protect you from all men. God does not guide those who reject faith."* (Verse 67)

It appears from the general context that what is meant here is that the Prophet would confront the people of the Scriptures with what they truly were. He would, thus, be telling them that they had no faith and indeed had nothing to stand on until they implemented the Torah and the Gospel and what had been revealed to them by their Lord. As such, their claims that they followed Scriptures and that they had a faith were false. *"Say: People of earlier revelations! You have no ground to stand upon unless you observe the Torah and the Gospel and that which has been revealed to you by your Lord."* (Verse 68)

At that time, when the Prophet was ordered to have such a confrontation with them, they used to recite their holy books and they claimed to be Jews or Christians and that they were believers. The orders given to the Prophet recognise nothing of these claims. Faith is not a word or a verbal statement or books that are recited or chanted, nor is it a quality that is passed on from parents to children. Faith is a way of life including personal beliefs, formal worship, and another important type of worship which is fulfilled through conducting all aspects of human life in accordance with faith. Since the people of the Scriptures did not establish their faith on such firm foundations, God's Messenger was ordered to confront them with the fact that they had no faith and that they had nothing to stand on.

The first practical result of implementing the Torah, the Gospel and what was revealed to the people of earlier revelations was the acceptance of the faith conveyed by the Prophet Muḥammad (peace be upon him). God had made a covenant with them to believe in every messenger He sends, and to give that messenger all their support. Their books, the Torah and the Gospel, included references and descriptions of the Prophet Muḥammad, as God, the most truthful of speakers, states. Hence, they would not be implementing the Torah and the Gospel and what was revealed to them by their Lord, (whether this phrase means the Qur'ān as some commentators say, or other Scriptures such as the Psalms, revealed to David), unless they followed the new faith which endorsed all that they had and superseded it.

Unless the Prophet confronted them with these facts, he would not have conveyed the message entrusted to him by his Lord.

God was certainly aware that to confront them with this decisive truth would make many of them grow in their arrogance and disbelief. That, however, did not prevent the Prophet from making such a confrontation, feeling no sorrow at their increased arrogance and deviation. It was Divine wisdom that he should proclaim the word of the truth, and allow it to produce its effect on people's hearts. This would provide anyone who follows right guidance with the truth. *"That which is revealed to you by your Lord is bound to make many of them even more stubborn in their arrogance and disbelief. But do not grieve for unbelieving folk."* (Verse 68)

By giving these instructions to the first advocate of the Divine faith, God delineated the method of advocacy and explained His purpose behind choosing this method. God also comforts His Messenger so that he does not grieve over what happens to those who reject the truth and grow even more stubborn in their arrogance and disbelief. They deserve their miserable end because their hearts cannot tolerate the word of truth. Hence, it is better to confront them with it in order to help their reality surface.

When the Truth is Advocated by the Few

These two verses with which the passage opens bring us back to the question of the possibility of forging an alliance or a relationship of patronage between Muslims and those who received revelations from God. We need to look afresh at this question in the light of the task assigned to God's Messenger of delivering His message in full and the expected result of his endeavours. This is expected to mean that many of them will grow even more stubborn in their arrogance and disbelief.

We find first of all that God Himself states that the people of earlier revelations have nothing to stand on until they have implemented the Torah and the Gospel and all that was revealed to them by their Lord. In other words, they have nothing to stand on until they have adopted the final religion as a logical consequence of their implementation of their Scriptures. This is made absolutely clear by calling on them, in several places in the Qur'ān, to believe in God and the Prophet. Hence, in their present status, they cannot be described as followers of a Divine faith and they do not have a religion acceptable to God. God knows that confronting them with this fact will cause many of them to be even more stubborn in their arrogance and in their disbelief. Nevertheless, God has commanded His Messenger to confront them with this fact in the frankest of manners, feeling no regrets as a result of what it may cause.

If we are to consider God's word in this matter to be final, as it clearly is, then there is no way that we can consider the people of earlier revelations as people of faith with whom Muslims can have a relationship of mutual support against atheists and atheism, as advocated by deluded people and those who delude them. It is not open for a Muslim to change what God has stated: *"It is not open for a believer, man or woman, once God and His Messenger have made judgement on a certain matter, to have any choice in that matter."* (33: 36) God's word remains valid for all time, unchanged by circumstances. Nor are we permitted to modify our attitude in order to prevent the likely outcome of confronting them with this fact, which is bound to make them even more aggressive against us. It is not open to us to try to gain favour with them by acknowledging that they have a faith which is acceptable to us. Nor can we support them in defending their faith against atheism in the same way as we defend our own faith, the only one acceptable to God, against atheism.

God's instructions do not mark out such a route for us to follow. Indeed, He neither accepts from us such a recognition of the beliefs of the people of earlier revelations, nor does He forgive us such an alliance or the concept on which it relies. When we choose for ourselves something other than He has chosen for us, we are in effect recognising deviant concepts as a Divine faith, akin to our own. But it is God who says that the people of earlier revelations have nothing to stand on until they observe the Torah, the Gospel and that which has been revealed to them by their Lord. It is sufficient for us to look at their situation to realise that they do nothing of the sort.

Those who claim to be Muslims but do not put into practice what their Lord has revealed to them are in the same position as those people of earlier revelations: they have nothing to stand on. Any person who wants to be a true Muslim must implement God's message in his life, and must follow this through with a clear address to those who do not follow suit, telling them that they have nothing to stand on until they have implemented their faith. Their claims to be religious are refuted by the One who has sent down the religion. Total clarity in this matter is imperative. It is also the duty of a Muslim who has implemented God's message in this life to call on such people to embrace Islam anew. To claim to be a Muslim merely by word of mouth or by belonging to a Muslim family signifies little. It does not give the claimant any endorsement to his assertion that he follows the Divine faith.

When either group have accepted faith and implemented it in their lives, a Muslim may forge out a relationship of patronage and support with them to defend faith against atheists and atheism. Without such a condition, all other attempts are futile.

Faith is not merely a banner or a slogan or something we inherit from our parents. It is a fact instilled in people's consciences and has practical implementation in life. It is a belief held deeply in a person's heart, combined with acts of worship, and a code of living. Divine faith must have all these elements. People do not follow Divine religion unless all these aspects are equally present in their hearts and minds as well as in their lives generally. Any other situation is an exercise in self-delusion which no true Muslim attempts. A Muslim must always make this fact plain and establish his relationship with people on its basis. He should not worry over the consequences because it is God who protects and it is God who denies true guidance to unbelievers.

An advocate of faith would not have conveyed what God has revealed and would not have made God's argument plain to mankind unless he explained to them the nature of faith in full, describing to them their own situation as it is, in all frankness, without hesitation. Indeed, he may do them a disservice, if he does not tell them that they have nothing to stand on and that all their beliefs and practices are false. He must tell them that he is calling on them to accept something totally different from what they have, and that they have to make a total departure from their concepts, systems and values. It is right that people should know from an advocate of faith where they stand in relation to the truth he is calling on them to accept, *"so that he who would perish might perish in clear evidence of the truth and that he who would live might live in clear evidence of the truth."* (8: 42)

When an advocate of faith minces his words and does not make the essential difference that separates the falsehood people follow and the truth to which he is calling them absolutely clear, he actually deceives them and causes them harm. Such equivocation does not tell people exactly what they are called upon to accept or what they are required to do. Moreover, such an advocate does not fulfil his duty of conveying what God requires of him.

Gentility in calling on people to come to God is confined to the approach an advocate of the truth employs, but not to the truth he is conveying to them. The approach may be modified according to circumstances, employing wisdom and kindly admonition, provided that the truth is stated completely and in full clarity.

Some of us may consider that the people of earlier revelations have the largest following and the greatest material power. Similarly, those who follow pagan faiths in various parts of the world number hundreds of millions, and have their say in international affairs. Some are also bound to see that the advocates of materialistic, atheist creeds command numerical strength and destructive power. On the other hand, they see that those who describe themselves as Muslims have nothing to boast of, simply because they do not implement the Book God has revealed to them. They may, thus, be overawed, feel unable to put a decisive word of truth to mankind's straying majority. They may think it useless to tell all those groups that they have nothing to stand on as also explain to them the religion of the truth.

But this is not the proper approach. *Jāhiliyyah*, or the state of ignorance of the truth, remains the same even though it may be widespread throughout the whole world. It does not matter what people follow. They continue to be in error, unless they follow the true faith. The duty of an advocate of the truth remains the same, and cannot be changed simply because those who have gone astray are too numerous or because falsehood appears too strong. Falsehood remains without foundation. The call to the truth should be resumed in the same fashion as it started: it must declare to all mankind that they have nothing to stand on. It must be clear to us that we now face a situation similar to that faced by God's Messenger, (peace be upon him), when God addressed him with these words: *"Messenger, proclaim what has been revealed to you by your Lord. For, unless you do it fully, you will not have delivered His message. God will protect you from all men. God does not guide those who reject faith. Say: People of earlier revelations! You have no ground to stand upon unless you observe the Torah and the Gospel and that which has been revealed to you by your Lord."* (Verses 67–8)

The Truth Versus People's Fancies

This first part of the present passage concludes with a clear statement of the faith which God accepts from people, regardless of what they were called before the message of the last Prophet. It was the faith which united people of all creeds and doctrines in ancient history. *"Those who believe, and those who are Jews, and the Sabians, and the Christians – anyone who believes in God and the Last Day and does what is right shall have no fear, nor shall they grieve."* (Verse 69)

The passage names four groups: "those who believe" refers to Muslims, and the Jews are the followers of the Prophet Moses. The term Sabians refers, most probably, to those who abandoned the worship of idols before the Prophet Muḥammad's message, worshiping God alone, following no particular creed. There were a handful of Arabs among them. The Christians are those who followed the Prophet Jesus Christ (peace be upon him).

This verse states that whatever their creed was, those who believe in God and the Last Day and do what is right – and it is implicitly understood here and explicitly elsewhere in the Qur'ān that they have done that in accordance with the final Prophet's message – will attain salvation: *"shall have no fear, nor shall they grieve."* (Verse 69) They need not worry about what they used to do or under what title they were classified. The most important title is the last one.

What we have been describing is implicitly understood from this Qur'ānic verse. It comes under that part of our faith which is essentially known to all people. It is a primary concept of this faith that the Prophet Muḥammad (peace be upon him) is the last of all prophets and a Messenger of God sent to all mankind. All people, regardless of their religion, creed, belief, race, and nationality, are called upon to believe in his message as he preached it in essence and detail. Anyone who does not believe in him as a Messenger and does not believe in the totality and the details of his message remains in error. God does not accept from him the religion he followed prior to the revelation of Islam. Nor is he included among those described by God as people who *"shall have nothing to fear, nor shall they grieve."* (Verse 69)

It is this primary concept of faith which a Muslim may not compromise on under the great pressure of the *jāhiliyyah* or darkness in which humanity lives today. Indeed, a Muslim cannot overlook this concept when he establishes his relations with other people of different creeds and religions. He cannot try to reduce the pressure of ignorance by coming to terms with the followers of other creeds or doctrines, giving them the privilege of having "a faith" acceptable to God and constituting grounds for mutual support.

It is God alone who is the patron of believers: *"Those who ally themselves with God and His Messenger and the believers (will find that) the party of God will be victorious."* (Verse 56) This is certainly true even though appearances may give a different impression. Moreover, those who believe in God and the Last Day and do what is right, on the basis of the religion of Islam, which is the religion acceptable to God, shall have nothing to fear and shall not grieve. They need have no fear of the forces of evil and darkness and they need have no fear of their own goodly, believing souls. Grief will remain unknown to them.

Following this, the *sūrah* gives us an account of a part of the history of the Children of Israel, the Jews, which shows that they have nothing to stand on and that the message of Islam must be conveyed to them so that they have a chance to believe in the Divine faith. On the other hand, this history shows the Muslims that the nature of the Jews has not changed. Hence, the importance of the Jews will be reduced in their minds and they will not condone any alliance or patronage when they have such an attitude to the truth and to faith: *"Surely, We accepted a solemn pledge from the Children of Israel, and We sent to them messengers. But every time a messenger came to them with something that was not to their liking, [they rebelled:] some they denounced as liars and some they put to death. They reckoned no harm would come to them, so they were wilfully blind and deaf [to the truth]. Thereafter, God accepted their repentance: still many of them acted blind and deaf. But God sees all that they do."* (Verses 70–1)

This is a fact of ancient history. Their attitude to the Prophet of Islam (peace be upon him) was neither the first nor the last. They have become immersed in sin and disobedience and they have repeatedly violated their covenant with God, taking their own caprice and fancies as their deity instead of obeying God, following Divine faith and the guidance of God's Messengers. Indeed, sin and aggression against the advocates of the truth has become part of their nature: *"Surely, We accepted a solemn pledge from the Children of Israel, and We sent to them messengers. But every time a messenger came to them with something that was not to their liking, [they rebelled:] some they denounced as liars and some they put to death."* (Verse 70) Indeed, the history of the Jews and their attitude towards their prophets is full of denunciation and rejection, as well as murder and aggression. It is, indeed, a history of following vain desire instead of Divine guidance.

Perhaps this is the reason for giving the Muslim community a long and detailed history of the Israelites. God's purpose is to warn the Muslim nation against following in the footsteps of the Israelites. In this way those who have good insight and who maintain their bond with God remain aware of these slips and follow the example of the Jewish prophets when they encounter similar experiences to theirs. This is bound to happen since some generations of Muslims will inevitably end up in the same situation as the Jews when the latter strayed away from Divine guidance and their hearts hardened. Such generations of Muslims will do likewise: follow the dictates of desire, reject guidance, treat some of the advocates of truth as liars and kill others.

The Jews committed all these sins, thinking that God would not put them to trial and that He would not punish them. They chose to overlook the laws set in operation by God, thinking all the time that they are "God's chosen people."

"They reckoned no harm would come to them, so they were wilfully blind and deaf [to the truth]." (Verse 71) God stamped their sight and hearing so that whatever they saw or heard was of no benefit to them. *"Thereafter, God accepted their repentance,"* and He granted them His mercy, but they did not desist, nor did they benefit by their experience. *"Still many of them acted blind and deaf. But God sees all that they do."* (Verse 71) He will give them, the reward they deserve according to what He sees of their actions and what He knows of their intentions. They will never he allowed to escape punishment

It is sufficient for the believers to know this old history of the Jews and their present situation to make their believing hearts disown any alliance with them, in the same way as did 'Ubādah ibn al-Ṣāmit. Only hypocrites like 'Abdullāh ibn Ubayy ibn Salūl could bring themselves to remain their allies.

Misconceptions Leading to Disbelief

Such was the situation with regard to the Jews among the people of earlier revelations. The situation with regard to Christians is explained in the *sūrah* in a most decisive manner which clearly fits with its general tone and with the question under discussion.

Early in the *sūrah*, those who claim that the Christ, son of Mary, was God are described as unbelievers. At this point, this description is re-emphasised with regard to those who claim that God is a third of a trinity or allege that Jesus Christ, son of Mary, was God Himself. The *sūrah* combines this with a testimony by Jesus (peace be upon him) that they are unbelievers. He warns them against ascribing Divinity to anyone other than God Almighty. He acknowledges very clearly that God is his Lord and their Lord. This is concluded by a warning by God Himself against continuing with their unbelief represented by their own statements which cannot be uttered by people who believe in God and in the right faith.

> *Unbelievers indeed are those who say: "God is the Christ, son of Mary." The Christ himself said: Children of Israel, worship God, my Lord and your Lord. Whoever associates partners with God, God shall forbid him entrance into Paradise and his abode will be the Fire. Wrongdoers will have no helpers. Unbelievers indeed are those who say: "God is the third of a trinity." Of certain, there is no god save the One God. Unless they desist from so saying, grievous suffering will surely befall those of them who are unbelievers. Will they not, then, turn to God in repentance and seek His forgiveness? God is Much-Forgiving, Merciful. The Christ, son of Mary, was but a Messenger: other messengers have passed away before him. His mother was a saintly woman. They both ate food [like other human beings]. Behold how clear We make [Our] revelations to them and behold how perverted they are. Say: Would you worship in place of God anything that has no power to harm or to benefit you? It is God alone who hears all and knows all. Say: People of earlier revelations! Do not overstep the bounds of truth in your religious beliefs, and do not follow*

199

the vain desires of those who have gone astray in the past, and
have led many others astray and are still straying from the right
path. (Verses 72–7)

We have already given a brief explanation of how and when these
deviant assertions crept into the Christian faith, which was preached
by Jesus (peace be upon him), a Messenger of God. Like his brothers,
God's Messengers, he preached the principle of God's oneness in
its purity, unadulterated by even the slightest shred of idolatry or
polytheism. All Divine messages had the common goal of
establishing the principle of God's oneness, calling on mankind to
believe in it, and reject all pagan beliefs. We will mention here briefly
the conclusions which those synods endorsed, advocating the
concept of trinity and that of the divinity of Jesus Christ and their
subsequent disagreements.

> Nawfal ibn Niʿmatullāh ibn Girgīs of Nazareth says: the Christian
> faith on which all churches agree and which represents the basis
> of the constitution agreed by the synod is to believe in the One
> God: a single father, the Almighty, the creator of the heavens and
> the earth and what is seen and what is unseen, and to believe in a
> single lord, Jesus, the only son born to the father prior to all
> times and created of God's light. He is a true god originating
> from a true god, born but not created, equal to the father in essence
> and from whom everything derives its existence. It is for the sake
> of us human beings and for the atonement of our sins he descended
> from heaven. He took shape from the Holy Spirit, and took form
> from the Virgin Mary, and was crucified on our behalf at the
> time of Pilate, and suffered and was buried and then rose from
> the dead on the third day according to what is written in the
> books. He then rose to heaven and sat to the right of the Lord.
> He will come down again with glory to make the living and the
> dead submit. His kingdom will be everlasting. The Christian faith
> also requires believing in the Holy Spirit, the lord who gives life
> and who comes from the father. Together with the son he submits
> to Him and glorifies Him. He speaks to prophets.

In *Muḥaḍarāt fī al-Naṣrāniyah*, Muḥammad Abū Zahrah quotes a
historian of christian Faith who mentions that the nature of God

comprises three equal consecutive elements: God the Father, God the Son and God the Holy Spirit. To the Father, all creation belongs through the Son; the Son has the atonement; and the Holy Spirit gives purification.

Because of the difficulty of formulating a clear concept which combines the three elements in one and reconciling God's oneness with the trinity, Christian theologians have always tried to evade rational discussion of this paradoxical question. The theologian Potter writes in a paper entitled "Principles and Details": "We have understood this as far as our reason can cope with it. We hope to understand it more clearly in future when everything in the heavens and on earth will be revealed to us. As for the present, the measure of our understanding is sufficient."

God, limitless is He in His glory, says that all these assertions are false and represent unbelief. As we have seen, they include the claim that the Christ has a Divine nature, and they claim that God is the third of a trinity. God has the final say on all questions. He always says the truth and He guides to the right path.

"Unbelievers indeed are those who say: "God is the Christ, son of Mary." The Christ himself said: Children of Israel, worship God, my Lord and your Lord. Whoever associates partners with God, God shall forbid him entrance into Paradise and his abode will be the Fire. Wrongdoers will have no helpers." (Verse 72) We see how Jesus Christ himself (peace be upon him) has warned them, but they paid no heed. After he departed from them, they followed the deviant path he warned them against, because it is certain to forbid them entrance into Paradise and make them suffer in the fire of Hell. They forgot what Christ told them: *"Children of Israel, worship God, my Lord and your Lord."* He declared to them that he and they stood in the same position of servitude to God, the One God who has no partners.

The Qurʾān makes a final judgement on all their blasphemous claims: *"Unbelievers are those indeed who say: 'God is the third of a trinity.'"* (Verse 73) It states the truth which constitutes the basis of every faith preached by every one of God's Messengers: *"Of certain, there is no god save the One God."* (Verse 73) It threatens them with the punishment prepared for those who make such blasphemous assertions and believe in them: *"Unless they desist from so saying, grievous suffering will surely befall those of them who are unbelievers."* (Verse 73) The unbelievers are the ones who continue to make such assertions which God has ruled to be a clear denial of faith.

These stern warnings are followed by encouragement and persuasion: *"Will they not, then, turn to God in repentance and seek His forgiveness? God is Much-Forgiving, Merciful."* (Verse 74) The door to repentance and forgiveness is, thus, left open. God's forgiveness and mercy are certain to be forthcoming, if sought before it is too late.

Mary, the Saintly Woman and Her Son

The *sūrah* then puts them face to face with this clear fact in the hope that they will reason properly and bring themselves to understand things as they are. This is coupled with amazement that even after this exposition, they continue to reject the facts: *"The Christ, son of Mary, was but a Messenger: other messengers have passed away before him. His mother was a saintly woman. They both ate food [like other human beings]. Behold how clear We make [Our] revelations to them and behold how perverted they are."* (Verse 75)

The verse describes both mother and son as people who ate ordinary food. This was a simple fact in the lives of Jesus Christ (peace be upon him) and his saintly mother. Eating food is a characteristic of living creatures which proves the humanity of Christ and his mother. Food is normally eaten to satisfy an undeniable physical need. Whoever needs to eat food in order to live cannot be a deity. God's life needs no food to support it because He lives and remains alive by Himself. He does not need to have any created thing like food to enter or leave his body. Limitless is He in His glory.

This logic is so clear and powerful that no one can deny the fact it states. It is followed, therefore, by a condemnation of the Christians' attitude in so far as they refuse to accept it: *"Behold how clear We make Our revelations to them and behold how perverted they are."* (Verse 75)

This ordinary human life which Christ lived has troubled those who wanted to make him a deity in spite of his teachings to the contrary. They went to a great deal of trouble and argument about Christ's nature and whether it was Divine or human, as we have already briefly explained.

Speaking from a different angle, but using the same clear logic, the *sūrah* wonders at their objectionable stance: *"Say: Would you worship in place of God anything that has no power to harm or to benefit you? It is God alone who hears all and knows all."* (Verse 76)

It should be noted that the Qur'ānic verse deliberately uses the word "anything" rather than "anyone" in order to group together all creatures that have been worshipped, including those who have reason. The Qur'ān here refers to the fact that they are creatures and, as such, they are far removed in nature from Divinity. Thus, Jesus, the Holy Spirit and Mary are included under "anything" because, by nature, they are some of God's creation. The expression contains its own powerful connotations implying that it is totally illogical for anything or anyone to be worshipped when they can neither harm nor benefit anyone.

"It is God alone who hears all and knows all." (Verse 76) As such, it is God who can cause harm and bring benefit. It is He who hears the supplication of His servants, accepts their worship and knows what they entertain in their minds and what intentions they have behind their supplication and worship. Other beings cannot answer prayers or supplication since they cannot hear or know everything.

This part is concluded with a general appeal the Prophet is required to make to the people of earlier revelations: *"Say: People of earlier revelations! Do not overstep the bounds of truth in your religious beliefs, and do not follow the vain desires of those who have gone astray in the past, and have led many others astray and are still straying from the right path."* (Verse 77) All these deviant beliefs have originated with trying to give Jesus (peace be upon him) a supreme position of honour, which caused them to *"overstep the bounds of truth".*

The vain desires of Roman rulers brought about idolatrous beliefs into Christianity and the clerical synods' same desires gave rise to all those allegations which have distorted the Christian faith. It should be remembered that Jesus Christ delivered his message in all honesty as a Messenger of God. He said: *"Children of Israel, worship God, my Lord and your Lord. Whoever associates partners with God, God shall forbid him entrance into Paradise and his abode will be the Fire. Wrongdoers will have no helpers."* (Verse 72) This last address is a final attempt to save the people of earlier revelations and to help them rid themselves of deviation, conflict and vain desire.

Before concluding our commentary on this section, we should refer briefly to three main facts. The first relates to the painstaking effort Islam makes in order to establish the correct concept of faith on the clear basis of God's absolute oneness, and to eradicate all the traces of polytheistic beliefs that distorted earlier religions. The true nature of Godhead is stated clearly and all Divine attributes are associated with God alone. No human being or other creature has any share in these attributes. Islam's great effort in this respect indicates that the correct concept of faith is of vital importance in imparting consistency and happiness to human life. It also indicates that Islam considers faith the basis for all human activities and relations.

The second fact is that the Qur'ān declares unequivocally that those who claim that the Christ, son of Mary, is God, or those who claim that God is the third of a trinity are unbelievers. Now that God has given His verdict, it is not open to any Muslim to consider such people as following a Divine faith. While Islam does not compel anyone to abandon his beliefs in order to embrace Islam, it does not approve of considering non-Islamic beliefs as a religion acceptable to God. It declares here that such beliefs will never be accepted by God, since they are, in their totality, a rejection of the Divine faith.

The third fact is a logical consequence of the preceding ones. It tells us that there can be no alliance or patronage with any of the people of earlier revelations who entertain such beliefs and a Muslim who believes in God's oneness as stated clearly by Islam. Every Muslim believes that Islam is the final form of the religion of submission to God, preached by the Prophet Muḥammad (peace be upon him), and that this is the only religion God accepts from mankind.

As such, any thought of mutual support between the followers of religions against atheism appears to be nonsensical. When beliefs differ so radically, there can be no meeting ground between them. From the Islamic point of view, everything in life is based essentially on faith.

When Wrongdoing is Condoned

These verses make a definitive statement of the Jewish Prophets' attitude towards the unbelievers from among the Children of Israel. It is represented by the attitude of the Prophets David and Jesus (peace be upon them). Both of them cursed the unbelievers among the Children of Israel and their prayers were answered because of the aggression of those unbelievers, the spread of immorality among them, their turning a blind eye to the spread of evil among themselves, and their patronising of other unbelievers. The outcome of all this was that they incurred God's displeasure and were cursed. Their punishment will be everlasting.

> *Those of the Children of Israel who disbelieved were cursed by David and Jesus, son of Mary. That was because they rebelled and persisted in their transgression. They would never restrain one another from wrongdoing. Vile indeed were the things they did. Now you can see many of them allying themselves with unbelievers. So evil is that which their souls make them do. They have incurred God's wrath and in suffering they shall abide. Had they truly believed in God and the Prophet and all that which was revealed to them, they would not have taken them for allies, but many of them are evildoers.* (Verses 78–81)

When we remember that it was Jesus and David who cursed the Children of Israel, we realise that theirs is a long history of unbelief, disobedience and rejection of the truth. Prophets who were sent to guide and save them were the ones who eventually condemned them so that they might not be guided to the truth. God answered their prayers and destined the Israelites to a perpetual curse.

The unbelievers among the Children of Israel were the ones who distorted their revealed Scriptures and refused to abide by the rulings of the Divine Code, as we are told in several Qur'ānic *sūrahs*. They violated their covenant with God in which they pledged themselves to support and follow every messenger He sent: *"That was because they rebelled and persisted in their transgression."* (Verse 78)

Jewish history is full of examples of such rebellion and aggression. These were not mere individual actions in the Jewish community. Indeed, they were so frequent they became characteristic of the whole community, and even those who did not perpetrate such crimes either turned a blind eye to them or did not speak out against them: *"They would never restrain one another from wrongdoing. Vile indeed were the things they did."* (Verse 79)

Rebellion and transgression can occur in any community by those who are corrupt and deviant. The world is never free from evil and communities will always contain people who transgress. But a good community, by nature, does not allow evil and transgression to become commonplace. When wrongdoing becomes more difficult than doing good in a community, and when deterrent punishments are prescribed and the whole community stands against evil and enforces such punishments, then evil shrinks and the motivation to commit it weakens. This gives the community stronger ties so that it is more closely knit together. Corruption becomes confined to a few individuals or groups who are rejected by the rest of the community and, hence, they hold no sway over it.

As the Qur'ān depicts this phenomenon of Israelite society, condemning it and showing it in a bad light, it wants for the Muslim community a solid structure which repels every aspect of rebellion and transgression. It wants the Muslim community to solidly defend the truth and to be sensitive to any aggression against it. It wants those who advocate the implementation of faith to discharge their responsibility by standing firm against evil, corruption, tyranny and transgression. The Muslims should pay no heed to anyone who blames them for their attitude. They maintain their opposition to evil whether it is practised by powerful rulers, influential men of wealth, evil people with physical power or the masses swayed by vain desires. God's system remains the true system and those who deviate from it are all alike, be they people of high or low position. Islam strongly emphasises the need to fulfil God's trust, and threatens a common punishment to the whole community if it allows evil to spread within it. The responsibility is shared by every individual and by the community as a whole.

'Abdullāh ibn Mas'ūd quotes the Prophet as saying: "When the Children of Israel began to commit sin, their scholars counselled them to desist, but they continued in their erring ways. Their scholars, nevertheless, continued to mix socially with them, and to eat and drink with them. God caused one group of them to stand against another and they were cursed by David and Jesus, son of Mary." *"That was because they rebelled and persisted in their transgression."* (Verse 78) The Prophet was reclining when he said this and at this point he sat up and said: "No! By Him who holds my soul in His hand, you must push them to follow the truth." (Related by Aḥmad.)

'Abdullāh ibn Mas'ūd quotes the following statement by the Prophet :

> The first defect which occurred in the community of the Israelites was that a man would see another and say to him: "Fear God and abandon what you have been doing because it

is not permissible for you." However, he meets him the following day but still the man persists in his erring ways, but this does not prevent the other from eating and mixing socially with him. When they did this, God caused division and conflict to occur among them.

The Prophet then read the Qur'ānic verses: *"Those of the Children of Israel who disbelieved were cursed by David and Jesus, son of Mary. That was because they rebelled and persisted in their transgression. They would never restrain one another from wrongdoing. Vile indeed were the things they did. Now you can see many of them allying themselves with unbelievers. So evil is that which their souls make them do. They have incurred God's wrath and in suffering they shall abide. Had they truly believed in God and the Prophet and all that which was revealed to them, they would not have taken them for allies, but many of them are evildoers."* (Verses 78–81)

The Prophet then said: "No! By God, you shall enjoin what is right, forbid what is wrong, stand up to those who are unjust and force them to follow the truth."

(Related by Abū Dāwūd.)

The matter is not then one of mere words which enjoin good actions and speak against bad ones. It cannot stop at this. It must hammer the point home, boycott the evildoer and check evil, corruption, and transgression, with force if need be. The Prophet is quoted as saying: "He of you who sees an evil action being committed should change it with his own hands. If he cannot, then with his tongue. If he still cannot, then with his heart. This last one is the weakest degree of faith." (Related by Muslim.)

Aḥmad relates a *ḥadīth* which quotes the Prophet as saying: "God does not punish the whole community for the actions of a section of it, until the community sees evil committed within its ranks and does not speak out against it when its people are able to do so. If the case reaches that stage, God punishes the whole community and the evildoers as well."

The Prophet is also quoted as saying: "The best type of *jihād* is to say a word of truth in front of a despotic ruler." (Related by Abū Dāwūd and al-Tirmidhī.)

There are plenty of Qur'ānic verses and *aḥādīth* which confirm this concept. It is necessary to establish a sense of common responsibility within the community so that none of its members turn a blind eye when they see evil being committed. No one just sits idle knowing that society is becoming corrupt and justifies their inaction by trying to avoid what may happen. Within the Muslim community, everyone is responsible for protecting and maintaining the bonds established by God.

All this requires the formulation of a proper concept of faith and knowledge of what believing entails. It also requires that we know the Divine system we are called upon to implement and that it encompasses all aspects of life. We further need to take our faith seriously and work hard to establish the Divine system in the life of our community. It is only a Muslim community which conducts its affairs on the basis of the Divine system and implements God's law that allows a Muslim individual to put into proper practice the principle of enjoining what is right and forbidding what is wrong. This principle no longer remains the action of an individual which has little impact, as is the case in all *jāhiliyyah* societies we see today. These societies have established social traditions of their own which condemn interference in other people's business and consider transgression and disobedience as personal matters. They further allow injustice and tyranny to suppress all opinions and voices and punish very severely everyone who declares the word of truth in the presence of a tyrant.

All efforts and sacrifices should be directed first of all to the establishment of a good and noble society which implements God's system. Efforts must not be wasted in attempting marginal improvements, which are largely individual in outlook, through enjoining what is right and forbidding what is wrong.

A Change That Must Be Total

Partial reforms are not sufficient when the whole of society has gone wrong and ignorance has prevailed. When society has adopted a law other than that of God, efforts must strike at the roots and *jihād* campaigns must have the clear aim to establish God's authority in society. When this is accomplished, there is a solid basis for the fulfilment of the all-important principle which is characteristic of the Muslim community: to enjoin what is right and to forbid what is wrong.

All this requires having strong faith and knowing the true nature of faith and the scope of its work in peoples' lives. It is through such understanding that advocates of the truth come to rely totally on God, confident in His support, hoping to receive reward from Him only. They do not look to have reward or appreciation from a society that has gone astray or to receive support from those people who choose to live in darkness.

All Qur'ānic statements and *aḥādīth* that speak of "enjoining what is right and forbidding what is wrong" actually refer to the duty of a Muslim individual in a Muslim community which acknowledges God's authority and enforces His law. Such a society may at times fall under dictatorship or witness the spread of some sinful practices. Hence, the Prophet (peace be upon him) says: "The best type of *jihād* is to say a word of truth in front of a despotic ruler." The Prophet uses the term "*Imām*" to refer to the ruler because, in the Islamic system, the ruler is the first *Imām*. No ruler can be described as *Imām* unless he acknowledges God's authority and his own duty to enforce God's law. A ruler who implements any other law is described in the Qur'ān differently: *"Those who do not judge in accordance with what God has revealed are indeed unbelievers."* (Verse 44) In ignorant societies which refuse to enforce God's law, the most important wrong which gives rise to all other wrongs is the rejection of God's Divinity through rejecting His law. It is to the changing of this basic wrong that the efforts of the Muslim community should be directed before tackling secondary wrongs. It is useless for good people to try to resist or forbid such small wrongs when they, by nature, emanate from the first wrong of attempting to usurp God's Divinity and which reject His authority by ignoring His law.

It is perhaps pertinent to ask here the following question: according to what measure do we describe people's actions as wrong and tell them to refrain from doing them? You may, for example, declare that a particular action is wrong and then find ten people rising up against you from different quarters to tell you that it is not wrong. They claim that it might have been considered wrong in previous generations, but with progress and development, things have to be looked at in a different light. It is important, therefore, to have a proper standard and sound values by which to judge matters and identify what is right and what is wrong. From where though can we derive such values and how do we establish such a standard? If we were to rely on the ever-changing judgement of people and societies, or their traditions and prejudices, we would end up in a maze where there are no sign posts or road markings. Nevertheless, it is so important to establish such a standard and that this standard should remain constant, unaffected by people's prejudices. The standard we require, then, is that which God lays down.

Now let us consider a situation where society does not recognise God's authority in the first place and does not implement His law. Or let us consider a situation where society ridicules and persecutes those who advocate the implementation of God's law. Would it not be a waste of our time and energy to try to correct certain details or side issues over which opinions, values and standards differ so widely? It is extremely important to reach an initial agreement on a basis, standard and authority to which we refer for arbitration over conflicting views.

We must begin with enjoining the most important "right" of all, namely, the acknowledgement of God's authority and the adoption of the way of life He has laid down. It is equally important to forbid the most serious of wrongs which amounts to a rejection of God's Divinity through the rejection of His way of life. When the foundation is established, the structure can be built. Let us, then, concentrate all our efforts on one front so that we can establish that foundation. It is sad to see good, well meaning people spending all their energy in a concerted attempt to correct certain details when the basic criterion for the establishment of an Islamic community is non-existent.

What use is it to try to persuade people not to accept or take earnings that are unlawful, in a society where the whole community is based on usury? In such a society, all money is unlawful and no one can make sure that what he earns is lawful, because the whole social and economic system is in conflict with God's law.

What use is it to try to persuade people not to be promiscuous in a society which does not consider adultery an offence except in cases of rape? Even in such cases, it does not enforce the punishment prescribed by God, because it rejects God's law and, consequently, rejects God as the Creator, Ruler and Legislator? It is futile to tell people not to drink when the law of the country permits drinking and punishes only those who go out in the street totally drunk. Even then, it administers a punishment other than that defined by God's law, which it does not recognise.

You may try to tell people not to abuse religion, but what good does that achieve in a society which does not recognise God's authority and in which God is not worshipped properly. Other deities are recognised and a different law and set of values, standards and systems are implemented. In such a situation, the whole society, including the person whose faith is abused, submits to those who enact laws and set values and standards for it.

We ask once again, what use is it to enjoin what is right and forbid what is wrong in these situations? What benefit do we gain when we tell people to refrain from doing these grave sins, let alone small ones, when the most cardinal sin of all, i.e. the rejection of God and His law, is not forbidden? The matter is far greater and wider than the questions which consume the efforts and energies of well meaning people. Details, however important, including cardinal sins, should take a secondary position at this stage. Unless God's authority to legislate is recognised and acted upon, all efforts directed to detail are wasted.

God's Messenger, (peace be upon him), says: "Anyone of you who sees something wrong being done should change it with his hand. If he cannot, then with a word of mouth and if he still cannot, then in his heart. This last one is the weakest degree of faith." Muslims may face a situation where they cannot change wrong physically with their own hands and cannot change it by speaking out against it. So what is left to them is the weakest degree of faith, which means that they should change it in their hearts. This is something that no one can prevent them from doing, if they are truly Muslims.

It should be explained that this is not a negative attitude to wrong, as may be thought. The fact that the Prophet describes it as "changing" what is wrong suggests that it is a positive action. To object to what is wrong, even in one's thoughts, means maintaining a positive attitude towards that wrong. It suggests that the person concerned rejects that wrong and tries to eradicate it and replace it with what is right at the first opportunity. A Muslim is required to maintain at least the weakest degree of faith which is to object to wrong in private. To submit to wrong, on the other hand, simply because it can exert enormous pressure, is to abandon even the weakest degree of faith. In such a situation, the same curse that has been incurred by the Children of Israel applies.

> *Those of the Children of Israel who disbelieved were cursed by David and Jesus, son of Mary. That was because they rebelled and persisted in their transgression. They would never restrain one another from wrongdoing. Vile indeed were the things they did.* (Verses 78–9)

An Essential Requirement of Faith

The real reason for this attitude of the Jews, despite their having received revelations from God, is that they do not really believe in God and His Messenger. They have not embraced God's final message. Hence, they are unbelievers. Had they believed, they would not have allied themselves to unbelievers: *"Now you can see many of them allying themselves with unbelievers. So evil is that which their souls make them do. They have incurred God's wrath and in suffering they shall abide. Had they truly believed in God and the Prophet and all that which was revealed to them, they would not have taken them for allies, but many of them are evildoers."* (Verses 80–1)

This statement which describes the position of the Jews at the time of God's Messenger (peace be upon him) also applies today, tomorrow and at all times. It is also true of all the peoples of earlier revelations in most parts of the world today. Hence, it is our duty to carefully study the Qur'ān and learn the lessons it has for every Muslim community throughout all generations.

It was the Jews who allied themselves to the unbelievers and incited them to attack the Muslims. God says of them in the Qur'ān: *"They say to the unbelievers that they are better guided than the believers."* (4: 51) This was most clearly apparent in the Battle of the Moat, but it was also clear both before and after it, up to our present time. Israel could not have come into existence in Palestine except through the Jews allying themselves to present-day unbelievers and atheists.

As for the other people of earlier revelations, they ally themselves with materialist atheism whenever they have to deal with Muslims. They even cooperate with people of pagan and idolatrous religions when they have to fight Muslims, even though those Muslims do not represent Islam in any way, except through being descendants of past

Muslim generations. All this goes to show how deeply rooted is the grudge against this faith and those who belong to it, though their claims of belonging to it may be false. God indeed tells the truth. He says: *"Now you can see many of them allying themselves with unbelievers. So evil is that which their souls make them do. They have incurred God's wrath and in suffering they shall abide."* (Verse 80) This is the net result of what they have done for themselves. Evil indeed is such an outcome. Bitter indeed are the fruits they reap from allying themselves with unbelievers.

Who of us reads or listens to God's description of those people and still takes decisions that cannot be sanctioned by God, concerning alliances and mutual support between the followers of this religion and its enemies who are allied with unbelievers? What motive could there be for those people to seek an alliance with unbelievers, unless it is lack of faith in God and His Messenger: *"Had they truly believed in God and the Prophet and all that which was revealed to them, they would not have taken them for allies, but many of them are evildoers."* (Verse 81) This is indeed the reason: they do not believe in God and the Prophet, and the majority of them are evildoers. They share the same feelings and directions with unbelievers. Hence, they prefer to be allied with them rather than with those who believe in God and His Messenger.

This Qur'ānic comment highlights three important facts. Firstly, that all the people of the Scriptures, with the exception of a few who believe in Muḥammad, God's Messenger (peace be upon him), do not believe in God because they do not believe in His last Messenger. The Qur'ān does not describe them as people who do not believe in the Prophet only, but describes them as non-believers in God as well: *"Had they truly believed in God and the Prophet and all that which was revealed to them, they would not have taken them for allies, but many of them are evildoers."* (Verse 81) This is a clear statement from God which does not admit any ambiguity or differing interpretation. No matter how strongly they claim that they believe in God, they are unbelievers, particularly when we take into consideration their deviant concepts of God as these have been outlined in this and other *sūrahs*.

Secondly, all the people of earlier revelations are required to embrace the Divine faith, as they have been called upon to do so by the Prophet Muḥammad (peace be upon him). If they respond, then they are believers and they follow a Divine faith. If they reject this call, God's description of them remains true.

Thirdly, there can be no bond of alliance or mutual support between them and Muslims in any matter, because all matters are, according to Islam subject to faith.

It is important, however, to point out that Islam instruct its followers to be kind to the people of earlier revelations and to extend to them benevolent treatment and to protect their lives, honour, and property when they are in the land of Islam. Muslims are also required to let them follow their religions, whatever they are, but to call on them gently to follow Islam and to argue with them over this in a reasonable manner. It is also the duty of Muslims to fulfil their covenants with them as long as they remain true to such covenants. They may not at any time be subjected to any form of compulsion in matters of faith.

Such is Islam: clear, straightforward, kind, tolerant.

God always tells the truth and He guides to the path that is straightest.

7

Relations with Other Faiths

You will certainly find that, of all people, the most hostile to those who believe are the Jews, and those who associate partners with God; and you will certainly find that the nearest of them in affection to the believers are those who say, "We are Christians." This is so because there are priests and monks among them and because they are not given to arrogance. (82)

۞ لَتَجِدَنَّ أَشَدَّ ٱلنَّاسِ عَدَاوَةً لِّلَّذِينَ ءَامَنُواْ ٱلۡيَهُودَ وَٱلَّذِينَ أَشۡرَكُواْ وَلَتَجِدَنَّ أَقۡرَبَهُم مَّوَدَّةً لِّلَّذِينَ ءَامَنُواْ ٱلَّذِينَ قَالُوٓاْ إِنَّا نَصَٰرَىٰ ذَٰلِكَ بِأَنَّ مِنۡهُمۡ قِسِّيسِينَ وَرُهۡبَانٗا وَأَنَّهُمۡ لَا يَسۡتَكۡبِرُونَ ۝

When they listen to what has been revealed to God's Messenger, you see their eyes overflow with tears because of the Truth they recognise. They say: "Our Lord, we do believe; so enrol us among those who bear witness to the truth. (83)

وَإِذَا سَمِعُواْ مَآ أُنزِلَ إِلَى ٱلرَّسُولِ تَرَىٰٓ أَعۡيُنَهُمۡ تَفِيضُ مِنَ ٱلدَّمۡعِ مِمَّا عَرَفُواْ مِنَ ٱلۡحَقِّ يَقُولُونَ رَبَّنَآ ءَامَنَّا فَٱكۡتُبۡنَا مَعَ ٱلشَّٰهِدِينَ ۝

"How could we fail to believe in God and the truth that has come to us when we dearly hope that our Lord will admit us among the righteous?" (84)

وَمَا لَنَا لَا نُؤۡمِنُ بِٱللَّهِ وَمَا جَآءَنَا مِنَ ٱلۡحَقِّ وَنَطۡمَعُ أَن يُدۡخِلَنَا رَبُّنَا مَعَ ٱلۡقَوۡمِ ٱلصَّٰلِحِينَ ۝

And for this their prayer God will reward them with gardens through which running waters flow, where they will abide. Such is the reward of those who do good; (85)

فَأَثَـٰبَهُمُ ٱللَّهُ بِمَا قَالُواْ جَنَّـٰتٍ تَجْرِى مِن تَحْتِهَا ٱلْأَنْهَـٰرُ خَـٰلِدِينَ فِيهَا ۚ وَذَٰلِكَ جَزَآءُ ٱلْمُحْسِنِينَ ﴿٨٥﴾

While those who disbelieve and deny Our revelations are destined for the blazing fire. (86)

وَٱلَّذِينَ كَفَرُواْ وَكَذَّبُواْ بِـَٔايَـٰتِنَآ أُوْلَـٰٓئِكَ أَصْحَـٰبُ ٱلْجَحِيمِ ﴿٨٦﴾

Overview

This short passage complements the discussion which has already taken place in this *sūrah* about the attitudes of the Jews, the Christians and those who associate partners with God towards His Messenger (peace be upon him) and the Muslim community. It includes statements explaining the deviation that has crept into the faiths of the Jews and Christians, the ill intentions and wickedness of the Jews towards their prophets and towards God's Messenger, and their support of the unbelievers against him. The discussion in this *sūrah* gives the final judgement on the Jews and Christians, describing them in terms of unbelief or "unfaith" because they have abandoned what their own Scriptures state and denied what God's Messenger has conveyed to them. This *sūrah* also confirms that the Jews and the Christians have nothing to stand on unless they implement the Torah and the Gospel and all that has been revealed to them by their Lord. Addressing the Prophet (peace be upon him), the *sūrah* requires him to convey what has been revealed to him by his Lord to all people: idolaters, Jews and Christians alike. All of them follow nothing of the Divine faith and all of them are called upon to believe in Islam. The *sūrah* also requires the Muslim community to be allied only with God, His Messenger and the believers and to seek no alliance with the Jews and the Christians because they are allies of one another. The Jews also ally themselves to unbelievers, and for this they have been cursed by David and Jesus, son of Mary.

This short passage explains the attitude of all these groups towards the Prophet and the Muslim community. They also state the different rewards awaiting them in the Hereafter.

Who Hates the Believers Most?

The Muslim community used to receive Qur'ānic revelations in order to determine, according to the directives of the Qur'ān, its plan of action, and to adopt according to these directives the proper attitudes towards all people. The Qur'ān is the Book which gives the Muslim community the guidance it needs and determines the course of action it should take. When the Muslim community implemented this method, it was able to overcome others and not be beaten by them. This is because it fought its enemies under direct Divine leadership, by virtue of the fact that the Prophet, its leader, followed Divine guidance and implemented Divine instructions.

The Divine directives included in the Qur'ān continue to be operative. The advocates of Islam today and tomorrow will do well if they listen to these directives and statements as if they are addressed to them now in order to determine on their basis their attitudes towards all groups of people and towards different beliefs and creeds, situations and systems, values and standards.

"You will certainly find that, of all people, the most hostile to those who believe are the Jews, and those who associate partners with God." (Verse 82) The way this statement is phrased makes it addressed either to the Prophet or to all believers because it states something that can be recognised by everyone. Arabic style admits both possibilities. In either case, it provides the same meaning. What is noteworthy about the phrasing of this statement is the fact that the Jews are mentioned ahead of the idolaters in being most hostile to the believers, and that their hostility is open and easily recognised by anyone who cares to pay attention.

It is true that in Arabic usage, the conjunction "and" simply denotes a combination without adding any ordering of those which are combined. By mentioning the Jews first in this instance, when it would be thought they would be less than the idolaters in their hostility to the believers as they have revealed Scriptures of their own, makes the ordering particularly significant. Because of the way it is phrased, the statement directs attention to the fact that their Scriptures have not

217

changed the Jews and that they are just the same as the unbelievers in their ardent hostility towards the believers. This is the least that can be said, although it is also possible that the statement means that in their hostility to believers, the Jews took the lead, their animosity greater than that of the idolaters.

When we look at the history of Islam ever since its very early days until the present moment, we have no doubt that the hostility of the Jews to the believers has always been more fierce, determined and longer lasting than the hostility of the idolaters and unbelievers. From the very first moment the Muslim state was established in Madinah, the Jews adopted a hostile attitude towards it. They schemed against the Muslim community from the outset of its very existence. Qur'ānic references to this hostility and scheming are sufficient to give a good idea of the unabating war the Jews have waged against Islam and its Messenger (peace be upon him), and the Muslim community throughout history. Indeed, this war has not abated for a single moment throughout fourteen centuries. It continues to rage throughout the world even today.

When the Prophet settled in Madinah, he concluded a treaty of peaceful coexistence with the Jews and called on them to believe in Islam, which confirmed the Torah that had been revealed to them before. They, however, did not fulfil their obligations under this treaty in the same way as they reneged on every pledge they made to their Lord or to their prophets. For this reason, God says to the Prophet about them: *"We have sent down to you clear revelations: none will deny them except the evildoers. Is it always to be the case that every time they make a solemn pledge some of them renege on it? The truth is that most of them do not believe. And now that a Messenger from God has come to them confirming what is already in their possession, some of those who had been given the Scriptures cast the Book of God behind their backs as though they know nothing [about it]."* (2: 99–101)

They harboured hostility towards Islam and the Muslims from the very first day when God united the two Arab tribes, al-Aws and al-Khazraj, under Islam, thus leaving no room for the Jews to play one group off against the other. They increased their hostility from the day the Prophet Muḥammad (peace be upon him) assumed leadership of the Muslim community denying the Jews any chance to impose their views. They have since then utilised all available weapons and all ways and means that their scheming ingenuity could identify to undermine Islam. In this they relied on their experience as slaves in Babylon and Egypt and their subservience to the Roman Empire. Although Islam was hospitable to them after their humiliation, they returned its favours with the most wicked scheming.

They incited all the forces of pagan Arabia against Islam, and they worked hard to forge an alliance with all previously hostile tribes to launch an offensive against the Muslim community. They even claimed that the Arab idolaters were a better guided people than the believers.

When Islam was able to overcome them with the force of the truth, they tried to scheme against it by incorporating fabrications into their books. The only book which remained pure was and is the Qur'ān, God's book which He has guaranteed to preserve intact. They also schemed against Islam by trying to sow discord within Muslim ranks and by creating trouble in which they managed to manipulate newcomers to Islam and those who had not acquired proper insight into Islamic principles or values. Their scheming also entailed inciting Islam's adversaries everywhere to come out in a joint effort against it.

In recent history, they have been the ones to lead the war against Islam throughout the world. It is they who utilised Christian and idolatrous forces in an all-out effort against Islam. It is they who create heroes who have Muslim names but try to suppress Islam with all their might. God tells the truth when He says: *"You will certainly find that, of all people, the most hostile to those who believe are the Jews, and those who associate partners with God."* (Verse 82)

An alliance of forces hostile to Islam was forged in order to launch a pincer attack against the newly-born Muslim state in Madinah. In an attempt to exterminate Islam altogether, this grouping consisted of the Jewish tribe of Qurayẓah as well as other Jews, the major Arab tribe of the Quraysh in Madinah and other major tribes in the rest of Arabia. The person who took it upon himself to bring about this alliance and who worked hard for its realisation was a Jew.

Thirty years later, a group of Jews started a mass uprising bringing together the remnants of hostile groups, and spreading all sorts of rumours. They succeeded in stirring up trouble to such an extent that it led to the assassination of 'Uthmān the third Caliph to rule the Muslim state after the Prophet. The Muslim world has often faced problems as a result of Jewish conspiracies ever since the early days of Islam.

The person who then took the lead in fabricating statements and attributing them to God's Messenger (peace be upon him), and fabricating reports about Islamic history and leading Muslim personalities was also a Jew.

In more recent history, it was a Jew who stirred nationalistic feelings and gave prominence to them in the last Islamic Caliphate. He was the schemer behind the rebellions and *coups d'etat* which began by replacing Islamic law with a "constitution" during the reign of Sultan 'Abd al-Ḥamīd prior to the abolition of Islamic rule altogether at the hands of the nationalist hero, 'Ataturk'.

The Jews have been the prime movers in the war declared on all fronts against the advocates of Islamic revival throughout the world. Moreover, the atheistic, materialistic doctrine in our world was advanced by a Jew, and the permissive doctrine which is sometimes called, "the sexual revolution", was advocated by a Jew. Indeed, most evil theories which try to destroy all values and all that is sacred to mankind are advocated by Jews.

The war that the Jews have launched against Islam has been much longer lasting and wider in spectrum than that launched against it by pagans and unbelievers both in old and modern times, although the latter has also been extremely ferocious. The fight with the Arabian idolaters in the early days of Islam did not last more than 20 years. Of similar duration was the battle against the Persian Empire. In modern times, we see that the war launched against Islam by paganism in India is and has been manifestly ferocious, but it does not equal the ferocity of the Zionist war against Islam. [Incidentally, Marxism is only an off-shoot of Zionism in this respect.] The only battle against Islam which is comparable to that of the Jews in respect of its duration and scope was that of the Crusades, to which we will presently refer.

We remind ourselves of this history in order to appreciate God's purpose in mentioning the Jews ahead of the idolaters in the ranking of those who are hostile to Islam: *"You will certainly find that, of all people, the most hostile to those who believe are the Jews, and those who associate partners with God."* (Verse 82) Theirs is a wicked nature which is full of hatred for Islam, its Prophet and its followers. Hence, God warns His Messenger and the believers against its designs. This wicked and most vile nature could only be defeated in past history by

Islam and its followers when they truly followed Islamic principles. Our modern world will not be saved from this wicked nature except by Islam, and only when its people implement Islam completely in their lives.

An Attitude Bringing Rich Rewards

"And you will certainly find that the nearest of them in affection to the believers are those who say, 'We are Christians.' This is so because there are priests and monks among them and because they are not given to arrogance." (Verse 82) This verse and the four verses that follow it describe a certain condition and make a judgement concerning it. The description applies to a group of the followers of Jesus (peace be upon him) who describe themselves as Christians, and it states that these are the nearest of all people in their affection to the believers.

Although these verses leave us in no doubt that they describe a particular case to which the whole statement applies, many are those who are mistaken in their understanding of it. Their mistake causes a serious error in determining the Muslims' attitude towards other camps. Hence, it is important to carefully study these verses and understand the particular case to which they apply.

That particular case applied to a certain group of Christians. They were closest in their affection to the believers, *"because there are priests and monks among them and because they are not given to arrogance".* (Verse 82) Among them were people who were fully aware of the true Christian faith, and were prepared to acknowledge the truth whenever they realised it.

The Qur'ān clarifies the fact that this description does not apply to all those who claim to be Christians. It provides more details of the attitude of this particular group: *"When they listen to what has been revealed to God's Messenger, you see their eyes overflow with tears because of the Truth they recognise. They say: 'Our Lord, we do believe; so enrol us among those who bear witness to the truth. How could we fail to believe in God and the truth that has come to us when we dearly hope that our Lord will admit us among the righteous?'"* (Verses 83–4)

This is a very vivid description of this group. They are so deeply touched when they listen to the Qur'ān that tears spring to their eyes in recognition of the truth they hear. In the first instance, they cannot express this recognition in any way better than allowing their eyes to overflow with tears. No words are adequate to describe their feelings. Such a response, indicative of profound effect, is a well-known human reaction.

Tearful eyes, however, are not enough. They do not wish to adopt a negative attitude to the truth they have recognised as a result of listening to the Qur'ān and its evident authoritativeness. They take a clear, positive attitude which accepts this truth, believes in it and submits to its authority. They declare their acceptance in a profound and frank manner, saying: *"Our Lord, we do believe; so enrol us among those who bear witness to the truth. How could we fail to believe in God and the truth that has come to us when we dearly hope that our Lord will admit us among the righteous?"* (Verses 83–4)

Firstly, they declare to their Lord that they believe in this truth they have recognised and pray to Him in His glory to include them among those who bear witness to this truth and with the community that seeks to implement it. That is the community of Muslims, which gives credence to its belief in this truth both by verbal declaration and by action to establish it in human life. Those new witnesses thus join the Muslim community that submits to the truth and they pray to God to witness their belief. Furthermore, they cannot accept that any obstacle should impede them from believing in God or submitting to the truth as they listen to it. After all, they hope that as a result of their acceptance of the faith, their Lord will be pleased with them, assign to them a higher rank and include them among the righteous: *"How could we fail to believe in God and the truth that has come to us when we dearly hope that our Lord will admit us among the righteous?"* (Verse 84)

This is, then, a definitive attitude towards the truth God has revealed to His Messenger. It is an attitude of careful listening, unbiased consideration, appropriate recognition, profound influence and unhesitating acceptance. The climax is to declare their total submission and their joining with the Muslim community, coupled with a prayer to God to include them among those who bear witness to the truth. This places on them a duty that their testimony should come in the form of action and struggle to implement the faith in human life, and a recognition that they can no longer adopt any way other than that of believing in God and the truth that He has revealed to His Messenger. It is this which causes them to hope that eventually they will win God's acceptance and His pleasure.

On Recognising the Truth of Islam

Having described their frank, positive attitude towards the truth revealed to God's Messenger and their declaration of their acceptance of Islam and their willingness to bear witness to it by sacrificing their wealth and lives for its cause, praying all the time that God may accept them as witnesses and admit them among the righteous, the *sūrah* describes their destiny: *"And for this their prayer God will reward them with gardens through which running waters flow, where they will abide. Such is the reward of those who do good."* (Verse 85)

God knows that what they have said is true and that they mean it seriously. They are determined to follow the path of faith and to bear witness to the truthfulness of the new religion they have adopted. He knows that they consider that bearing such testimony with all that it requires of personal and financial sacrifice is a favour which God grants to those of His servants who He chooses. He also knows that they realise that they have no way to follow other than the one they have chosen, hoping that their Lord will include them among the righteous. As God knows all this about them, He accepts their statement and grants them Heaven as a reward, describing them as people who do good and granting them the reward He keeps in reserve for such people: *"And for this their prayer God will reward them with gardens through which running waters flow, where they will abide. Such is the reward of those who do good."* (Verse 85) Doing good is the highest grade of faith and submission to God. This group of people have earned God's own acknowledgement that they do good.

The *sūrah* has given us a very clear description of this group of people who are *"nearest in affection to the believers"*, giving prominence to the fact that they are far from arrogant and that they respond to the truth once they recognise it. Moreover, they are honest, serious and willing to fulfil the requirements of faith. But the *sūrah* does not stop at that in identifying this group. It goes on to distinguish them from the rest of those who say, *"We are Christians"*. This latter group listen to the truth, but they deny it, turn away from it and have no interest in bearing witness to its truthfulness. Indeed, they claim it to be false: *"While those who disbelieve and deny Our revelations are destined for the blazing fire."* (Verse 86)

There is no doubt that the description, *'those who disbelieve and deny Our revelations'*, refers here to those who claim to be Christians, yet listen to the truth and refuse to respond to it. The Qur'ān describes them as unbelievers as long as they adopt this attitude. The description applies to the Jews and Christians who are joined with the idolaters in being unbelievers as long as they continue to deny that what God revealed to His Messenger as the truth, and as long as they continue to refuse to accept Islam which is the only religion acceptable to God. Statements to this effect are found in the Qur'ān: *"Those who disbelieve among the people of earlier revelations and the idolaters could have never departed [from their erring ways] until there had come to them the Clear Proof... Those who disbelieve among the people of earlier revelations and the idolaters shall be in the fire of hell, wherein they will abide. They are the worst of all creatures."* (98: 1 and 6) *"Unbelievers indeed are those who say: 'God is the Christ, son of Mary.'"* (Verse 72) *"Unbelievers indeed are those who say: 'God is the third of a trinity.'"* (Verse 73) *"Those of the Children of Israel who disbelieved were cursed by David and Jesus, son of Mary."* (Verse 78)

It is, then, a description repeatedly used in the Qur'ān and a judgement endorsed on several occasions. It is used here to distinguish between two groups of those who describe themselves as Christians as they adopt opposing attitudes towards believers. It also distinguishes the destiny of one group to that of the other. The first group will dwell in Heaven forever, since this is the reward of those who do good, while the other will end up in Hell.

In conclusion, we say that not all those who describe themselves as Christians are included among those who are *"nearest in affection to the believers"*. Anyone who suggests otherwise simply tries to make his judgement on the basis of only one part of the Qur'ānic statement, paying little attention to the rest. God's judgement applies only to a particular group of Christians of whom God has given us a full description, leaving no room for ambiguity or confusion.

But who are the Christians about whom this statement is made? We have several reports which identify them. The first one is given by al-Qurṭubī, a renowned scholar, who includes the following in his well-known commentary on the Qur'ān:

This verse refers to Negus, the ruler of Abyssinia, and his people. When a group of Muslims arrived in their land after the first emigration, as reported in detail in biographies of the Prophet, to save themselves from persecution by the unbelievers in Makkah.

The emigrants were a good number of people. God's Messenger later migrated to Madinah and the unbelievers were unable to capture him. Subsequently, war broke out between the two camps and the unbelievers were unable to harm the Prophet. When the Battle of Badr took place and God caused many of the stalwarts among the unbelievers to be killed in that Battle, the unbelievers of the Quraysh thought that they could pursue their revenge against the Muslim emigrants in Abyssinia. Some of them suggested that they should send two wise men to Negus with rich presents to request him to extradite the Muslims who had taken refuge in his land. If he responded favourably to this request, they would kill those Muslims in revenge for those unbelievers killed at the Battle of Badr.

The Quraysh sent 'Amr ibn al-'Āṣ and 'Abdullāh ibn Abī Rabī'ah with rich gifts. When God's Messenger heard of this, he sent 'Amr ibn Umayyah al-Ḍamrī who carried a letter from the Prophet to Negus. When Negus read the Prophet's letter, he called in Ja'far ibn Abī Ṭālib and his fellow immigrants. He also called in his priests and monks. He asked Ja'far to recite a passage from the Qur'ān and Ja'far recited *Sūrah* 19, entitled Mary. When they listened to it, their eyes were full with tears. It is to those people that reference is made by God in the following verses: *"You will certainly find that, of all people, the most hostile to those who believe are the Jews, and those who associate partners with God; and you will certainly find that the nearest of them in affection to the believers are those who say, 'We are Christians.' This is so because there are priests and monks among them and because they are not given to arrogance. When they listen to what has been revealed to God's Messenger, you see their eyes overflow with tears because of the Truth they recognise. They say: 'Our Lord, we do believe; so enrol us among those who bear witness to the truth.'"* (Verses 82–3) (This report is mentioned in a *ḥadīth* related by Abū Dāwūd.]

A different report is given by al-Bayhaqī on the authority of Ibn Isḥāq:

Twenty people or so of Abyssinian Christians came to meet the Prophet (peace be upon him) when he was still in Makkah. They found him in the Mosque and they talked to him and asked him questions. Several groups of people from the Quraysh were sitting in their usual places around the Ka'bah. When the Abyssinians had put all their questions to the Prophet, he called on them to believe in his message. He recited to them passages of the Qur'ān. When they listened to them, their eyes were tearful. They responded positively and declared that they believed in him as God's Messenger. They recognised him as the Prophet described in their Scriptures. When they left the Prophet, Abū Jahl, [the most hostile opponent of Islam in Makkah], and a number of Quraysh men stopped them and said, 'What a gullible group of people you are! Your people back home have sent you to gather information about this man. But you have not been long with him when you disowned your own faith and declared your belief in what he said to you. We have never seen a more feeble-minded group than you.' They replied, 'We leave you in peace, as we do not wish to have a slanging match with you. We are responsible for our deeds and you for yours. We will let no chance to do ourselves good slip away without making use of it.' It is also said that this group of Christians came from Najrān in Southern Arabia. It is reported that other verses of the Qur'ān commending their attitude were also revealed including the following verses: *"Those to whom We have vouchsafed revelations in the past believe in it [i.e. the Qur'ān]; and when it is read out to them, they say, 'We believe in it, for it is the truth from our Lord. Indeed even before this have we surrendered ourselves to Him. These shall receive a twofold reward for having been patient in adversity, and having repelled evil with good, and having spent in charity out of what We provided for them, and whenever they heard frivolous talk, having turned away from it and said: We are responsible for our deeds and you for yours. Peace be to you. We do not seek out ignorant people.'"* (28: 52–5)

A third report suggests that Ja'far ibn Abī Ṭālib, the Prophet's cousin, and his fellow immigrants in Abyssinia, came back to join the Prophet accompanied by 70 men wearing woollen clothes. Sixty-two of them were from Abyssinia and the other eight from Syria. The latter group included a monk called Baḥīrā and the other seven were Idrīs, Ashraf,

Abrahah, Thumāmah, Qutham, Durayd and Ayman. The Prophet recited to them the full text of *Sūrah* 36. When they listened to the Qur'ān, their eyes were full of tears and they declared that they believed in its truth. They said, 'This is very similar to the revelations given to Jesus Christ.' It is in reference to them that the following verses were revealed: *"You will certainly find that, of all people, the most hostile to those who believe are the Jews, and those who associate partners with God; and you will certainly find that the nearest of them in affection to the believers are those who say, 'We are Christians.' This is so because there are priests and monks among them and because they are not given to arrogance. When they listen to what has been revealed to God's Messenger, you see their eyes overflow with tears because of the Truth they recognise. They say: 'Our Lord, we do believe; so enrol us among those who bear witness to the truth. How could we fail to believe in God and the truth that has come to us when we dearly hope that our Lord will admit us among the righteous?'"* (Verses 82–4) This delegation was sent by the Abyssinian ruler, Negus, and they were the ones who dedicated themselves to worship in isolated places, such as caves.

Sa'īd ibn Jubayr says that God also revealed other verses of the Qur'ān, such as verses 52–5 of *Sūrah* 28, quoted above, about this group of people. Muqātil and al-Kalbī report that they were 40 Christians from Najrān and 32 from Abyssinia together with 68 from Syria. Qatādah says that these verses were revealed in reference to a group of Christians who followed the authentic Christian revelations. When God sent the Prophet Muḥammad with His last message, they believed in him and God praised them for this.

A Positive Response to God's Revelations

What we have stated in respect of the meaning of these verses, as suggested by the general sequence of the *sūrah* and confirmed by these reports, fits in well with other statements in this *sūrah* and in the Qur'ān as a whole concerning the attitudes of Jews and Christians in general towards the Islamic faith and its followers. Moreover, it fits in with the history of the Muslim community throughout the fourteen centuries of its history.

The *sūrah* maintains the same trend, atmosphere and objectives throughout. Moreover, God's revelations do not contradict each other:

*"Had it issued from any but God, they would surely have found in it
many an inner contradiction!"* (4: 82) In this same *sūrah* various
statements have been given which confirm the import of this text
which is the subject of our discussion. Of these we may quote:
*"Believers, do not take the Jews and the Christians for your allies.
They are allies of one another. Whoever of you allies himself with
them is indeed one of them. God does not bestow His guidance on the
wrongdoers."* (Verse 51) *"Say: People of earlier revelations! You have
no ground to stand upon unless you observe the Torah and the Gospel
and that which has been revealed to you by your Lord. That which is
revealed to you by your Lord is bound to make many of them even
more stubborn in their arrogance and disbelief. But do not grieve for
unbelieving folk."* (Verse 68)

Similarly in *Sūrah* 2, The Cow, we read: *"The Jews and the
Christians will never be pleased with you [Muḥammad] unless you
follow their faith. Say, 'God's guidance is the only true guidance.' And
if after all the knowledge you have received you yield to their desires,
there shall be none to help you or protect you from God."* (2: 120)

The events of history have confirmed God's warnings to the
Muslim community against the designs of both the Jews and
Christians. History has recorded the wicked opposition of the Jews
to Islam right from its first day in Madinah. Their scheming against
Islam has continued since then to the present moment, and they
continue to be its leaders, nursing their wicked grudges and always
resorting to treacherous schemes to undermine Islam. History has
also recorded that the crusading Christians have taken a hostile
attitude to Islam ever since the Battle of al-Yarmūk between the
Muslim army and the forces of the Byzantine Empire. It must be
mentioned here that there were exceptional cases such as those
described in the verses we have been discussing, when some
Christians responded to the call of Islam and embraced it. There
were also other groups of Christians who preferred to live under
Islamic justice in order to save themselves from the oppression of
their co-religionists. The general Christian trend towards Islam,
however, is epitomised by the Crusades which have continued in
different shades from the day of the Battle of al-Yarmūk up to the
present day, although they may occasionally seek to take a low
profile.

The Crusades, which lasted for two centuries, epitomise the Christian grudge against Islam. Their attitude is also reflected by the war of extermination launched against Islam and Muslims in the Andalus, in the colonisation of Muslim areas in Africa and throughout the world, as well as in missionary campaigns throughout the Muslim world.

Despite their mutual hatred of each other, Zionism and the Christian world continue to maintain their alliance against Islam. In their campaign against it, they have given practical proof to what God, who knows all, has said about them: *"They are allies of one another."* (Verse 51) They continued their campaigns until they were able to break up the state of the last Caliphate and they went on to erode all aspects of Islam, one after the other. They managed to undermine the Islamic system of government, and they are trying now to undermine the ties generated by Islamic prayer, as the Prophet himself has forewarned.

Moreover, today, they adopt the attitude of the Jews, lending support to paganism against Islam, wherever the two are in confrontation. They do this through direct aid or through the international organisations which they control. The attitude of Christian powers to the conflict between India and Pakistan over Kashmir is proof positive of all this.

In addition, they continue to patronise and lend support to regimes which undertake to crush the Islamic revivalist movement everywhere. They try to impart a heroic character to these regimes in order to enable them to crush Islam. This is a brief summary of what the history of fourteen centuries of Islam tell us about the attitude of the Jews and Christians towards Islam. Both are in the same camp, hostile to Islam, always trying to undermine it. It is extremely important that the advocates of Islam who fight for it today and in the future should realise this, so that they are not deceived by reconciliatory calls which take up the first part of the Qur'ānic statement and abandon its end, without picking up the thread of the whole *sūrah* or the evidence provided by other Qur'ānic statements, or without benefiting from historical events that confirm all this. Such movements use the preamble of the Qur'ānic text in order to calm the Muslims' legitimate feelings towards those who are hostile to them and scheme against them. All these forces mobilise their efforts in order to level a final, devastating blow at the roots of the Islamic faith.

These forces fear nothing as much as they fear enlightened minds among the believers, even though they may be small in number. Those who try to suppress this awareness are the worst enemies of Islam. Some of them may be deluded victims but the harm they cause is in no way less than the harm which the worst enemies of Islam try to inflict. Indeed, it may be even more harmful.

This Qur'ān guides to the way that is straightest. It is highly consistent, showing no contradiction whatsoever. Therefore, we must try to understand its message with open minds.

8

Detailed Legislation for Believers

Believers, do not forbid your-selves the good things God has made lawful to you. Do not transgress; God does not love the transgressors. (87)

يَـٰٓأَيُّهَا ٱلَّذِينَ ءَامَنُوا۟ لَا تُحَرِّمُوا۟ طَيِّبَـٰتِ مَآ أَحَلَّ ٱللَّهُ لَكُمْ وَلَا تَعْتَدُوٓا۟ إِنَّ ٱللَّهَ لَا يُحِبُّ ٱلْمُعْتَدِينَ ۝

Eat of what God has provided for you of lawful and wholesome things, and have fear of God in whom you believe. (88)

وَكُلُوا۟ مِمَّا رَزَقَكُمُ ٱللَّهُ حَلَـٰلًا طَيِّبًا وَٱتَّقُوا۟ ٱللَّهَ ٱلَّذِىٓ أَنتُم بِهِۦ مُؤْمِنُونَ ۝

God will not take you to task for those of your oaths which you may utter without thought, but He will take you to task for oaths which you have sworn in earnest. The breaking of an oath must be atoned for by the feeding of ten needy persons with more or less the same food as you normally give to your own families, or by clothing them, or by the freeing of one slave. He who cannot afford any of these shall fast three days instead. This shall be the atonement for your oaths when

لَا يُؤَاخِذُكُمُ ٱللَّهُ بِٱللَّغْوِ فِىٓ أَيْمَـٰنِكُمْ وَلَـٰكِن يُؤَاخِذُكُم بِمَا عَقَّدتُّمُ ٱلْأَيْمَـٰنَ فَكَفَّـٰرَتُهُۥٓ إِطْعَامُ عَشَرَةِ مَسَـٰكِينَ مِنْ أَوْسَطِ مَا تُطْعِمُونَ أَهْلِيكُمْ أَوْ كِسْوَتُهُمْ أَوْ تَحْرِيرُ رَقَبَةٍ فَمَن لَّمْ يَجِدْ فَصِيَامُ ثَلَـٰثَةِ أَيَّامٍ ذَٰلِكَ كَفَّـٰرَةُ أَيْمَـٰنِكُمْ إِذَا حَلَفْتُمْ وَٱحْفَظُوٓا۟ أَيْمَـٰنَكُمْ

you have sworn [and broken them]. But be mindful of your oaths. Thus God makes clear to you His revelations, so that you may give thanks. (89)

كَذَلِكَ يُبَيِّنُ ٱللَّهُ لَكُمْ ءَايَٰتِهِ لَعَلَّكُمْ تَشْكُرُونَ ۝

Believers, intoxicants, games of chance, idolatrous practices and divining arrows are abominations devised by Satan. Therefore, turn away from them so that you may be successful. (90)

يَٰٓأَيُّهَا ٱلَّذِينَ ءَامَنُوٓا۟ إِنَّمَا ٱلْخَمْرُ وَٱلْمَيْسِرُ وَٱلْأَنصَابُ وَٱلْأَزْلَٰمُ رِجْسٌ مِّنْ عَمَلِ ٱلشَّيْطَٰنِ فَٱجْتَنِبُوهُ لَعَلَّكُمْ تُفْلِحُونَ ۝

Satan seeks only to stir up enmity and hatred among you by means of intoxicants and games of chance, and to turn you away from the remembrance of God and from prayer. Will you not, then, desist? (91)

إِنَّمَا يُرِيدُ ٱلشَّيْطَٰنُ أَن يُوقِعَ بَيْنَكُمُ ٱلْعَدَٰوَةَ وَٱلْبَغْضَاءَ فِى ٱلْخَمْرِ وَٱلْمَيْسِرِ وَيَصُدَّكُمْ عَن ذِكْرِ ٱللَّهِ وَعَنِ ٱلصَّلَوٰةِ فَهَلْ أَنتُم مُّنتَهُونَ ۝

Obey God, and obey the Messenger, and be ever on your guard. But if you turn away, then know that Our Messenger's only duty is a clear delivery of the message [entrusted to him]. (92)

وَأَطِيعُوا۟ ٱللَّهَ وَأَطِيعُوا۟ ٱلرَّسُولَ وَٱحْذَرُوا۟ فَإِن تَوَلَّيْتُمْ فَٱعْلَمُوٓا۟ أَنَّمَا عَلَىٰ رَسُولِنَا ٱلْبَلَٰغُ ٱلْمُبِينُ ۝

Those who believe and do righteous deeds shall have no blame attached to them for any food they may have eaten, so long as they fear God and truly believe and do righteous deeds, and continue to fear God and believe, and remain God-fearing and persevere in doing good. God loves those who do good. (93)

لَيْسَ عَلَى ٱلَّذِينَ ءَامَنُوا۟ وَعَمِلُوا۟ ٱلصَّٰلِحَٰتِ جُنَاحٌ فِيمَا طَعِمُوٓا۟ إِذَا مَا ٱتَّقَوا۟ وَّءَامَنُوا۟ وَعَمِلُوا۟ ٱلصَّٰلِحَٰتِ ثُمَّ ٱتَّقَوا۟ وَّءَامَنُوا۟ ثُمَّ ٱتَّقَوا۟ وَّأَحْسَنُوا۟ وَٱللَّهُ يُحِبُّ ٱلْمُحْسِنِينَ ۝

Believers, God will certainly try you by means of game which may come within the reach of your hands or your spears, so that God may mark out those who truly fear Him in their hearts. Whoever transgresses after all this will have grievous suffering. (94)

يَـٰٓأَيُّهَا ٱلَّذِينَ ءَامَنُوا۟ لَيَبْلُوَنَّكُمُ ٱللَّهُ بِشَىْءٍ مِّنَ ٱلصَّيْدِ تَنَالُهُۥٓ أَيْدِيكُمْ وَرِمَاحُكُمْ لِيَعْلَمَ ٱللَّهُ مَن يَخَافُهُۥ بِٱلْغَيْبِ فَمَنِ ٱعْتَدَىٰ بَعْدَ ذَٰلِكَ فَلَهُۥ عَذَابٌ أَلِيمٌ ۝

Believers, kill no game while you are on pilgrimage. Whoever of you kills game by design shall make amends in cattle equivalent to what he has killed, adjudged by two persons of probity among you, to be brought as an offering to the Ka'bah; or else he may atone for his sin by feeding needy persons, or by its equivalent in fasting, so that he may taste the evil consequences of his deeds. God has forgiven what is past; but whoever repeats his offence, God will inflict His retribution on him. God is Almighty, Lord of retribution. (95)

يَـٰٓأَيُّهَا ٱلَّذِينَ ءَامَنُوا۟ لَا تَقْتُلُوا۟ ٱلصَّيْدَ وَأَنتُمْ حُرُمٌ وَمَن قَتَلَهُۥ مِنكُم مُّتَعَمِّدًا فَجَزَآءٌ مِّثْلُ مَا قَتَلَ مِنَ ٱلنَّعَمِ يَحْكُمُ بِهِۦ ذَوَا عَدْلٍ مِّنكُمْ هَدْيًۢا بَٰلِغَ ٱلْكَعْبَةِ أَوْ كَفَّٰرَةٌ طَعَامُ مَسَٰكِينَ أَوْ عَدْلُ ذَٰلِكَ صِيَامًا لِّيَذُوقَ وَبَالَ أَمْرِهِۦ عَفَا ٱللَّهُ عَمَّا سَلَفَ وَمَنْ عَادَ فَيَنتَقِمُ ٱللَّهُ مِنْهُ وَٱللَّهُ عَزِيزٌ ذُو ٱنتِقَامٍ ۝

Lawful to you is all water-game, and whatever food the sea brings forth, as a provision for you and for travellers. However, you are forbidden land-game as long as you are in the state of consecration [or *ihrām*]. Be conscious of God, to whom you shall all be gathered. (96)

أُحِلَّ لَكُمْ صَيْدُ ٱلْبَحْرِ وَطَعَامُهُۥ مَتَٰعًا لَّكُمْ وَلِلسَّيَّارَةِ وَحُرِّمَ عَلَيْكُمْ صَيْدُ ٱلْبَرِّ مَا دُمْتُمْ حُرُمًا وَٱتَّقُوا۟ ٱللَّهَ ٱلَّذِىٓ إِلَيْهِ تُحْشَرُونَ ۝

God has made the Ka'bah, the Inviolable House of Worship, a symbol for all mankind; and so too the sacred month and the garlanded sacrificial offerings. This, so that you may know that God is aware of all that is in the heavens and the earth, and that God has full knowledge of everything. (97)

Know that God is severe in retribution and that God is Much-Forgiving, Merciful. (98)

The Messenger's duty is but to deliver the message [entrusted to him]. God knows all that you reveal, and all that you conceal. (99)

Say: Evil and good are not equal, even though the abundance of evil may be pleasing to you. Have fear of God, you who are endowed with understanding, so that you may triumph. (100)

Believers, do not ask about matters which, if made known to you, may cause you hardship. If you should ask about them while the Qur'ān is being revealed, they shall be made plain to you. God will forgive you these; for God is Much-Forgiving, Forbearing. (101)

﴿جَعَلَ ٱللَّهُ ٱلْكَعْبَةَ ٱلْبَيْتَ ٱلْحَرَامَ قِيَٰمًا لِّلنَّاسِ وَٱلشَّهْرَ ٱلْحَرَامَ وَٱلْهَدْىَ وَٱلْقَلَٰئِدَ ذَٰلِكَ لِتَعْلَمُوٓا۟ أَنَّ ٱللَّهَ يَعْلَمُ مَا فِى ٱلسَّمَٰوَٰتِ وَمَا فِى ٱلْأَرْضِ وَأَنَّ ٱللَّهَ بِكُلِّ شَىْءٍ عَلِيمٌ ۞﴾

﴿ٱعْلَمُوٓا۟ أَنَّ ٱللَّهَ شَدِيدُ ٱلْعِقَابِ وَأَنَّ ٱللَّهَ غَفُورٌ رَّحِيمٌ ۞﴾

﴿مَّا عَلَى ٱلرَّسُولِ إِلَّا ٱلْبَلَٰغُ وَٱللَّهُ يَعْلَمُ مَا تُبْدُونَ وَمَا تَكْتُمُونَ ۞﴾

﴿قُل لَّا يَسْتَوِى ٱلْخَبِيثُ وَٱلطَّيِّبُ وَلَوْ أَعْجَبَكَ كَثْرَةُ ٱلْخَبِيثِ فَٱتَّقُوا۟ ٱللَّهَ يَٰٓأُو۟لِى ٱلْأَلْبَٰبِ لَعَلَّكُمْ تُفْلِحُونَ ۞﴾

﴿يَٰٓأَيُّهَا ٱلَّذِينَ ءَامَنُوا۟ لَا تَسْـَٔلُوا۟ عَنْ أَشْيَآءَ إِن تُبْدَ لَكُمْ تَسُؤْكُمْ وَإِن تَسْـَٔلُوا۟ عَنْهَا حِينَ يُنَزَّلُ ٱلْقُرْءَانُ تُبْدَ لَكُمْ عَفَا ٱللَّهُ عَنْهَا وَٱللَّهُ غَفُورٌ حَلِيمٌ ۞﴾

People before your time inquired about them, and on that account they came to deny the truth. (102)

قَدْ سَأَلَهَا قَوْمٌ مِّن قَبْلِكُمْ ثُمَّ أَصْبَحُواْ بِهَا كَـٰفِرِينَ ۝

It was not God who instituted [superstitions like those of] a slit-ear she camel, or a she-camel let loose for free pasture, or idol sacrifices for twin-births in animals, or stallion-camels freed from work. It is unbelievers who attribute their own lying inventions to God. Most of them never use their reason. (103)

مَا جَعَلَ ٱللَّهُ مِنۢ بَحِيرَةٍ وَلَا سَآئِبَةٍ وَلَا وَصِيلَةٍ وَلَا حَامٍ وَلَـٰكِنَّ ٱلَّذِينَ كَفَرُواْ يَفْتَرُونَ عَلَى ٱللَّهِ ٱلْكَذِبَ وَأَكْثَرُهُمْ لَا يَعْقِلُونَ ۝

When they are told, "Come to that which God has revealed and to the Messenger," they reply, "Sufficient for us are the ways we found our fathers following." Why, even though their fathers knew nothing and were devoid of all guidance? (104)

وَإِذَا قِيلَ لَهُمْ تَعَالَوْاْ إِلَىٰ مَآ أَنزَلَ ٱللَّهُ وَإِلَى ٱلرَّسُولِ قَالُواْ حَسْبُنَا مَا وَجَدْنَا عَلَيْهِ ءَابَآءَنَآ أَوَلَوْ كَانَ ءَابَآؤُهُمْ لَا يَعْلَمُونَ شَيْئًا وَلَا يَهْتَدُونَ ۝

Believers, it is but for your own souls that you are accountable. Those who go astray can do you no harm if you [yourselves] are on the right path. To God you all must return. He will then make you understand all that you were doing [in life]. (105)

يَـٰٓأَيُّهَا ٱلَّذِينَ ءَامَنُواْ عَلَيْكُمْ أَنفُسَكُمْ لَا يَضُرُّكُم مَّن ضَلَّ إِذَا ٱهْتَدَيْتُمْ إِلَى ٱللَّهِ مَرْجِعُكُمْ جَمِيعًا فَيُنَبِّئُكُم بِمَا كُنتُمْ تَعْمَلُونَ ۝

Believers, let there be witnesses to what you do when death approaches you and you are about to make bequests: two persons of probity from among your own people, or two others from outside, if the pangs of death come to you when you are travelling through the land. Detain them both after prayer, and if you have any doubt in mind, let them swear by God, "We shall not sell this [our word] for any price, even though it were for a near kinsman; and neither shall we conceal anything of what we have witnessed before God; for then we should be among the sinful." (106)

يَـٰٓأَيُّهَا ٱلَّذِينَ ءَامَنُوا۟ شَهَٰدَةُ بَيْنِكُمْ إِذَا حَضَرَ أَحَدَكُمُ ٱلْمَوْتُ حِينَ ٱلْوَصِيَّةِ ٱثْنَانِ ذَوَا عَدْلٍ مِّنكُمْ أَوْ ءَاخَرَانِ مِنْ غَيْرِكُمْ إِنْ أَنتُمْ ضَرَبْتُمْ فِى ٱلْأَرْضِ فَأَصَٰبَتْكُم مُّصِيبَةُ ٱلْمَوْتِ تَحْبِسُونَهُمَا مِنۢ بَعْدِ ٱلصَّلَوٰةِ فَيُقْسِمَانِ بِٱللَّهِ إِنِ ٱرْتَبْتُمْ لَا نَشْتَرِى بِهِۦ ثَمَنًا وَلَوْ كَانَ ذَا قُرْبَىٰ وَلَا نَكْتُمُ شَهَٰدَةَ ٱللَّهِ إِنَّآ إِذًا لَّمِنَ ٱلْءَاثِمِينَ ۝

But if afterwards it should come to light that the two [witnesses] have been guilty of [this very] sin, then two others should replace them from among those immediately concerned. Both shall swear by God, "Our testimony is indeed truer than that of these two. We have not transgressed the bounds of what is right; for then we should be among the evil-doers." (107)

فَإِنْ عُثِرَ عَلَىٰٓ أَنَّهُمَا ٱسْتَحَقَّآ إِثْمًا فَـَٔاخَرَانِ يَقُومَانِ مَقَامَهُمَا مِنَ ٱلَّذِينَ ٱسْتَحَقَّ عَلَيْهِمُ ٱلْأَوْلَيَٰنِ فَيُقْسِمَانِ بِٱللَّهِ لَشَهَٰدَتُنَآ أَحَقُّ مِن شَهَٰدَتِهِمَا وَمَا ٱعْتَدَيْنَآ إِنَّآ إِذًا لَّمِنَ ٱلظَّٰلِمِينَ ۝

Thus it will be more likely that people will offer testimony in accordance with the truth; or else they will fear that the oaths of others may be taken after their oaths. Have fear of God and hearken [to Him]. God does not guide those who are iniquitous. (108)

ذَٰلِكَ أَدْنَىٰ أَن يَأْتُوا بِٱلشَّهَٰدَةِ عَلَىٰ
وَجْهِهَآ أَوْ يَخَافُوٓا أَن تُرَدَّ أَيْمَٰنُۢ بَعْدَ
أَيْمَٰنِهِمْ وَٱتَّقُوا ٱللَّهَ وَٱسْمَعُوا وَٱللَّهُ
لَا يَهْدِي ٱلْقَوْمَ ٱلْفَٰسِقِينَ ١٠٨

Overview

This long passage makes it clear that the authority to legislate belongs only to God who alone determines what is permissible and what is forbidden. Once this basic rule is established, it becomes applicable in all matters, regardless of their degree of importance. Anyone who claims the authority to legislate, by word or deed, is actually claiming Godhead, which belongs only to God Himself. In other words, he does not simply transgress the bounds of what is permitted, he also assaults God's authority. If any legislation is enacted on the basis of social traditions or people's views, then, in practical terms, these are preferred to what God revealed to His Messenger. As such, it constitutes a departure from faith altogether.

This passage provides a long list of legislation in different areas. Every piece begins with an address to those who believe. It is a reminder to them of their essential quality, which implies unqualified acknowledgement of God's supremacy, sovereignty and authority to legislate. As such, it is an address which re-emphasises the basic quality of faith. This is coupled with a commandment to obey God and His Messenger and to beware of turning one's back on God's legislation. A warning against God's punishment is added, only to be followed with the prospect of earning His forgiveness and mercy. The believers are then told that they have their own way to follow. They are to pay no heed to anyone who does not submit to God's authority.

Then, a clear distinction is drawn between the believers who acknowledge that the authority to legislate belongs to God alone on the one hand and on the other those who follow a different line, claiming for themselves the right to legislate: *"Believers, it is but for your own souls that you are accountable. Those who go astray can do you no harm if you [yourselves] are on the right path. To God you all must return. He will then make you understand all that you were doing [in life]."* (Verse 105)

This makes the believers a community on their own, with its independent course of action, code and legal source. When the Muslim community outlines its own course of action and declares its determination to follow it, it knows that other people's disagreement and error will not cause it any harm. All will eventually return to God.

Such is the central theme of this long passage. We will look at its detailed points as we proceed with our commentary.

Prohibiting What is Lawful

The first address in this passage to the believers reminds them that they may not exercise any of God's attributes, since these belong totally to God. As such, they may not forbid themselves any of the wholesome and good things that God has made lawful to them. It is not open to them to make a demonstration of self-imposed prohibition, refusing to eat of such good food God has given them. They must remember that it is God who has provided them with such lawful and wholesome sustenance. It is only He who may designate things as permissible or forbidden: *"Believers, do not forbid yourselves the good things God has made lawful to you. Do not transgress; God does not love the transgressors. Eat of what God has provided for you of lawful and wholesome things, and have fear of God in whom you believe."* (Verses 87–8)

The whole question of legislation is closely linked to that of Godhead. It is God alone who has the sole authority to regulate for people's lives. His authority is derived from the fact that it is He who has created human beings and provided them with food and sustenance. Hence, to Him alone belongs the right to make permissible to them whatever He pleases of His own provisions and to declare any part of such provisions forbidden to them. Human beings themselves acknowledge this logic. Whoever owns something enjoys the right to dispose of it in any way he pleases. Anyone who violates this basic principle is undoubtedly a transgressor. It is only to be expected that believers do not make an assault on God in whom they believe. It is inconceivable that a believer could ever assault God's authority.

These two short verses state this principle in absolute clarity. No one may argue against this principle unless he is a transgressor, and God does not love transgressors. This is a general question which establishes a general principle relating to the significance of Godhead and what rights God has against His servants. It also relates to the effect of believing in God with regard to the behaviour and practices of believers. We have a number of reports which suggest that these two verses and the one which follows them (relating to oaths and the various atonements for breaking them) were revealed by way of comment on a particular incident that took place during the Prophet Muḥammad's lifetime. While knowledge of the circumstances of revelation of a particular verse can throw light on its meaning and significance, we have to remember that in general, Qur'ānic statements have a universal application. They do not relate to particular incidents only, unless there is a specific case with which they deal.

One report by Ibn Jarīr mentions that the Prophet (peace be upon him) one day sat to speak with his Companions, reminding them of their duties and the reckoning on the Day of Judgement. He did little more than to warn them of the punishment of the Hereafter and then left. Some of his Companions then said to each other: "We must do something of substance. The Christians forbid themselves certain things and we should do likewise." Some of them declared that they would abstain from eating meat or eating any part of the leg of certain animals. While others declared that they would not eat during the day and some said they forbade themselves marriage. When the Prophet was told of this, he spoke to them again and said: "How is it that some people have forbidden themselves marriage, or food or sleep? As for me, I sleep and worship at night, and I fast on some days and abstain from fasting on others, and I marry women. Whoever chooses a path other than mine does not belong to me." It is in connection with this incident that this Qur'ānic verse was revealed: *"Believers, do not forbid yourselves the good things God has made lawful to you. Do not transgress; God does not love the transgressors. Eat of what God has provided for you of lawful and wholesome things, and have fear of God in whom you believe."* (Verses 87–8)

Another report confirming the one just quoted is given by Anas, one of the Prophet's Companions, and is related by both al-Bukhārī and Muslim: "Three people came to the home of God's Messenger (peace be upon him), enquiring of his wives about his worship. When

239

they were told of it, they felt that it was less than expected. Then one of them said: "How can we compare ourselves to God's Messenger (peace be upon him) when God has already forgiven him any sin that he might have committed and any which he may commit in future." Hence, one of them declared: "I shall spend all night, every night, in prayer." The second said: "As for me, I shall fast every day of my life." The third one said: "I shall stay away from women and will never get married." The Prophet went to them and said: "Are you the ones who said so and so. You should know that I am the one who fears God most among you. Nevertheless, I fast on some days and abstain from fasting on others; I pray, but I also go to sleep; and I do get married. Whoever abandons my path does not belong to me."

Al-Tirmidhī relates on the authority of 'Abdullāh ibn 'Abbās that a man came to the Prophet (peace be upon him) and said: "If I eat meat, I want to be with women and I am motivated by desire. Therefore, I have forbidden myself eating meat." God revealed the Qur'ānic verse: *"Believers, do not forbid yourselves the good things God has made lawful to you..."* (Verse 87)

Atonement for Breaking an Oath

The verse that follows, which refers to oaths and their atonement, appears to have been revealed in order to deal with such cases when people make an oath in order to solemnise their abstention from something permissible, as was done by those Companions of the Prophet. The Qur'ān also makes it clear that it is not up to human beings to declare things forbidden or permissible. That authority belongs to God, in whom those Companions of the Prophet believed. This Qur'ānic verse also deals with all vows of abstention from doing something good or vows to undertake something evil. Whenever it is clear to a person who has made an oath that breaking it is better and more conducive to earning God's pleasure, he should break it and atone for it in one of the methods defined by this Qur'ānic verse.

'Abdullāh ibn 'Abbās says that it was revealed in connection with those people who forbade themselves wholesome types of food and clothes as well as appropriate marriages. They had vowed to abide by these restrictions. When the commandment, *"Believers, do not forbid yourselves the good things God has made lawful to you,"* was revealed, they asked: "What shall we do with our oaths?" This verse giving the necessary verdict was then revealed. It makes clear that God does not take people to task for oaths which they may utter without thought, or those which they may pronounce "off the cuff," as it were, without consciously deciding to make an oath. At the same time, Muslims are urged not to devalue their oaths by uttering too many of them without thought. An oath by God is a very serious statement. Hence, it must not be uttered without thought.

An oath made solemnly and deliberately requires an atonement if it is to be broken. The atonement is given in detail in this Qur'ānic verse: *"The breaking of an oath must be atoned for by the feeding of ten needy persons with more or less the same food as you normally give to your own families, or by clothing them, or by the freeing of one slave. He who cannot afford any of these shall fast three days instead. This shall be the atonement for your oaths when you have sworn [and broken them]. But be mindful of your oaths. "*(Verse 89) The Arabic term which is used to describe the type of food which should be offered to the ten needy persons means literally either "the average" or 'the best' food a person gives to his own family. However, we can combine both aspects of the meaning because the average is normally preferred in Islam. It also applies to clothing the ten needy persons which means giving them some of the average type of clothes one gives to one's family.

An alternative is to free a person from slavery, but it is not specified here whether that slave should be a believer. Hence, scholars have different views concerning this point, but we will not discuss the details of these views. *"He who cannot afford any of these shall fast three days instead. "* (Verse 89) It is only when a person is unable to meet the requirements of any of the above types of atonement that he may atone for his broken oath by fasting. Again, scholars have varying views with regard to whether these three days must be consecutive or not. Our own approach in this commentary is not to discuss such varying views or to evaluate them. Anyone who wishes to study them may do so by referring to books of fiqh which discuss them in detail. All views of scholars are in agreement on the essential purpose of the atonement, namely, attaching proper value to the breached contract and giving proper respect to oaths which are pledges or forms of contracts which God has ordered to be honoured. Hence, if anyone of us makes an oath and finds out subsequently that it is better, from the Islamic point of view, to do otherwise, he both breaks his oath and atones for it. The same applies if he makes an oath which he has no authority to make, such as an oath of prohibition or permissibility of a particular thing. In this case, he breaks the oath and atones for it.

Let us now talk about the subject matter of these verses. As for the particular circumstances, God makes it plain that what He has made lawful is wholesome and what He has forbidden is foul. Hence, it is not for people to choose something different from what God has chosen for them, for two basic reasons: firstly, the authority to forbid or make lawful belongs to God alone. Any violation of that is a transgression which displeases God and contradicts faith. Secondly, God makes lawful only what is good and wholesome. Therefore, people may not forbid themselves such wholesome things that are beneficial to them and to life in general. A human being's knowledge of life and of himself cannot be matched with God's knowledge who combines perfect wisdom with absolute knowledge. Since God has made these things lawful, then they must be good and wholesome. God's knowledge is perfect, based on absolute certainty. Hence we say: had God known that these matters were foul or evil, He would have spared His servants their consequences. Had He known that abstention from them would be better, He would not have made them lawful.

This religion has been revealed so that it brings about goodness in human life and achieves perfect balance and complete harmony between all aspects of human life. It does not overlook any natural human need, nor does it suppress any constructive human activity within appropriate limits. Hence, Islam denounces monastic aestheticism because it amounts to a suppression of nature and an impediment to the development of life. Similarly, Islam speaks out against the forbidding of wholesome lawful things, because these help the development of life. It must be remembered that God has created this life so that it may flourish and develop in accordance with the constitution He has laid down for it. Monastic aestheticism and the forbidding of wholesome things come into direct conflict with God's method for human life because they bring life to a stop at a certain point under the pretext of seeking something more sublime. It should be stated here that attaining the sublime is feasible within the system God has laid down and made easy through its compatibility with human nature.

The fact that this verse was revealed to deal with particular circumstances does not restrict its general applicability because it relates to the question of Godhead and legislation. This is not confined to the statement of which types of food, drink and marriage are lawful and which are forbidden. It applies to the authority to legislate in all matters of life.

We try to emphasise this message as much as we can, because the fact that Islam has not been allowed to regulate human life for a long while has enabled the tendency in people to give Qur'ānic statements a restricted applicability. Thus, many people think that terms like "permissible" and "forbidden" apply only to the slaughtering of animals, to the types of food, drink and clothing a Muslim may have, and to how marriages should be conducted. Many people tend to refer to Islam only within this area. Other general and more substantive matters are considered in light of theories, constitutions and laws which have nothing to do with Islam. A community's social set-up, political system and international relations are only some examples of serious matters that are determined without reference to Islam.

Islam is a constitution which regulates all of human life. A person who accepts Islam in full and follows all its commandments is a believer, while a person who follows some other method, even though this may be in a single question or issue, is one who rejects faith and transgresses against God's authority. As such, he is not a believer, although he may profess to respect faith and claims to be a Muslim. When he follows a law other than that of God, he falsifies all his claims and takes himself out of the realm of faith altogether.

It is to this central issue that these Qur'ānic verses refer. It puts the question of believing in God above all other considerations. As such, it gives it the seriousness which it should always enjoy.

A Categorical Prohibition of Intoxicants

It is within the context of legislation, permissibility and prohibition, as well as the moulding of the Muslim community in Madinah, purging it from all remaining traces of past tradition of the dark days, that a clear and decisive verdict is given on intoxicating drinks and gambling, coupled with practices of associating partners with God.

> *Believers, intoxicants, games of chance, idolatrous practices and divining arrows are abominations devised by Satan. Therefore, turn away from them so that you may be successful. Satan seeks only to stir up enmity and hatred among you by means of*

intoxicants and games of chance, and to turn you away from the remembrance of God and from prayer. Will you not, then, desist? (Verses 90–1)

Drinking, gambling, idols and divining arrows were important aspects of pre-Islamic Arabia. They were closely related in both practice and tradition. The Arabs used to drink to the point of extravagance. They considered that drinking afforded people distinction. They often mention drinking in their poetry as a practice to be proud of or to praise others with. In social gatherings, drinking was coupled with the slaughter of animals which were immediately cooked to provide food to those who took part in these drinking bouts, those who served wine and those who frequented such gatherings. The animals were slaughtered at the feet of idols which were sprayed with the blood of their sacrifice. In such social events, the act of divining arrows was practised in order to determine the sharing out of the sacrificial meat. Everyone's share was determined by his arrow, with the highest arrow giving the largest share, and the lowest giving no share whatsoever, even though it might have been the arrow of the person who provided the animal for slaughter. This gives us an idea of how traditions were intertwined with ignorant ideological concepts.

Islam did not address such traditions at the start, because they are based on mistaken beliefs. To try to reform them at the surface level before establishing the right foundation of faith was bound to be a wasted effort, and this a Divine system would not even consider. Islam begins its reform with the paramount question for every human being, namely, faith. It uproots the very basic ideological concepts of ignorance in order to put in place the Islamic concept, which is in complete harmony with human nature. It explains to people how grossly mistaken their concepts of God are and guides them to recognise their true Lord and Creator. Once they know Him, they begin to listen with great attention in order to find out what pleases and displeases their Lord. Prior to this they are not even ready to listen or obey an order or commandment. They are not prepared to abandon their ignorant practices no matter how often they are advised against them. The key to human nature is that of faith. Unless the right key is used, nothing of morality or social reform will take root in human nature. Thus, it remains closed, unenlightened, and unfathomable.

The Islamic method of reform did not start with correcting the deviations and abominations of the dark ages, or *Jāhiliyyah*. It addressed the question of faith, beginning with the declaration that there is no deity save God. It took around 13 years to establish this concept of God's oneness, with all that it entails, in the hearts of the early Muslims. In this period, the only aim was its establishment, so that people could know their Lord and submit themselves to His authority. When faith was clearly established in their hearts and they recognised that they could have no choice other than what has been chosen for them by God, then the next phase of outlining their duties, including worship, began. This was combined with the process of eradicating the social, economic, moral and behavioural traces of ignorance. It began in effect at the moment when God's order could be obeyed without hesitation because people realised that God could only order them to do what is good for them.

In other words, commandments were issued after submission had become clear, when every Muslim realised that he had no say other than the say of God. Shaikh Abu'l Ḥasan ʿAlī al-Nadwī describes this stage succinctly and clearly in his invaluable book *Islam and the World,* under the subtitle "Highest Pinnacle of Development":

> Once the Gordian knot of unbelief had been cut, it was easy to unfasten the other knots that bound them (meaning the early Muslims). Once the Prophet had opened their hearts to Islam, he did not have to struggle at each step to make them reject the Wrong and accept the Right. They had entered into the new faith heart and soul and submitted themselves without demur to what the Prophet decreed. They unhesitatingly confessed before the Prophet such crimes as were not known to anyone but themselves. If they committed any crime, they voluntarily submitted themselves for punishment. Many of them actually had wine cups in their hands when the Qurʾānic injunction against the use of intoxicants was revealed, but the Word of God came between them and the cups. They threw away the cups at once and broke their wine barrels so that the drains of Madinah literally overflowed with their detestable contents.[1]

---

1. Abul Ḥasan Ali Nadwī, *Islam and the World.* Tr. M.A. Kidwai, Lucknow, Academy of Islamic Research, 1980, pp. 53–4

Yet, the prohibition of intoxicants and games of chance did not come as a surprise. Before this categorical prohibition, some steps were taken to loosen the hold of such social traditions which were closely intertwined with personal habits as well as with economic aspects. Indeed, this was the third or fourth step Islam took to solve the problem of intoxicant drinks.

The first step was no more than firing a shot in the right direction, when God (limitless is He in His Glory) says in *Sūrah* 16, The Bee, revealed in Makkah: *"And from the fruit of date palms and vines you derive intoxicants as well as wholesome food."* (16: 67) This was the first indication to Muslims whereby intoxicants were placed in opposition to wholesome sustenance.

The second step addressed the Muslims' religious conscience through legislative logic, with the verse revealed in *Sūrah* 2, The Cow: *"They ask you about intoxicants and games of chance. Say: In both there is great evil although they have some benefits for people; but their evil far exceeds their benefit."* (2: 219) The import here is clear: since the evil of a particular practice is far greater than its benefit, then it is better to abandon it altogether. Hardly anything is totally devoid of benefit, but its permissibility or prohibition depends on how far its evil outweighs its benefit.

The third step broke the habit of drinking and put it on a collision course with attendance to obligatory prayer. Here we have the verse revealed in *Sūrah* 4, Women: *"Believers, do not attempt to pray when you are drunk, [but wait] until you know what you are saying."* (4: 43) Since Muslims offer five obligatory prayers every day, with a close time range between them, which is not sufficient to get drunk in and then regain sobriety, this instruction practically restricted the times available for drinking. This, in effect, abolished the habits of mid-morning and mid-afternoon drinking, which were part of the traditions of pre-Islamic Arabia. Moreover, it militated against addiction, which is closely related to the amount of time available for drinking. In this way, it became practically impossible for a Muslim to attend to his prayers on time, and to drink at his usual times.

The fourth and final stage was this categorical prohibition which came after people had become fully ready to accept it. It needed only a clear order and the Muslims were sure to obey it without hesitation.

Obedience: A Main Characteristic of Muslim Society

It seems that the first of these verses, i.e. the one in *Sūrah* 16, caused 'Umar ibn al-Khaṭṭāb, who described himself prior to embracing Islam as a man of drink, some worry and he wished for a clear-cut ruling on drinking. That verse makes a distinction between what people use dates and grapes for, as it describes them as "intoxicants and wholesome food." (16: 67)

'Umar ibn al-Khaṭṭāb [may God be pleased with him] reports that he said: "My Lord, give us a clear-cut ruling on drinking." The verse in *Sūrah* 2 was then revealed, stating: *"They ask you about intoxicants and games of chance. Say: In both there is great evil although they have some benefits for people; but their evil far exceeds their benefit."* (2: 219) 'Umar was called in and the verse was recited to him. He said: "My Lord, give us a clear-cut ruling on drinking." The verse in *Sūrah* 4 was then revealed: *"Believers, do not attempt to pray when you are drunk, [but wait] until you know what you are saying."* (4: 43) 'Umar was called in and the verse was recited to him. He once again said: "My Lord, give us a clear-cut ruling on drinking." The verse in this *sūrah*, The Repast, was then revealed, stating: *"Satan seeks only to stir up enmity and hatred among you by means of intoxicants and games of chance, and to turn you away from the remembrance of God and from prayer. Will you not, then, desist?"* (Verse 91) 'Umar was called in once more and the verse was recited to him. He said: "We do desist, my Lord! We do desist." (Related by al-Nasā'ī, Abū Dāwūd, al-Tirmidhī, and Ibn Mājah.)

When these two verses which make intoxicants absolutely forbidden were revealed in the third year of the Islamic calendar, shortly after the Battle of Uḥud, the matter did not require more than sending someone around the places where people gathered in Madinah to announce: "All intoxicants are forbidden." Everyone who had a glass of wine in his hand broke it and everyone who was in the actual process of drinking threw out what was in his mouth. Barrels and bottles of wine and other intoxicants were broken. The whole matter was over as if the people had never before drunk intoxicants.

Let us now look at the way the Qur'ānic statement is phrased, because it tells us much about the Qur'ānic method of cultivating people's minds and reforming their behaviour. It begins with the address so familiar in this part of the *sūrah*: *"Believers."* This address awakens the

247

hearts of believers on the one hand and reminds them, on the other, of the basic requirement of faith, namely, obedience and submission.

This is followed by a decisive statement on the nature of those practices which admit no counter argument: *"Intoxicants, games of chance, idolatrous practices and divining arrows are abominations devised by Satan."* (Verse 90) These are, then, foul practices and cannot be included among good and wholesome things which God has permitted. Moreover, they have been devised by Satan, man's old enemy. It is sufficient for a believer to know that something is devised by Satan to make it totally repugnant to him.

At this point, the prohibition is issued, but is combined with the prospect of attaining success, which itself has its profound effect on the human mind: *"Therefore, turn away from them so that you may be successful."* (Verse 90) The Qur'ānic verses go on to further expose Satan's scheme behind the devising of these abominations: *"Satan seeks only to stir up enmity and hatred among you by means of intoxicants and games of chance, and to turn you away from the remembrance of God and from prayer."* (Verse 91) Satan's aim and the purpose of his scheming are thus exposed before every Muslim. Satan seeks nothing except the stirring up of enmity and hatred among believers so as to turn them away from their worship. What a wicked scheme!

Satan's aims can easily be recognised in our practical life after we have accepted them as true, since God has stated them so. It does not take anyone with an open mind long to recognise how Satan actually stirs up enmity and hatred, utilising for this purpose intoxicants and gambling. Intoxicants weaken one's consciousness and self-control, heighten tempers and stir up whims and impulses. Gambling and all games of chance leave people with a sense of loss and grudges. It is natural that a losing gambler nurses a strong grudge against the winner who takes away his money from under his nose and leaves him empty handed. It is only natural that such matters stir up enmity and hatred, regardless of the impression of happiness they initially give off.

The fact that intoxicants and gambling do turn people away from their remembrance of God and from prayer is too clear to require elaboration. Drinking makes people forget and gambling makes them oblivious to everything else. Indeed, games of chance keep gamblers in a state of intoxication which is not dissimilar to that produced by drink. The world of a gambler is akin to that of a drunk: tables, glasses and a strike of fortune or misfortune.

As this clear reference to Satan's aim in devising these abominations produces its effect and awakens the hearts of those who believe, the question is then put which admits only the sort of answer 'Umar gave when he heard it for the first time: *"Will you not, then, desist?"* His immediate response was: "We do desist, my Lord! We do desist."

The *sūrah* goes on to put the whole matter in its proper perspective: *"Obey God, and obey the Messenger, and be ever on your guard. But if you turn away, then know that Our Messenger's only duty is a clear delivery of the message [entrusted to him]."* (Verse 92)

This is the basic rule to which all matters are referred: obedience to God and His Messenger, i.e. submission which leaves no room except for absolute obedience and total compliance. There is also an implicit warning in this statement: *"If you turn away, then know that Our Messenger's only duty is a clear delivery of the message [entrusted to him]."* (Verse 92) He has certainly conveyed God's message with absolute clarity. Anyone who disobeys bears full responsibility for his disobedience. This warning, implicitly as it is expressed, is indeed very strong. The believers are made aware that should they slip into disobedience they only harm themselves. God's Messenger has fulfilled his trust and conveyed his message. Hence, he is no longer responsible for them. Nor will he shield them from punishment, since they have disobeyed him. Their faith is in the hands of God, who is able to punish those who disobey. Thus does the Qur'ānic method open up our hearts and penetrate our depths.

Why Intoxicants Are So Repugnant

It is useful to explain here the nature of intoxicants which are meant in this prohibition. Abū Dāwūd relates this *ḥadīth* on the authority of 'Abdullāh ibn 'Abbās: "Everything that is brewed is wine, and every intoxicant is forbidden." 'Umar addressed the Muslims, standing on the Prophet's pulpit, with a group of the Prophet's Companions in attendance. He said: "When the Qur'ānic verse was revealed prohibiting drinks, intoxicants were derived from five types of produce: grapes, palm dates, honey, wheat and barley. Wine refers to everything that blurs the mind." These statements clearly indicate that intoxicants include every brewed drink which causes intoxication. It is not restricted to a particular type. Whatever intoxicates is forbidden.

The lack of consciousness, whichever intoxicant produces it, is diametrically opposed to the state of alertness which Islam requires of every Muslim so that he consciously feels his link with God at every moment, making sure that all his thoughts and actions are of the sort that please God. By being so alert and conscious, the Muslim plays a positive role in the proper development of life and in protecting it against weakness and corruption. He further protects himself, his property and honour and he helps to protect the Muslim community and its system and law against all types of aggression. A Muslim is not abandoned so that he cares only for himself or his enjoyments. On the contrary, at every moment he has duties to fulfil which require that he be always alert. These include duties towards his Lord, himself, his family and the Muslim community of which he is a member and towards humanity at large. Even when he enjoys the wholesome pleasures Islam permits, he must retain his full consciousness so that he is not enslaved by any type of pleasure or desire. He is in control of all his desires and he fulfils them as one who is totally in control. Drunkenness is the opposite state.

Moreover, seeking such unconsciousness is simply an attempt to escape from the reality of life at a particular moment in time and a preference for the sort of visions which accompany drunkenness. Islam disapproves of all this because it wants people to see the realities as they are, to look them in the face and to conduct their lives on the basis of reality, not imagination. It is through facing reality that man proves his will-power. To escape to the realm of imagination is to prove one's weakness and lack of will. Islam wants its people to have a strong will, unfettered by habit or addiction. From the Islamic point of view, this is enough reason to forbid intoxicants and all drugs. All these are abominations devised by Satan and their effect is only the corruption of human life.

Scholars have different views with regard to whether intoxicants are impure in themselves like other physical impurities, or whether the prohibition applies only to drinking them. The majority of scholars are of the first view, while the second view is that of Rabī'ah, al-Layth ibn Sa'd, al-Muznī of the Shafi'ī school and a number of later scholars of Baghdad. Perhaps this reference to scholarly views on this point is adequate for our purposes.

Self-Surrender and Obedience

When these verses were revealed totally prohibiting all intoxicants, and describing them as an abomination devised by Satan, two groups of people raised a query in the same wording but for totally different reasons. A few of the Prophet's Companions who were very scrupulous said: "What about our Companions who died when intoxicants were still lawful to drink?" Some of them said: "What about those killed in the Battle of Uḥud, with intoxicants in their bellies?" i.e. before they were forbidden to drink. Another group who were keen to seize every chance to sow the seeds of doubt among the Muslim community said similar things. Their aim was to try to weaken the Muslims' trust in the reasoning behind Islamic legislation. They also wanted to convey the feeling that those who died before the prohibition of intoxicants were totally lost, since they died with this abomination in their bodies. Hence, the purpose behind the following verse: *"Those who believe and do righteous deeds shall have no blame attached to them for any food they may have eaten, so long as they fear God and truly believe and do righteous deeds, and continue to fear God and believe, and remain God-fearing and persevere in doing good. God loves those who do good."* (Verse 93)

This verse states that what has not been forbidden is lawful and that prohibition begins with its statement, not at any moment prior to this. There can be no retrospective prohibition and punishment, cannot be inflicted without a clear statement of ruling. Those who died before the prohibition of intoxicants had nothing to fear, because they did not drink any forbidden thing and did not commit any act of disobedience. They feared God and did righteous deeds, knowing that He was totally aware of their intentions and actions. Such a person neither disobeyed nor drank something forbidden.

We have no intention of taking part in the controversy raised by the Mu'tazilah group concerning the ruling that intoxicants are abominations. What we will say, however, is that they raised the question about whether this is a result of its prohibition or because of the inherent quality of intoxicants. They also posed the question about whether what is forbidden is so ruled because of its inherent qualities, or because this quality is attached to it as a result of its prohibition. In my view all this controversy is futile and alien to the Islamic approach. When God forbids something, He knows why He forbids it, whether He states that reason or not. Whether the prohibition is based on the quality of what is prohibited, or on something that relates to the individual partaking of it personally, or to the interests of the whole community, it is God who knows the whole truth. Obeying His orders is an undeniable duty of every Muslim. Any subsequent controversy addresses no real need. Realism is an essential aspect of the Divine method. No one can say: "If prohibition is the result of an inherent quality in the thing prohibited, how can it be permitted in the period leading up to its prohibition?" God must have had a good reason for leaving it permissible for a while. After all, this is always determined by God alone. This is, indeed, an essential quality of Godhead. Whether man considers something to be good or bad is not the determining factor because man can consider something to be the determining reason for prohibition when in actual fact it is not. The appropriate attitude is to accept God's legislation and to carry it out whether we know the reasons behind them or not. God knows everything and we know little.

The implementation of God's law must be based in the first instance on submission to Him. This is, indeed, the very meaning of Islam. When man has shown his obedience, he can use his mind to identify, as much as he is able to, God's purpose behind His commandment or prohibition, whether this purpose is stated by God or not, understood by human intellect or not. It must be remembered, however, that God, not man, is the final arbiter on whether something should be included in His law. When God has issued His decree, all arguments must stop. His decree must be implemented. If a decision is left to human intellect, people become the final arbiter on God's legislation. How then can this fit in with God's position as the ultimate authority, or with man's submission to Him?

Let us now consider the phraseology of this verse: *"Those who believe and do righteous deeds shall have no blame attached to them for any food they may have eaten, so long as they fear God and truly believe and do righteous deeds, and continue to fear God and believe, and remain God-fearing and persevere in doing good. God loves those who do good."* (Verse 93)

I admit that I have not found anything stated by commentators on the Qur'ān to be totally satisfactory in explaining the way this Qur'ānic verse is phrased, and why fear of God is mentioned once in combination with both faith and righteous deeds, and repeated once more in

252

combination with faith and on a third occasion combined with doing good. Nor do I consider now as satisfactory my own comments on this repetition which are included in the first edition of this book. The best that I have read, although it too remains somewhat unsatisfactory to me, is that written by al-Ṭabarī: "The first reference to fearing God equates this fearing of God to total acceptance of His commandment, submission to it and an acting upon it. The second reference equates it with an unshakeable acceptance of faith while the third mention represents a God-fearing person as always being ready to do good work voluntarily."

I will quote here what I have written on this particular point in the first, shorter edition of this work: "This is a method of confirmation by way of following a general statement with a detailed one. The first reference is a general, comprehensive one which includes God-fearing, strong faith and righteous deeds. The aspect of God-fearing is then repeated once in combination with faith and another with doing good, righteous deeds, in order to emphasise this sense and to highlight the important rule that actions are judged by the inner feelings that accompany them. God-fearing is the best expression of a fine sensitivity towards God's commandments and a constant relationship with Him that combines belief in Him with acceptance of His orders. Righteous deeds are the practical translation of inner faith. It is interaction between deeds and beliefs that is the criterion for judgement. Appearances provide no such criterion. It is this basic rule which requires repetition and emphatic statements."

At this moment in time I do not find my own words satisfactory, but I cannot come up with anything better. I seek God's help.

Consecration and Game Killing

The *surah* continues to elaborate on further prohibitions, speaking about game when one is in the state of consecration, or *iḥrām*, and what compensates for its killing. It further speaks of the purpose of the sanctity of the House of Worship in Makkah, the sacred months, dedicated and garlanded cattle which must not be touched as the *surah* makes clear in its opening verses. This part concludes with the establishment of a clear standard of values for Muslim individuals and Muslim society. According to this standard, a small amount of good is far more valuable than evil, plentiful as it may be.

Believers, God will certainly try you by means of game which may come within the reach of your hands or your spears, so that God may mark out those who truly fear Him in their hearts. Whoever transgresses after all this will have grievous suffering. (Verse 94) Believers, kill no game while you are on pilgrimage. Whoever of you kills game by design shall make amends in cattle equivalent to what he has killed, adjudged by two persons of probity among you, to be brought as an offering to the Ka'bah; or else he may atone for his sin by feeding needy persons, or by its equivalent in fasting, so that he may taste the evil consequences of his deeds. God has forgiven what is past; but whoever repeats his offence, God will inflict His retribution on him. God is Almighty, Lord of retribution. (Verse 95) Lawful to you is all water-game, and whatever food the sea brings forth, as a provision for you and for travellers. However, you are forbidden land-game as long as you are in the state of consecration [or iḥrām]. Be conscious of God, to whom you shall all be gathered. (Verse 96) God has made the Ka'bah, the Inviolable House of Worship, a symbol for all mankind; and so too the sacred month and the garlanded sacrificial offerings. This, so that you may know that God is aware of all that is in the heavens and the earth, and that God has full knowledge of everything. (Verse 97) Know that God is severe in retribution and that God is Much-Forgiving, Merciful. (Verse 98) The Messenger's duty is but to deliver the message [entrusted to him]. God knows all that you reveal, and all that you conceal. (Verse 99)

At the beginning of this *sūrah*, God says: "*Believers, do not offend against the symbols set up by God, or against the sacred month, or the offerings or the garlands, or against those who repair to the Sacred House, seeking God's grace and pleasure. Only when you are released from the state of consecration may you hunt.*" (Verse 2) However, this early prohibition of killing game during consecration, or the violation of God's rites, the sacred months, garlanded sacrificial animals, or intercepting those who are on their way to the Sacred House did not specify any punishment to be inflicted on perpetrators in this life. They only incurred a sin. Now a punishment is outlined in the form of an atonement which is sufficient to make the offender taste the evil of what he has perpetrated. The verses declare that past offences have been forgiven, but anyone who commits fresh violations is threatened with God's vengeance.

Like all the other sections of this long passage, this part opens with an address to the believers. They are then told that they are about to be set a test concerning game that has been prohibited to them while they are in the state of consecration, or *iḥrām*: "*Believers, God will certainly try you by means of game which may come within the reach of your hands or your spears, so that God may mark out those who truly fear Him in their hearts. Whoever transgresses after all this will have grievous suffering.*" (Verse 94)

It is a very easy game that is brought within their vicinity. They could easily grab it with their hands, or with their spears. Some reports suggest that such game would come as close as the doors of their tents or homes. This, then, was a trial of temptation. Similar in nature to that which the Children of Israel were asked to endure in former times, but in which they failed. They had pleaded with their Prophet, Moses (peace be upon him), to appoint a day when they would not have to attend to any aspect of their daily affairs. Rather, they would rest and spend the whole day in worship. Thus, the Sabbath was established for them. They were then tempted with water game, whereby fish of all types came right to the sea shore on the day of the Sabbath. On other days, it went far into the water in the normal behaviour of fish. The Children of Israel, however, could not resist the temptation, could not keep their covenant with God. In the end, they resorted to playing tricks holding the fish in enclosures without actually taking them out of the water. They only captured the fish from those enclosures on the following morning, when the Sabbath was over. Indeed, God instructs the Prophet Muḥammad to question them about this, confronting them with their trickery: "*Ask them about the town which stood facing the sea: how its people broke the Sabbath. Each Sabbath their fish appeared before them, breaking the water's surface, but they would not come near them on other than Sabbath days. Thus did We try them because of their disobedience.*" (7: 163)

It is this same trial which the Muslim community came through successfully, while the Jews did not. This is the proof of God's description of the Muslim community: "*You are the best community that has ever been raised for mankind; you enjoin the doing of what is right and forbid what is wrong, and you believe in God. Had the people of earlier revelations believed, it would have been for their own good. Few of them are believers, while most of them are evildoers.*" (3: 110)

In fact the Muslim community has passed the test on numerous occasions whereas the Jews did not pass any similar tests. Hence, God deprived them of their leadership role and assigned it to the Muslim community, giving it more power to establish its entity on earth than He has given to any other community. The fact remains that the code of living laid down by God was never implemented in a practical system regulating the whole of human life until it was put into practice by the Muslim community. But that was when that community was truly Islamic, when it knew and accepted that Islam means that the Divine religion and its laws must be implemented in human life. It also realised that it was placed in a position of trust, undertaking the fulfilment of that great task and providing leadership for mankind in implementing the Divine law.

The Purpose of the Trial

The trial of providing easy game at the time when it was prohibited to kill during the period of consecration, or *iḥrām*, was one of the numerous tests that the Muslim community successfully passed. The care God took of this Muslim community and its education is reflected in such tests. In this particular incident, God tells the believers of the purpose beyond His test: "*So that God may mark out those who truly fear Him in their hearts.*" (Verse 94) Being truly God-fearing, or fearing Him in one's heart, is the solid basis on which faith is established in a person's conscience. It mould's one's behaviour and it is the essence of putting man's vicegerency on earth into practice.

Human beings do not see God, but they feel His presence in their hearts when they truly believe in Him. To them, He is beyond the reach of all their faculties of perception, but their hearts know and fear Him. The certainty of this great truth in a firm, unshakeable belief in God, and achieving, without seeing Him or feeling His presence with our senses, a strength of belief equal, if not superior, to that based on one's senses is something great indeed. A believer declares that "there is no deity other than God" without having seen Him. To have such belief is indicative of a huge step forward towards a superior level of humanity that taps man's natural faculties and makes the best use of all his natural abilities. This represents a great departure away from the realm of animal existence that cannot look up to anything beyond its immediate perception. On the other hand, when man bars his soul from looking up to what lies beyond the reach of his faculties of perception and confines his feelings to the material world surrounding him, he shuts down his superior faculties and lingers permanently in his material and sensual world.

Hence, God makes this quality of fearing Him in our hearts the crucial point of this test, making it clear to the believers so that they are able to use all their powers to achieve it. God certainly knows, initially, who fears Him in his heart, but He does not hold people to account on the basis of His initial knowledge. They are accountable only for what they actually do, which God also knows on the basis of its taking place.

"*Whoever transgresses after all this will have grievous suffering.*" (Verse 94) Man is thus told of the trial to which he is being put. He is informed of its purpose and warned against yielding to temptation. All means of success have been given to him. Hence, should he transgress after all this, it is only fair that he should be made to endure grievous suffering. This is his own choice.

Details of the atonement for violation are then given. This starts with a firm prohibition and ends with a second warning: "*Believers, kill no game while you are on pilgrimage. Whoever of you kills game by design shall make amends in cattle equivalent to what he has killed, adjudged by two persons of probity among you, to be brought as an offering to the Ka'bah; or else he may atone for his sin by feeding needy persons, or by its equivalent in fasting, so that he may taste the evil consequences of his deeds. God has forgiven what is past; but whoever repeats his offence, God will inflict His retribution on him. God is Almighty, Lord of retribution.* (Verse 95)

The prohibition applies to killing game deliberately when a person is in the state of consecration, or *iḥrām*. If a game animal is killed by accident, the person in consecration neither incurs a sin nor has to give any compensation. For deliberate killing, the compensation is an offering of cattle or other animals equivalent to the game he has killed. Thus, if a person in consecration kills a deer, the compensation may be an offering of a sheep or a goat; for a camel, a cow or an ox is appropriate; for an ostrich or a giraffe or a similarly large animal, a camel may be offered; for a rabbit or a cat the offering may be a rabbit. What has no equivalent among animals however, an offering of its cash value is acceptable in compensation.

The compensation is adjudged by two Muslim men of probity. Should they rule that a particular type of animal be slaughtered, that animal is set loose until it reaches the Ka 'bah where it is slaughtered and given to the poor to eat. If such an animal is not available, the arbiters may rule that the compensation be given in the form of food given to the poor, provided that its quantity is equivalent to the value of either the animal to be slaughtered or the game animal killed. If the offender who has to make this compensation cannot afford this, he should fast a number of days to be decided as fair compensation. To do so, the value of the animal is first estimated, then the number of poor people that could be fed by this amount is determined. He fasts one day for every poor person. As for how much money is sufficient to feed one poor person, this is a matter on which scholars have differed. However, it cannot be a fixed sum, as it differs according to place, time and conditions.

The verse states the purpose of this compensation: "*So that he may taste the evil consequences of his deeds.*" (Verse 95) The requirement of compensation implies punishment. The offence is a breach of a strict prohibition. Hence, it cannot be left unpunished. However, God makes it clear that He has forgiven offences of the past, but He threatens those who do not desist from committing such violations with severe punishment: "*God has forgiven what is past; but whoever repeats his offence, God will inflict His retribution on him. God is Almighty, Lord of retribution.*" (Verse 95) Thus, if the killer of game wants to boast of his hunting ability by killing game animals which God wants to enjoy security in the vicinity where all are secure, he should know that it is God who is almighty and who exacts retribution.

All this applies to hunting on land. Fishing, on the other hand, is permissible in all situations: "*Lawful to you is all water-game, and whatever food the sea brings forth, as a provision for you and for travellers.*" (Verse 96) This means that all types of water animals are permissible to catch and use for food whether a person is in the state of consecration or not. With this mention of the permissibility of water-game and food from the sea, the verse restates the prohibition of killing game on land during consecration: "*However, you are forbidden land-game as long as you are in the state of consecration [or* iḥrām*].*" (Verse 96)

All scholars are unanimous that killing animal game is forbidden for any person in consecration. However, scholars have differing views as to the permissibility of eating game, should the animal be killed by another person who is not in consecration. Moreover, scholars disagree as to the referent of the term "game" as used in this verse: does it apply only to animals that are normally pursued as game; or does the prohibition apply to all animals, including those which are not normally considered game and are not referred to as game.

These rules of permissibility and prohibition are concluded with a statement that appeals to the believers' sense of fearing God and reminds us of the Day of Judgement and the reckoning we will then have to face: *"Be conscious of God, to whom you shall all be gathered."* (Verse 96)

The Reason for Prohibition

It is perhaps pertinent to ask here about the purpose behind these prohibition rules. Well, God wishes to provide a security zone for mankind, where they seek refuge from life's worries. This zone is represented by the Ka'bah, the Inviolable House of Worship, and the sacred months. They offer a haven of peace in the midst of the raging battle between those in combat through life, regardless of their race and ethnic origin. Their desires, ambitions and needs continue to fuel their struggle, but this security zone beckons to them so that it may substitute reassurance for their worries, love for conflict, brotherhood and security for hostility and fear. What is more is that such concepts are not confined to the realm of theories and ideals; people are given practical training in real life to grab such feelings and maintain them. Thus, they are seen as a reality, not mere words and visions that have no bearing on real life.

> God has made the Ka'bah, the Inviolable House of Worship, a symbol for all mankind; and so too the sacred month and the garlanded sacrificial offerings. This, so that you may know that God is aware of all that is in the heavens and the earth, and that God has full knowledge of everything. Know that God is severe in retribution and that God is Much-Forgiving, Merciful. The Messenger's duty is but to deliver the message [entrusted to him]. God knows all that you reveal, and all that you conceal. (Verses 97–9)

God has made the sanctity of the Ka'bah applicable to man, animals, birds, insects and all creatures. They all feel secure there. In the period of consecration, the prohibitions apply even before someone reaches the Ka'bah. God has also prohibited all fighting and killing in the four sacred months of Dhu'l-Qa'dah, Dhu'l-Ḥijjah, Muḥarram and Rajab. Even in pre-Islamic days, God made the Arabs highly respectful of the sanctity of those sacred months. Thus, they would not frighten anyone or seek any vengeance during those times. A man would meet the killer of his father, son, or brother and would not take any action against him. Thus, those four months became a season for travel and seeking one's livelihood. God's purpose has been that the Ka'bah should be a place of peace and security, where people are not troubled by fear and anxiety. Similarly, He made those four months a time-zone of security. He then extended the cover of peace and security beyond geographical and time zones so that it included sacrificial animals let loose during the pilgrimage and 'umrah. None could intercept such animals until they reached the Ka'bah. The same security being extended to any person or animal wearing a garland taken from the trees of the Ḥaram area; this by way of declaring the protection granted by the Ka'bah.

These sanctities were put in place at the time when the Ka'bah was built by the Prophets Abraham and Ishmael. It was then that God made the Ka'bah a haven for people and a sanctuary. In fact, He reminds the idolatrous Arabs of His favour in placing them close to the House which provides security and sanctuary while people all around them live in fear. Yet still they do not give thanks or express real gratitude. They do not address their worship to God alone even in the House that was built as a symbol for God's oneness. They further said to God's Messenger who called on them to attribute all Godhead to God alone: *"If we were to follow the guidance you bring us, we will be snatched away from our land."* God reports their claim and confronts them with the security and peace they enjoy in the vicinity of the Ka'bah, the Sacred Mosque God has sanctified: *"They say: If we were to follow the message to which you invite us, we would be snatched away from our land! Why – have We not established for them a secure sanctuary, to which are brought the fruits of all good things, as provision from Ourself? But most of them are ignorant."* (28: 57)

An authentic *ḥadīth* related by both al-Bukhārī and Muslim quotes the Prophet as saying on the day Makkah fell to Islam: "This city is a forbidden city: its trees may not be cut, nor its plants sheared; its game may not be deliberately scared, and whatever is dropped by people may not be picked up except for identification." Of all living things, only five may be killed in the vicinity of the Ka'bah or by a person in consecration. These are: a raven, kite, scorpion, mouse and a biting dog. Al-Bukhārī and Muslim relate, on the authority of 'Ā'ishah, that "the Prophet ordered the killing of five harmful creatures in the Ḥaram and outside it: ravens, kites, scorpions, mice and biting dogs." Snakes were also added in an authentic *ḥadīth* related by Muslim on the authority of 'Abdullāh ibn 'Umar.

Madinah was similarly declared a place of sanctity. 'Alī quotes the Prophet as saying: "Madinah is a sanctuary between 'Īr and Thawr." A *ḥadīth* related by al-Bukhārī and Muslim on the authority of 'Abbād ibn Tamīm states that the Prophet said: "Abraham has consecrated Makkah and prayed for it. I am consecrating Madinah just like Abraham consecrated Makkah."

Furthermore, it is not merely a time and place security zone for humans and animals alone. It is also a security zone for the human conscience, that vast arena of the human soul attendant with all its struggles and strains. It is like a volcano that sends its smoke, fire and lava to burn the land and mar the clarity of time, harming man and animal alike. The Ka'bah and its environs provides the perfect sanctuary in the midst of all this conflict. This sanctuary extends its peace and security so as to make a person in consecration unwilling to chase an animal or a bird, which would otherwise be lawful for them to slay. However, here they are in a sanctuary, in a place of security for animals and humans alike. The whole place is a stage for training the human soul so that it is purged of all its shady traces and so that it is able to attain a standard of clarity and sublimity that enables it to deal with the Supreme Society of Heaven.

Man, terrified, worried and engaged in endless strife as he is, is always in dire need of such a security zone which God has provided in the Islamic faith and outlined its boundaries in the Qur'ān.

"*This, so that you may know that God is aware of all that is in the heavens and the earth, and that God has full knowledge of everything.*" (Verse 97) This may sound a rather strange comment at this particular juncture, but it is perfectly understandable. God has laid down this faith and established this sanctuary so that people may know that He knows everything that is in the heavens and the earth and that He is fully aware of all things. Thus, they know that God is fully cognizant of human nature, as well as people's aspirations, needs and spiritual longings. He enacts legislation in order to satisfy natures, meet needs, fulfil aspirations and answer longings. When people feel in their hearts how God's compassion is evident in His law and appreciate the harmony between their nature and God's law, they realise that God is fully aware of all that is in the heavens and the earth and that His perfect knowledge encompasses everything.

It is most remarkable how this religion of Islam meets all the needs and aspirations of human nature. It has been moulded in a way that perfectly fits human nature. When a person's heart is responsive to the Islamic faith, it finds in it beauty, serenity, comfort and an ease of standards unknown except to those who have experienced them.

The discussion of the permissible and the prohibited, both in consecration and at other times, is brought to its conclusion with a clear warning against incurring punishment, while at the same time offering the prospect of forgiveness and mercy: *"Know that God is severe in retribution and that God is Much-Forgiving, Merciful."* (Verse 98) The warning is coupled with pointing out that responsibility lies clearly with the one who breaches sanctities and does not regret or repent: *"The Messenger's duty is but to deliver the message [entrusted to him]. God knows all that you reveal, and all that you conceal."* (Verse 99)

Foul and Wholesome

At the concluding part of this passage God provides us with a standard so that we may give correct judgement of all things. In these scales, only what is good and wholesome is weighty, while that which is foul and evil carries no weight. This prevents a Muslim from being deceived when he finds that the foul is plentiful and the evil too numerous. *"Say: Evil and good are not equal, even though the abundance of evil may be pleasing to you. Have fear of God, you who are endowed with understanding, so that you may triumph."* (Verse 100)

Evil and good are mentioned here within the context of elaborating which food and game are permissible and which are forbidden. What is forbidden is evil, while everything that is permissible is good. Certainly the good and the evil cannot be equal, even though the evil may come in such plenty that it attracts and tempts people. That which is good provides enjoyment that is not followed by foul consequences, such as regret, waste, pain or disease. The pleasure gained out of evil things cannot be matched even by a modicum of the good things in life. What is more is that with the good things, man enjoys safety in this life and in the life to come. When the human mind is free of the shackles of desire as a result of its being God-fearing and when it has attained a keen watchfulness, it will inevitably prefer good to evil. This is bound to end in success and triumph, both in this world and in the Hereafter: "*Have fear of God, you who are endowed with understanding, so that you may triumph.*" (Verse 100)

This verse especially suits the present occasion, but it has a much wider implication. It looks to a broad horizon, encompassing life in its totality.

God, who has raised this community as the best model for mankind, wants it to undertake the great trust of establishing His system and constitution on earth, so that it maintains it in practical life as no previous community ever did. Hence, this community has been in need of long and sustained training that purges it from all traces of past ignorance and takes it by the hand from the low ebb of material life along the incline of an Islamic life. The training then continues to purify the concepts, habits, practices and feelings of the Muslim community, strengthening its will and determination to advocate only the truth. What is more is that it takes place amidst all the adversity it has to face and the responsibility it has to shoulder in so doing. The final stage is that the Muslim community has to shape and mould its whole life in accordance with Islamic values. This places the Muslim community truly on God's side. It gives it the fairest form of humanity, upholding a standard that will never equate evil with good, even though the evil is plentiful and replete with temptation. The ability to distinguish evil from good and to give each its proper value as shown in God's system makes evil very light in God's scale and good very much heavier, even though it may be much smaller in quantity. When the Muslim community attains such a standard, it becomes worthy of shouldering God's trust, providing leadership for humanity, weighing things up according to God's scales, choosing what is good for mankind, and refusing to be tempted by an abundance of evil.

Another situation in which this standard is found to be most suitable is that when falsehood puts on airs and graces so that people think it mighty, plentiful and powerful. But a believer looks at such rising falsehood with a firm gaze, remains unaffected by its apparent might, and chooses, in preference to it, the truth which displays no apparent strength and commands no ready forces. He prefers it only because it is the truth, plain and simple, carrying no weight or authority other than its being true in God's measure.

God subjected the first Muslim community to the Qur'ānic system of education, under the supervision of His Messenger (peace be upon him), until it attained the standard which He had determined to be necessary for its role as trustee of the Divine faith. This standard does not merely apply to conscience and inner belief, but also to practices and life affairs. It looks at all desires, attractions, aspirations, and conflicting interests with which human life abounds, whether these belong to individuals or the community as a whole and then evaluates them by God's standard. This makes it worthy of shouldering the heavy responsibility of trusteeship over human life as a whole.

In His education of the Muslim community, God used all sorts of directives, influences, tests, trials and legislation, placing them all in one bunch to fulfil a single role, namely, the preparation of this community for its role as guardian of God's faith on earth. This preparation required equipping it with the right concepts, formulating the right reactions and responses, adopting the proper morality, legal code and system, and following the right practices, etc. When that preparation was completed, God achieved with that community whatever He willed. God certainly is able to accomplish His purpose at all times. Thus, the earth witnessed a sublime model of the Divine faith in practice. Humanity can always emulate that model, provided it realises that it has to struggle hard for that purpose. When it is determined to go ahead with such a struggle, God will give it His help and support.

Politeness in Dealing with the Prophet

The *sūrah* moves on to draw the attention of the early Muslims to the standard of politeness they must adopt with the Prophet. They are told not to ask him about matters on which he remains silent, particularly such matters which, should they be tackled, may cause hardship or embarrassment to the person raising the question, or may impose on him heavy tasks or restrictions that God, out of His mercy, has chosen not to impose on the Muslims.

> *Believers, do not ask about matters which, if made known to you, may cause you hardship. If you should ask about them while the Qur'ān is being revealed, they shall be made plain to you. God will*

264

forgive you these; for God is Much-Forgiving, Forbearing. People before your time inquired about them, and on that account they came to deny the truth. (Verses 101–2)

Some people used to put numerous questions to the Prophet (peace be upon him) asking him about matters on which no order or prohibition had been given. Some were always asking about the details of matters that the Qur'ān gave in general terms, to make them easier for people. Some asked about matters which need not be exposed, because exposure would cause a problem either to the person putting the question or to others. It is reported, for example, that when the verse establishing the duty of pilgrimage was revealed, a man asked the Prophet whether pilgrimage was a duty every year. The Prophet disliked the question because the Qur'ānic verse left the matter unspecified: *"Pilgrimage to this House is a duty owed to God by all people who are able to undertake it."* (3: 97) To offer the pilgrimage once is sufficient for this duty to be fulfilled. To ask whether it is a duty required every year is to give the text a much harder interpretation and one which God has not imposed.

A *ḥadīth* attributed to 'Alī, without quoting the Prophet, says: "When the verse stating that 'pilgrimage is a duty owed to God by all people who are able to undertake it,' was revealed, some people asked the Prophet: 'Is it every year?' He did not answer. They repeated the question and he said: 'No.' Had I said, 'yes,' it would have become an obligation." Then God revealed the verse stating: *"Believers, do not ask about matters which, if made known to you, may cause you hardship."* (Verse 101) (Related by al-Tirmidhī and al-Dāraquṭnī)

Al-Dāraquṭnī relates a similar *ḥadīth* on the authority of Abū Hurayrah who says: "The Prophet said: 'Mankind, Pilgrimage has been made a duty of yours.' A man stood up and asked, 'Is it every year, Messenger of God?' The Prophet did not answer him, so the man repeated the question. The Prophet asked who the man was putting the question. When he was told his name, he said: 'By Him who holds my soul in His hand, had I said, "Yes", it would have become binding. Had it been made binding, you would not be able to fulfil it, and if you were not able to fulfil it, you would be guilty of disbelief.'" Then God revealed the verse stating: *"Believers, do not ask about matters which, if made known to you, may cause you hardship."* (Verse 101)

According to al-Ṭabarī, on one occasion people asked the Prophet a great many questions. In reference to that occasion Muslim relates in his *Ṣaḥīḥ* on the authority of Anas that "the Prophet said: 'By God I will answer any question you put to me, as long as I am in this position.' A man stood up and asked: 'Which will be my place of entry?' The Prophet said, 'The Fire.' 'Abdullāh ibn Ḥudhāfah asked: 'Who is my father, Messenger of God?' The Prophet said to him, 'Your father is Ḥudhāfah.' His mother said to him: 'I have never heard of a more undutiful son. How could you be sure that your mother might not have done something which women prior to Islam did? You would have, then, exposed her in front of all people.' He said: 'Had he said that I belonged to a black slave, I would have affiliated myself to him.'" It should be added here that the second man mentioned in this *ḥadīth*, 'Abdullāh ibn Ḥudhāfah, was among the early Muslims in Makkah. He went to Abyssinia with the second group of emigrants and took part in the Battle of Badr. He was known for his sense of humour.

Another report by al-Ṭabarī on the authority of Abū Hurayrah states: "The Prophet came out angry, with his face red, and sat on the pulpit. A man rose and asked him: 'Where will I be?' He said, 'In the Fire.' Another man asked him: 'Who is my father?' The Prophet said: 'Your father is Ḥudhāfah.' 'Umar ibn al-Khaṭṭāb stood up and said: 'We acknowledge God as our Lord, Islam as our faith, and Muḥammad (peace be upon him) as God's Prophet, and the Qur'ān as our constitution. Messenger of God, we only recently abandoned idolatry, and God knows best who were our fathers.' The Prophet's anger cooled down. "Then the verse was revealed stating: "*Believers, do not ask about matters which, if made known to you, may cause you hardship.*" (Verse 101)

Mujāhid quotes Ibn 'Abbās as saying that this verse was revealed in answer to people who asked about certain superstitious practices involving animals. He quotes another scholar, Sa'īd ibn Jubayr, as citing in support the verse that follows, stating: "*It was not God who instituted [superstitions like those of] a slit-ear she camel, or a she-camel let loose for free pasture, or idol sacrifices for twin-births in animals, or stallion-camels freed from work.*" (Verse 103)

All these reports and similar ones give us a clear picture of the type of questions which believers have been ordered not to ask.

The Qur'ān was revealed from on high not merely to establish a faith or outline a legal code, but also to educate a community and establish a society. It also aims to reform the attitudes of individuals and to set for them a logical and moral system of its own. Here the

Qur'ān is teaching Muslims how and when to put their questions, demarcating the boundaries of investigation and the system through which to acquire knowledge. Since God is the source of the Islamic code and the One who reveals what is unknown, it is only good manners that His servants should leave it to His wisdom whether to provide details of the legal provisions or to state them in general terms only, and whether to inform them of what is unknown to them or keep it hidden away from them. It behoves them well to stop at the limits determined by God whose knowledge encompasses all things. It is not in their interest to set for themselves stricter limits, through the pursuit of different possibilities. It is wrong that they should try to seek to know things that lie beyond the reach of their powers of perception when God has determined not to reveal these to them. Their attempts are bound to be fruitless, for God knows well the limits of human power and potential. He gives them the law that suits them, revealing only that measure of knowledge with which they are able to cope.

Choosing the Hard Way

God has kept certain matters unknown to man, or He might have expressed certain matters in general terms. It does not harm people to leave such matters in the form God has left them. To question these at the time of the Prophet might have provided them with distressing answers, or might have overburdened both them and future generations. Hence, God tells the believers not to ask about certain matters which if revealed might be harmful. He also warns them that should they ask about these during the Prophet's lifetime, when the Qur'ān was being revealed, for then they would have their answers, but these would impose on them obligations that God did not originally make binding: "*Believers, do not ask about matters which, if made known to you, may cause you hardship. If you should ask about them while the Qur'ān is being revealed, they shall be made plain to you. God will forgive you these; for God is Much-Forgiving, Forbearing.*" (Verse 101) The verse carries a clear instruction not to inquire about matters which God has left out or stated without details in order to keep duties lighter, as in the case of pilgrimage.

God then gives the example of former communities that were given revelations. Some of them made things harder for themselves by numerous questions about rulings and duties. When, as a result, God made new obligations binding on them, they failed to perform these, thus rejecting them. Had they left matters as God stated them originally, they would have been able to benefit by the easier tasks God wanted to assign to them. They would not have had to cope with their failure to fulfil their responsibilities.

We have seen how the Jews asked too many questions when they were ordered to slaughter a cow (Volume I, pp. 75–80). They were not given any conditions initially, and as such, slaughtering any cow would have been good enough. However, they asked for a description, and then details of that description. With every question, the choice before them was narrowed down and the task became harder. Had they refrained from putting these questions, the matter would have remained much easier. The same was the case when they asked for the Sabbath. When it was granted to them, at their request, they could not cope with its obligations. They followed the same pattern time and time again, until God forbade them many things either for educational purposes or as a punishment.

An authentic *ḥadīth* quotes the Prophet as saying: "Whatever I leave out, do not pursue it with me. Communities before you were ruined as a result of asking too many questions and disputing with their prophets." In another authentic *ḥadīth* the Prophet states: "God has imposed certain obligations; so do not neglect them. He set certain boundaries; so do not transgress them. Furthermore, He has forbidden certain things; so do not violate these. And He has left out certain matters as an act of grace, forgetting none of them; so do not ask about these."

In his authentic collection of *aḥādīth* Muslim relates that the Prophet said: "Among all Muslims, the worst offender against the Muslim community is one who asks about something which has not been forbidden them, and as a result of his question, it has been made forbidden."

A Practical Approach to Knowledge

Perhaps these *aḥādīth* we have quoted, together with statements in the Qur'ān, delineate the Islamic system of pursuing knowledge. The first point to make clear is that, from the Islamic point of view, knowledge is sought to face a real need and to satisfy that need. Human powers and faculties are too precious to expend in pursuing detailed matters of what

Islam calls *ghayb*, a term which refers to what lies beyond the reach of human perception. That is because such knowledge is not sought to meet any real or practical need in human life. It is sufficient for the human mind to believe in that *ghayb* as described by the One who has described it. When the human mind goes beyond that belief in order to investigate its nature and details, it will not attain any true results, because it is simply not equipped with the necessary faculties to achieve that knowledge. God has given us all that we need to know about it. Any further pursuit is a waste of effort; it is no more than trying to walk in the desert without a guide. It is bound to end in total loss.

As for Islamic rulings, these are sought when needed, to face practical situations as and when these take place. This is the proper Islamic approach.

Throughout the Makkan period of Islamic revelations, not a single administrative ruling was outlined, although orders were given to do certain things and to refrain from others. Detailed rulings, such as mandatory and discretionary punishments, atonements and the like were only revealed after the establishment of the Islamic state in Madinah, because that state was able to carry out these details and put them into practice.

The first generation of Muslims was fully abreast of this approach. Hence, they would not give a judgement on any question unless it had taken place. Even then, they would only give a judgement within the context of the question, and without trying to apply texts to assumed events that had not taken place. They wanted to maintain seriousness in both questions and rulings. Al-Dārimī, a leading scholar of *Ḥadīth*, reports that 'Umar ibn al-Khaṭṭāb used to rebuke anyone who asked about things that had not taken place. He also mentions that Zaid ibn Thābit, a learned scholar among the Prophet's Companions, used to say when a question was put to him: "Has this taken place yet?" If he was told that it had, he would give an answer on the basis of his knowledge. If he was told that it had not taken place, he would say: "Leave it, then, until it takes place."

Another report by al-Dārimī mentions that 'Ammār ibn Yāsir, a Companion of the Prophet, was asked about a particular matter. He said: "Has it taken place?" They answered, "No." He said: "Do not trouble us with it, then. Should it take place, we will look into it for you."

Al-Dārimī also mentions a report by Ibn 'Abbās, stating: "I have never seen a community better than the Prophet's Companions. They asked him only about 13 matters, the answers for them all are given in the Qur'ān. Among these are, '*They ask you about fighting in the sacred month...*' (2: 217), and, '*They ask you about menstruation...*' (2: 222), and the like. They only asked about what would benefit them."

Imām Mālik says: "I have lived in this city, [meaning Madīnah], and the only knowledge available to its people is the Qur'ān and the *Sunnah*. Should something unusual take place, the Governor would call in all scholars available. Whatever view they approved, he would implement. But you ask too many questions, a habit the Prophet disapproved of."

Al-Qurṭubī, a commentator on the Qur'ān, says in his explanation of this verse [i.e. Verse 101] that the Prophet says: "God has forbidden you to be undutiful to your mothers, burying your daughters alive, stinginess and greed. He also dislikes three qualities: idle speech, asking too many questions and wasting money." Many scholars are of the view that "asking too many questions" refers to asking many hypothetical questions about Islamic rulings on theoretical and imaginary matters and trying to deduce unnecessary rulings for them. The early Muslims disliked this exercise, considering it to be a pursuit leading to nothing beneficial. They would say that should something take place, a scholar would be guided to its ruling.

This shows the Islamic system to be serious and practical. It provides practical rulings deduced from the principles of Divine law for practical problems in life. In its approach to these problems, it studies each one according to its circumstances and conditions in order to give for it a ruling that covers all its aspects and applies to it fully. To ask for rulings on hypothetical questions is neither useful nor necessary. Since a matter has not taken place, it is impossible to measure it properly. To issue a ruling for it is not suitable, because it cannot cover its aspects which remain unknown. In fact, both question and answer in this case imply a loose attitude to Islamic law and are in breach of the proper Islamic approach.

The same applies to questions asking for Islamic rulings in countries which do not implement Islamic law, and to the answers given to such questions. Divine law is asked for rulings only when these are meant for implementation. Therefore, when both the one who asks the question and the one who answers it are aware that they live in a country where God's authority over human life is denied, then what is the purpose of the whole process of seeking an Islamic ruling? Such a country does not recognise that Godhead means submission to God, His law and authority in this life. So, in such a situation, the two parties to the process of deducing an Islamic ruling on a particular question are involved in degrading Islamic law, whether they are aware of the fact or not.

We may say the same concerning purely theoretical studies of details of Islamic law concerning aspects that remain unimplemented. Such studies are no more than an idle pursuit, aiming to give a false impression that Islamic law occupies a place in the land where it is studied in academic institutes, although it remains unimplemented in the courts. Anyone who is party to giving such a false impression may be guilty of sinful action.

This religion of Islam is serious indeed. It has been revealed so that it governs human life. Its aim is to help people so that they submit to God alone and to deprive those who usurp God's authority of what they claim to be theirs so that all authority is given to God's law. It must be remembered that Islamic law is devised to govern all aspects of human life. It issues its rulings to deal with practical questions and real needs. Hence, it gives a ruling only for questions that actually take place and only when they do take place. Its rulings take into account all the aspects and circumstances of every problem. This religion of Islam has not been revealed so that it becomes a mere slogan, or that its law becomes a subject for academic, theoretical study that has no bearing on practical life. It does not indulge in solving hypotheses and providing hypothetical answers to them.

That is the practical meaning of the seriousness of Islam. Any Islamic scholar who wishes to follow its system, with such seriousness, should work hard for the implementation of Islamic law in practical life. Otherwise, he should at least refrain from issuing theoretical rulings that have no place in reality.

Freedom for the Human Mind

We have already mentioned a report in which Mujāhid quotes Ibn 'Abbās and Sa'īd ibn Jubayr's comments on the immediate reason for revealing the verse instructing the believers not to put questions concerning certain matters which would cause them difficulty or distress should they be stated in detail. The same report mentions that their questions included things and practices known in pre-Islamic days.

We have not been able to determine which particular things and practices were referred to, but the fact that the *sūrah* mentions the dedication of certain types of cattle immediately after the instruction not to ask unnecessary questions of detail suggests that the two are somehow linked. This is all that we need to say before discussing the verse that refers to such idolatrous practices.

> *It was not God who instituted [superstitions like those of] a slit-ear she camel, or a she-camel let loose for free pasture, or idol sacrifices for twin-births in animals, or stallion-camels freed from work. It is unbelievers who attribute their own lying inventions to God. Most of them never use their reason. When they are told, "Come to that which God has revealed and to the Messenger," they reply, "Sufficient for us are the ways we found our fathers following." Why, even though their fathers knew nothing and were devoid of all guidance?* (Verses 103–4)

The human mind finds itself at a crossroads: it either maintains its proper nature with which God has equipped it or takes a different route. Should it take this way, it will recognise its one Lord, God, the Lord of the universe. It will submit to Him and accept His legislation, rejecting all other types of lordship. This means that it will reject any law other than God's. In this case, the human mind will find contact with its Lord to be so easy and worshipping Him to be so simple and clear. Alternatively, the human mind could lose its way in the maze of ignorance, facing darkness in every way and a myth at every junction. Tyrannical deities demand all sorts of worship rituals and sacrifices, which, in time, increase and multiply. An idolater will then forget their origins, but continue to offer them by force of habit. He will writhe under the demands of worshipping a multitude of deities, which will deprive him of all dignity that God has bestowed on man.

Islam declares that the authority to which all people must submit is the One God. In doing so, it liberates people from bondage to one another, restores man's dignity and frees the human mind from the fetters of rituals offered to multiple deities. Hence, Islam fights to eradicate idolatry in all its shapes and forms, pursuing it wherever it settles or manifests itself: deep in the human conscience, in worship rituals, in social practices, or in government and political systems.

At this point, the *surah* pays attention to one aspect of idolatry in pre-Islamic, pagan Arabia. It brings it into focus so as to refute all legends surrounding it. It states the basic principles of rational thinking, as well as the principles of law and faith at the same time: "*It was not God who instituted [superstitions like those of] a slit-ear she-camel, or a she-camel let loose for free pasture, or idol sacrifices for twin-births in animals, or stallion-camels freed from work. It is unbelievers who attribute their own lying inventions to God. Most of them never use their reason.*" (Verse 103)

Superstitious Practices

There were certain types of cattle people consecrated for their deities on conditions based in their inherited myths and which people accepted blindly. What were these? Who made the regulations concerning them? We have widely differing reports explaining each type of cattle. We will mention only a couple of these definitions to give an idea of such practices.

Al-Zuhrī quotes Sa'īd ibn al-Musayyb who says that the *baḥīrah*, or "a slit-ear she-camel" was one whose milk was dedicated for deities. [Needless to say, the milk was taken and used by the custodians of the temples.] The second type, *sā'ibah*, was a she-camel dedicated to deities and let loose to graze wherever it wanted. The third type, *waṣīlah*, was a she-camel that gave birth to two she-camels consecutively. This they would sacrifice for their deities. The fourth type, *ḥāmī*, was a male camel kept for breeding. When he had ensured conception for a set number of she-camels, they said that his back had warmed and he was freed and let loose.

Linguists have similar definitions. The first type, *baḥīrah*, is a she-camel whose ear has been widely slit. When a she-camel has given birth five times, producing in the fifth a male camel, the Arabs would slit its ear as a mark of consecration, prohibiting anyone from riding or slaughtering it for food. It would never be turned away from pasture or water. Even when a man suffering from fatigue saw it, he would not ride it. The second type, *sā'ibah*, was a she-camel let loose. When a person wanted to make an offering as a gesture of gratitude after his recovery from illness or return from a long journey or the like, he would say, "My she-camel is free." It would, thus, be consecrated in the same fashion as the first type.

273

According to a number of linguists, the third type of cattle, *wasīlah*, referred to a female sheep being a twin of a male sheep. The female would, then, be spared slaughter. Others say that when a sheep gives birth to a female, they took it. Should it give birth to a male, they would slaughter it as an offering to their deities. Now if she gave birth to twins: a male and a female, they would say that the female had spared its brother and they would not slaughter the male as an offering. The fourth type, *ḥāmī*, was a male camel when it fathered no less than ten different pregnancies. They would say that his back had warmed. Thus, he would not be used to carry anything, and he would be let free to drink and graze wherever he wanted.

Other reports give similar or different definitions but they are all of the same nature based in the same superstitious beliefs. It is clear that these are no more than idolatrous myths. When myth and personal desire are the ultimate arbiter, there can be no logic or proper limits. Rituals will soon diverge, with omissions and additions made at will. This took place in pre-Islamic Arabia and it can happen anywhere, at any time, once human conscience deviates from absolute, straight and clear monotheism. Appearances may differ, but the essence of ignorance remains, allowing guidance to be derived from any source other than God Almighty.

When we speak of the state of ignorance we are not referring to a certain period of time. We mean a state that may take different shapes at any time. There can only be belief in one God, with total submission to Him, acknowledging His total authority, addressing all actions, emotions, thoughts and intentions to Him and deriving all values, standards, concepts and laws from Him and setting all systems and situations on His guidance. Or else, there will be a state of ignorance, in one form or another, characterised by submission to other people or different creatures, without limits or controls. The point here is that the human mind cannot, on its own, be the source of proper control, unless it is controlled by true faith. We see at all times that the human mind is easily influenced by desires. It loses its power of resistance when it is subjected to different pressures, unless it refers to a well-defined standard of control.

Today, 14 centuries after the revelation of the Qur'ān, we observe that whenever the bond that links the human mind to the One God becomes loose, the human mind finds itself lost in an endless labyrinth. It then submits to different deities and loses its freedom, dignity and strength. I personally have seen in the Egyptian countryside numerous forms of myth, in which certain types of animals are consecrated for alleged saints and shrines, in the same way as they were consecrated for false deities in olden times.

At the core of such rituals in any state of ignorance we find the basic question that sets the starting point: Who is the ultimate judge in human life? Is it God alone, as He has stated? Or are there other judges, as people may decide for themselves, setting their own values, standards, systems, laws and rituals? In other words: To whom does Godhead belong? To God alone, or to some of His creatures, whoever they may be?

Contradiction in Terms

As the Qur'ān deals with these aspects, it states first of all that God has not initiated those practices of consecrating cattle. Who, then, has set those practices for the unbelievers? *"It was not God who instituted [superstitions like those of] a slit-ear she-camel, or a she-camel let loose for free pasture, or idol sacrifices for twin-births in animals, or stallion-camels freed from work."* (Verse 103) Those who follow any code or doctrine other than the one God has laid down are unbelievers, making false claims against God. They may enact their own laws and claim that these are God's law. Or they may claim for themselves the right to promulgate their own laws, allowing no room for God's law in their system, but at the same time, they claim that they do not disobey God. All this is no more than fabricating lies against God. *"It is unbelievers who attribute their own lying inventions to God. Most of them never use their reason."* (Verse 103)

The pagan Arabs used to believe that they were following the faith of Abraham, as revealed to him by God. They did not deny God altogether. Indeed they acknowledged Him, His power and control over the universe. Nevertheless, they enacted their own laws and legislation, claiming that these were all part of God's law. As such they were unbelievers. The same description applies to all people in any state of ignorance, when they make their own laws, whether they claim them to be part of God's law or not.

God's law is that which He has stated in His book, and which was outlined by His Messenger. It is neither vague nor ambiguous. It does not admit, as ignorant people claim everywhere, that anyone may invent something and claim it to be part of God's law. Hence, God brands those who make such claims as unbelievers, and then describes them as devoid of reason. Had they used their reason, they would not have fabricated lies and attributed them to God. Had they had any logic, they would not have imagined that their lies could be accepted.

The irony of what they say and do is made even clearer: *"When they are told, 'Come to that which God has revealed and to the Messenger,' they reply, 'Sufficient for us are the ways we found our fathers following.' Why, even though their fathers knew nothing and were devoid of all guidance?"* (Verse 104)

Divine law is well-defined in God's revelations, and clarified by the *Sunnah.* This is the point at which Islam takes its course, which is totally different from that of unbelief. When people are called to implement what God has revealed and His Messenger has explained, they either respond positively and in this case they are Muslims, or they reject the call, and in this case they are unbelievers. There is no other choice. Some Arabs, however, used to respond to such a call by saying that they were satisfied with what they had inherited from their fathers. Thus, they followed laws enacted by human beings in preference to those enacted by the Lord of all human beings. They turned a deaf ear to the appeal to free themselves from submission to other people. By choice, they made their reason and conscience subservient to their forefathers.

In response to such an attitude the Qur'ān makes this reproachful comment: *"Why, even though their fathers knew nothing and were devoid of all guidance?"* (Verse 104) This denunciation of their following their forefathers, even though they were devoid of all knowledge, does not mean that had their forefathers had a wealth of knowledge, they would be right to follow them in abandoning what God has revealed. The verse merely makes a statement of fact, describing their situation and that of their predecessors. Yet surely no one would take up his own laws or those of his father, when he has access to God's law and the *Sunnah* of God's Messenger unless he is totally devoid of all knowledge and all guidance. Let such a person claim what he may about his knowledge and enlightenment. God's statement expresses the truth, which is further confirmed by reality. Only an ignorant, deviant unbeliever prefers human law to God's law.

Individual Responsibility

When the situation of the unbelievers was explained, the *sūrah* makes a statement showing the believers as a separate group, distinguished by the duties and obligations they have to fulfil. It defines for them what attitude they should take to other people. It tells them that they may look forward to no reward other than that of God. They should aspire to no reward in this life. "*Believers, it is but for your own souls that you are accountable. Those who go astray can do you no harm if you [yourselves] are on the right path. To God you all must return. He will then make you understand all that you were doing [in life].*" (Verse 105)

It is a case of a complete break between them and those who are hostile to their cause. Moreover, they should have a relationship of mutual support among themselves, since they form one community: "*Believers, it is but for your own souls that you are accountable. Those who go astray can do you no harm if you [yourselves] are on the right path.*" (Verse 105)

What this verse says to the believers is that they should take care of themselves, purifying their souls and committing themselves wholly to their community, paying no attention to what others may say or do, even though they may go far astray. As believers, they are a separate unit, independent of all others. In this unit, they take care of one another, in complete mutual solidarity. Other than this, they have no need for any bonds or ties of loyalty with anyone.

This single verse establishes some highly important principles with regard to the Muslim community and its relations with other communities. The Muslim community constitutes God's party, while those who are opposed to it belong to Satan's party. Hence, no ties of loyalty or solidarity may exist between the two, as they do not have any ideology in common, nor do they share in any goal, responsibility, means of action or result and reward.

The Muslim community must demonstrate total solidarity within its ranks, where all its members exchange good and sincere counsel, following Divine guidance. This makes them a community apart. When this becomes a reality, the Muslim community need not worry if everyone else goes astray, since it is committed to following God's guidance.

This, however, does not mean that the Muslim community should abandon its task of calling on all people to follow Divine guidance, represented in its own faith, law and system. Once the Muslim community has established its system in its land, its continuing duty is to call on all mankind, urging them to follow the guidance God has provided for their happiness. It should also discharge its trust, ensuring justice among all people, and steering them away from error.

The fact that the Muslim community is accountable only for itself and that it suffers no harm as the result of anyone going astray as long as it follows God's guidance does not mean that it is not accountable if it fails to enjoin what is good and forbids what is wrong. This is certainly a task that it must fulfil within its own ranks first, and then throughout the whole earth. The first thing in "what is right" is submission to God, or Islam, and implementing His law, while the first thing in "what is wrong" is to sink into a state of ignorance and usurp God's authority, abandoning His law. Any judgement of ignorance is a judgement of tyranny, which is defined as an authority at variance with God's authority. The Muslim community is in a position of trust over its own affairs in the first instance, then over the affairs of all humanity.

The purpose in defining the limits of responsibility in this verse is not to say, as some people of old understood and some today understand, that a believer is not required individually, to enjoin what is right and forbid what is wrong when he or she has ascertained that they follow the right guidance. Nor does it mean that, once the Muslim community has set itself on its course following Divine guidance while others remain astray, it is not required, collectively, to establish God's law in the land. This verse of the Qur'ān does not absolve Muslim individuals or the Muslim community of their ongoing responsibility to combat evil and error and to resist tyranny. The worst form of tyranny is to usurp God's authority and Godhead and to force people to be subservient to any law other than His own. In fact no following of guidance whether by individuals or the community is sufficient while such evil exists.

Al-Nasā'ī, al-Tirmidhī, Abū Dāwūd and Ibn Mājah all report that Abū Bakr once said after praising God and glorifying Him: "People often read this verse, *'Believers, it is but for your own souls that you are accountable,'* but they misunderstand it. I have heard God's Messenger (peace be upon him) say: When people see evil and take no action to alter it, they render themselves exposed to God's punishment that encompasses them all." Thus, the first Caliph corrected what some of his contemporaries imagined the verse to mean. Today, we are in much greater need for this correction, because changing an evil situation has become much harder. Hence, it is all too easy for the weak to interpret the verse in a way that exempts them from putting up any struggle against evil.

For certain, this religion cannot establish its roots without effort and struggle. It needs followers who spare no effort to guide people to it in order to liberate them from subservience to other people so that they may submit to God alone. Such followers will do their utmost to establish the right concept of Godhead and to repel those who usurp God's authority so that God's law is seen to be implemented in human life. Such efforts are peaceful when the misguided ones are individuals in need of direction. However, force will be needed when there is a tyrannical power turning people away from God's guidance, and standing in the way of establishing the Islamic faith and implementing God's law. It is only then that the believers will have fulfilled their responsibility and those who persist in error are punished by God: "*To God you all must return. He will then make you understand all that you were doing [in life].*" (Verse 105)

Witnesses at the Time of Death

The passage is concluded with an outline of the rulings applicable to witnesses to a will, when the testator is away from home and from his society. These are the final rulings given in this *sūrah* on certain transactions in Islamic society. They provide guarantees to ensure that people receive what is rightly theirs.

Believers, let there be witnesses to what you do when death approaches you and you are about to make bequests: two persons of probity from among your own people, or two others from outside, if the pangs of death come to you when you are travelling through the land. Detain them both after prayer, and if you have any doubt in mind, let them swear by God, "We shall not sell this [our word] for any price, even though it were for a near kinsman; and neither shall we conceal anything of what we have witnessed before God; for then we should be among the sinful." But if afterwards it should come to light that the two [witnesses] have been guilty of [this very] sin, then two others should replace them from among those immediately concerned. Both shall swear by God, "Our testimony is indeed truer than that of these two. We have not transgressed the bounds of what is right; for then we should be among the evil-doers." Thus it will be more likely that people will offer testimony in accordance with the truth; or else they will fear that the oaths of others may be taken after their oaths. Have fear of God and hearken [to Him]. God does not guide those who are iniquitous. (Verses 106–8)

The process outlined in these three verses indicates that a person who feels the end to be near and wants to make bequests assigning any money he has to his relatives should call in two Muslim witnesses of probity and give them what property he has so that they may give it to his relatives who are not present. This applies when the person concerned is in his hometown. If he is travelling and does not find two Muslim witnesses to entrust his property to, then it is permissible to have two non-Muslim witnesses.

Should the Muslim community, or the family of the deceased, doubt the honesty of what the witnesses hand over, or they have reason to suspect that the witnesses have been unfaithful to their trust, then the following procedure applies. The witnesses are brought forward after having offered prayers, according to their faith, and they are asked to testify by God that they would not swear to make any gain for themselves or for anyone else, even a close relative, and that they would not conceal anything entrusted to them. Should they do so, they acknowledge that they would be guilty of committing a sin. Thus, their testimony is approved.

However, if it later appears that the witnesses have been guilty of a breach of trust, giving false testimony under oath, another procedure takes place. The two closest heirs of the deceased who have suffered as a result of the false testimony come forward and swear that their own testimony is truer than that of the two witnesses, and that by stating this fact, they are guilty of no iniquity. Should this take place, then the statement of the first two witnesses is considered null and void, while the statement of the second two witnesses is upheld.

The Qur'ānic verses state that these procedures ensure that witnesses remain true in their testimony, fearing that the first witnesses are rejected. Hence, they try hard to be true to their trust. *"Thus it will be more likely that people will offer testimony in accordance with the truth; or*

AL-MĀ'IDAH (The Repast) 5

else they will fear that the oaths of others may be taken after their oaths."
(Verse 108) These verses are concluded with a reminder to all people
to remain God-fearing, and to watch God and obey His
commandments. They are further reminded that God will not give
His guidance to anyone who turns away from His path. *"Have fear of
God and hearken [to Him]. God does not guide those who are iniquitous."*
(Verse 108)

Al-Qurṭubī, a leading commentator on the Qur'ān, relates the
occasion that led to the revelation of these three verses:

> I do not know of any disagreement among scholars that these
> three verses were revealed in connection with Tamīm al-Dārī and
> 'Adī ibn Baddā'. Al-Bukhārī, al-Dāraquṭnī and others quote this
> report by Ibn 'Abbās: Tamīm al-Dārī and 'Adī ibn Baddā' used to
> go frequently to Makkah. Once a young man from the Sahm
> clan went with them and he died in a place where there was no
> Muslim. Just before his death, he put them in charge of his
> property, which they delivered to his family, but they retained a
> silver article with a gold covering. God's Messenger (peace be upon
> him) asked them by God whether they had withheld or concealed
> anything. Later on, that silver article was found in Makkah. People
> there said that they bought it from 'Adī and Tamīm. Two men
> who were heirs of the man from Sahm stated under oath that the
> article belonged to their relative and that their testimony was truer
> than that of the two witnesses. They also confirmed that they
> had not transgressed. [The Prophet] then took the silver article
> [to give to the deceased man's relatives]. It was in relation to those
> people that these verses were revealed... [The text quoted here is
> the one related by al-Dāraquṭnī.]

It is clear that the nature of the society in which these rulings were
laid down has a bearing on the procedures outlined. The calling of
witnesses and entrusting things to their care, the taking of an oath in
public after offering prayers to enhance one's religious consciousness,
the fear of being found out, should one be tempted to lie or to act
dishonestly, are all measures which suggest their effectiveness in a
particular type of society. Modern societies may have different methods
and measures of proof, such as documentation, registration, and bank
deposits, etc.

The question then which can be posed here is: has this text lost its operational validity in today's society? The fact is that we may often be misguided by the circumstances that prevail in a particular society. We may think that some recommended measures may have lost their validity or effectiveness, or that they have become unnecessary, or that they were more suited to past communities. Such thoughts may be the result of developments that have taken place in society.

When we are so misguided, we simply forget that this religion of Islam is meant for all mankind, in all places and for all generations. We also forget that a huge number of people today still live in semi-primitive or underdeveloped conditions. Such communities are in need of legal provisions and procedures to suit their needs in all their forms and stages of development. They find in this religion of Islam what suits their needs in all situations. When they move up along the ladder of development and progress, they will still find in it what satisfies their needs in the same way. They also find that its legal provisions satisfy their present needs and the needs of their development. This is one miracle of this religion and its law. It is a proof that it is laid down by God who knows all.

We may also be misguided when we forget that individuals today living in societies that have attained a high standard of development may find themselves in some emergency situation when they could rely on the simplicity and comprehensiveness of Islamic law. We must not forget that the tools employed by the Islamic faith have been devised so that they are effective in all environments, applicable to all cases, in bedouin and urban communities, in the desert and the jungle, as well as in the town and city. It is a faith for mankind in all ages and societies. Again, this is one of its great miracles.

We are even more grossly misguided when we think that we, human beings, know what suits us better than God, our Creator. But we are often reminded by the realities that we should be more humble in our approach. We should better remember before we face the shock of His reality. We should know what manners we should adopt when we refer to God. We should behave like the obedient servants of God, the Master of all.

9

About Jesus and the Repast

On the day when God will gather all [His] messengers and ask them, "What response did you receive?" – they will answer, "We have no knowledge. Indeed, it is You alone who has full knowledge of all that lies beyond the reach of human perception." (109)

۞ يَوْمَ يَجْمَعُ ٱللَّهُ ٱلرُّسُلَ فَيَقُولُ مَاذَآ أُجِبْتُمْ قَالُواْ لَا عِلْمَ لَنَآ إِنَّكَ أَنتَ عَلَّمُ ٱلْغُيُوبِ ﴿١٠٩﴾

God will say: "Jesus, son of Mary! Remember the blessings which I bestowed on you and your mother: how I strengthened you with the Holy Spirit, so that you could speak to people in your cradle, and as a grown man; how I instructed you in the Book and in wisdom, in the Torah and in the Gospel; how, by My leave, you fashioned from clay the figure of a bird and breathed into it so that, by My leave, it became a living bird; how, by My leave, you healed the blind man and the leper, and by My leave, restored the dead to life; how I prevented

إِذْ قَالَ ٱللَّهُ يَعِيسَى ٱبْنَ مَرْيَمَ ٱذْكُرْ نِعْمَتِي عَلَيْكَ وَعَلَى وَٰلِدَتِكَ إِذْ أَيَّدتُّكَ بِرُوحِ ٱلْقُدُسِ تُكَلِّمُ ٱلنَّاسَ فِي ٱلْمَهْدِ وَكَهْلًا وَإِذْ عَلَّمْتُكَ ٱلْكِتَٰبَ وَٱلْحِكْمَةَ وَٱلتَّوْرَىٰةَ وَٱلْإِنجِيلَ وَإِذْ تَخْلُقُ مِنَ ٱلطِّينِ كَهَيْـَٔةِ ٱلطَّيْرِ بِإِذْنِي فَتَنفُخُ فِيهَا فَتَكُونُ طَيْرًا بِإِذْنِي وَتُبْرِئُ ٱلْأَكْمَهَ وَٱلْأَبْرَصَ بِإِذْنِي وَإِذْ تُخْرِجُ ٱلْمَوْتَىٰ بِإِذْنِي

283

the Children of Israel from harming you when you came to them with all evidence of the truth: when those of them who disbelieved declared: 'This is plain sorcery.' (110)

وَإِذْ كَفَفْتُ بَنِىٓ إِسۡرَٰٓءِيلَ عَنكَ إِذۡ جِئۡتَهُم بِٱلۡبَيِّنَٰتِ فَقَالَ ٱلَّذِينَ كَفَرُواْ مِنۡهُمۡ إِنۡ هَٰذَآ إِلَّا سِحۡرٌ مُّبِينٌ ۝

And when I inspired the disciples to have faith in Me and in My Messenger; they said: "We believe; and bear you witness that we have surrendered ourselves [to God]." (111)

وَإِذۡ أَوۡحَيۡتُ إِلَى ٱلۡحَوَارِيِّـۧنَ أَنۡ ءَامِنُواْ بِى وَبِرَسُولِى قَالُوٓاْ ءَامَنَّا وَٱشۡهَدۡ بِأَنَّنَا مُسۡلِمُونَ ۝

The disciples said: "Jesus, son of Mary! Can your Lord send down to us a repast from heaven?" He answered: "Fear God, if you are truly believers." (112)

إِذۡ قَالَ ٱلۡحَوَارِيُّونَ يَٰعِيسَى ٱبۡنَ مَرۡيَمَ هَلۡ يَسۡتَطِيعُ رَبُّكَ أَن يُنَزِّلَ عَلَيۡنَا مَآئِدَةً مِّنَ ٱلسَّمَآءِ قَالَ ٱتَّقُواْ ٱللَّهَ إِن كُنتُم مُّؤۡمِنِينَ ۝

Said they: "We desire to eat of it, so that our hearts are reassured and that we know that you have spoken the truth to us, and that we may be witness of it." (113)

قَالُواْ نُرِيدُ أَن نَّأۡكُلَ مِنۡهَا وَتَطۡمَئِنَّ قُلُوبُنَا وَنَعۡلَمَ أَن قَدۡ صَدَقۡتَنَا وَنَكُونَ عَلَيۡهَا مِنَ ٱلشَّٰهِدِينَ ۝

"God, our Lord," said Jesus, son of Mary, "send down upon us a repast from heaven: it shall be an ever-recurring feast for us – for the first and the last of us – and a sign from You. And provide us our sustenance, for You are the best provider." (114)

قَالَ عِيسَى ٱبۡنُ مَرۡيَمَ ٱللَّهُمَّ رَبَّنَآ أَنزِلۡ عَلَيۡنَا مَآئِدَةً مِّنَ ٱلسَّمَآءِ تَكُونُ لَنَا عِيدًا لِّأَوَّلِنَا وَءَاخِرِنَا وَءَايَةً مِّنكَ وَٱرۡزُقۡنَا وَأَنتَ خَيۡرُ ٱلرَّٰزِقِينَ ۝

God replied: "I am sending it down to you. But whoever of you disbelieves after this, I shall inflict on him suffering the like of which I have not inflicted on anyone in the world." (115)

قَالَ ٱللَّهُ إِنِّي مُنَزِّلُهَا عَلَيْكُمْ فَمَن يَكْفُرْ بَعْدُ مِنكُمْ فَإِنِّي أُعَذِّبُهُۥ عَذَابًا لَّآ أُعَذِّبُهُۥٓ أَحَدًا مِّنَ ٱلْعَٰلَمِينَ ۝

And God will say: "Jesus, son of Mary! Did you say to people, 'Worship me and my mother as deities beside God?'" [Jesus] answered: "Limitless are You in Your glory! I could never have claimed what I have no right to [say]! Had I said this, You would certainly have known it. You know all that is within myself, whereas I do not know what is in Yourself. Most certainly, it is You alone who fully knows all that lies beyond the reach of human perception. (116)

وَإِذْ قَالَ ٱللَّهُ يَٰعِيسَى ٱبْنَ مَرْيَمَ ءَأَنتَ قُلْتَ لِلنَّاسِ ٱتَّخِذُونِي وَأُمِّيَ إِلَٰهَيْنِ مِن دُونِ ٱللَّهِ قَالَ سُبْحَٰنَكَ مَا يَكُونُ لِيٓ أَنْ أَقُولَ مَا لَيْسَ لِي بِحَقٍّ إِن كُنتُ قُلْتُهُۥ فَقَدْ عَلِمْتَهُۥ تَعْلَمُ مَا فِي نَفْسِي وَلَآ أَعْلَمُ مَا فِي نَفْسِكَ إِنَّكَ أَنتَ عَلَّٰمُ ٱلْغُيُوبِ ۝

Nothing did I tell them beyond what You bade me [to say]: 'Worship God, who is my Lord and your Lord.' I was witness to what they did as long as I lived in their midst. Then when You took me to Yourself, You have been watching over them. You are indeed a witness to all things. (117)

مَا قُلْتُ لَهُمْ إِلَّا مَآ أَمَرْتَنِي بِهِۦٓ أَنِ ٱعْبُدُوا۟ ٱللَّهَ رَبِّي وَرَبَّكُمْ وَكُنتُ عَلَيْهِمْ شَهِيدًا مَّا دُمْتُ فِيهِمْ فَلَمَّا تَوَفَّيْتَنِي كُنتَ أَنتَ ٱلرَّقِيبَ عَلَيْهِمْ وَأَنتَ عَلَىٰ كُلِّ شَىْءٍ شَهِيدٌ ۝

If You punish them, they are Your servants; and if You forgive them, You are indeed Almighty, Wise." (118)

إِن تُعَذِّبْهُمْ فَإِنَّهُمْ عِبَادُكَ وَإِن تَغْفِرْ لَهُمْ فَإِنَّكَ أَنتَ ٱلْعَزِيزُ ٱلْحَكِيمُ ۝

God will say: "This is the day
when their truthfulness shall
benefit all who have been
truthful. Theirs shall be gardens
through which running waters
flow, where they will abide for
ever. God is well-pleased with
them, and they are well-pleased
with Him. That is the supreme
triumph." (119)

قَالَ ٱللَّهُ هَٰذَا يَوْمُ يَنفَعُ ٱلصَّٰدِقِينَ صِدْقُهُمْ
لَهُمْ جَنَّٰتٌ تَجْرِى مِن تَحْتِهَا ٱلْأَنْهَٰرُ
خَٰلِدِينَ فِيهَآ أَبَدًا رَّضِىَ ٱللَّهُ عَنْهُمْ وَرَضُواْ عَنْهُ
ذَٰلِكَ ٱلْفَوْزُ ٱلْعَظِيمُ ﴿١١٩﴾

To God belongs all sovereignty
over the heavens and the earth
and all they contain. He has the
power over all things. (120)

لِلَّهِ مُلْكُ ٱلسَّمَٰوَٰتِ وَٱلْأَرْضِ وَمَا فِيهِنَّ
وَهُوَ عَلَىٰ كُلِّ شَىْءٍ قَدِيرٌ ﴿١٢٠﴾

Overview

This whole passage serves as a complement to the efforts undertaken
in this *sūrah* to keep faith pure and to purge it from all the errors and
deviations Christians have introduced. They forced their faith away
from its Divine origins and fundamental principles when they diverted
it from belief in the absolute oneness of God. That was the belief
preached by Jesus (peace be upon him) and by every former messenger
of God. They introduced into it certain aspects of disbelief which had
nothing to do with Divine faith.

As such, this passage aims to establish the truth about Godhead and
servitude to God, as these are conceived by Islam. This truth is presented
through a great scene portrayed here in which Jesus states in front of
all God's messengers and all humanity that he never said to his people
anything of what they have alleged that both he and his mother were
deities. He declares that he could have never said any such blasphemy.

The *sūrah* presents this truth in a vivid scene taken from the Day of
Judgement in the same way as the Qur'ān presents various scenes of
that great day. In all such presentations, the picture is portrayed in
such an inspiring, vivid and effective way that we almost see it before
our very eyes. We are moved by each such scene as though it were

taking place here and now. We see what is taking place, hear what is being said and feel every reaction and response. So, what does this scene at the end of this *sūrah* present?

When All Messengers Are Gathered Together

On the day when God will gather all [His] messengers and ask them, "What response did you receive?" – they will answer, "We have no knowledge. Indeed, it is You alone who has full knowledge of all that lies beyond the reach of human perception. (Verse 109)

Those messengers were sent at different times to their respective people, each going his own way to his city or village, and belonging to different races and nations, all preaching the same message to their communities. Then, the last of them, Muḥammad, is given a single message addressed to all people of all races in all generations. Those messengers are gathered together by the One who sent them individually, and as they come together they bring with them the different responses they received. Now, in this scene, those messengers, representing humanity throughout its life span on earth, come together and stand before God, the Lord of all mankind on an awesome day.

The scene is full of life: *"On the day when God will gather all [His] messengers and ask them: 'What response did you receive?'"* (Verse 109) Today, everything is brought together, and messengers account for their messages. The results are declared before all humanity.

"What response did you receive?" Messengers are human. They know what they see and feel with their senses, but they have no knowledge of what lies beyond. They had called on their peoples to follow Divine guidance. Some responded positively while others turned away. A messenger does not know the full truth about a person responding positively, even though he may know the truth of the one turning away. He can only tell by appearances; it is God who knows the full truth and what is concealed. Those messengers are now in the presence of God and, among all human beings, they know God best, fear Him most and are too modest to speak out, in His presence, on the basis of their limited knowledge when He knows all.

This is an awesome interrogation, on the day when all creatures are gathered, the Supreme Company is present and all humanity is looking on. This is a confrontation, when all humanity is put face to face with the Messengers, and especially the unbelievers who are now arrayed before those Messengers to whom they used to lie. Then the declaration is made that those noble messengers simply preached the Divine faith, and that they are now in His presence stating what happened to their messages and giving an account of the reaction of their communities which denied them. Those messengers declare that true knowledge belongs to God alone. Whatever they knew should not, in all modesty and humility, be stated by them to God whose knowledge is perfect, absolute. *"They will answer: 'We have no knowledge. Indeed, it is You alone who has full knowledge of all that lies beyond the reach of human perception.'"* (Verse 109)

Those messengers who were sent before the time of Jesus were believed by some people and denied by others. Their account is thus completed with this general answer that they give, leaving all knowledge to God and putting the whole matter into His hands. Hence, the *sūrah* adds nothing here about them. The address is made to Jesus alone, who was a total wonder to his people. It was Jesus who was surrounded with mystery and around whom all sorts of myth and superstition have circulated. A great deal of confusion has been made about his qualities, nature, birth and end.

A Hard Confrontation

The account given in this *sūrah* addresses Jesus, son of Mary, in front of all those who attributed to him Divine status, worshipped him and weaved around him and his mother all sorts of exaggerated stories. The address reminds him of the grace God bestowed on him and on his mother, enumerating the miracles God gave him to help people to believe in his message. Yet some people denied his message most violently, while others were dazzled with the miracles he was given. On account of such miracles they elevated him to the status of a deity, when all miracles are given by God, who created him, gave him a message and supported him.

God will say: "Jesus, son of Mary! Remember the blessings which I bestowed on you and your mother: how I strengthened you with the Holy Spirit, so that you could speak to people in your cradle, and as a grown man; how I instructed you in the Book and in wisdom, in the Torah and in the Gospel; how, by My leave, you fashioned from clay the figure of a bird and breathed into it so that, by My leave, it became a living bird; how, by My leave, you healed the blind man and the leper, and, by My leave, restored the dead to life; how I prevented the Children of Israel from harming you when you came to them with all evidence of the truth: when those of them who disbelieved declared: 'This is plain sorcery.' And when I inspired the disciples to have faith in Me and in My Messenger; they said: 'We believe; and bear you witness that we have surrendered ourselves [to God].'" (Verses 110–11)

Here we have a full account of the various aspects of grace bestowed by God on Jesus and his mother, Mary. To start with, he was supported by the Holy Spirit in his infancy. Then, he was talking to people long before children normally start to talk, absolving his mother of all suspicion raised around her on account of his miraculous birth that had no parallel in history. He also talked to them later when as a grown man he was again supported by the Holy Spirit, Gabriel. He was also given knowledge of the Book and wisdom. He was born without knowledge of reading and writing, but God gave him that knowledge, as He imparted to him wisdom in order to deal with different situations in the best way. God also taught him the Torah which had been given to the Children of Israel and the Gospel which God gave him to confirm the Torah.

Furthermore, God gave Jesus several miraculous things that no human being could accomplish without God's support. Thus, he could fashion a bird shape of clay and breathe into it, and all at once it became a living bird. How did this happen? We do not know, because we still do not know how God creates life. Moreover, he adds quality to life: he cures a person born blind, by God's leave, when medicine does not know how to give eyesight to such a person. God, who gives human beings their faculty of seeing, is able to open a blind person's eyes to see the light. Jesus also cured the leper without using any medicine. Medication is merely a tool for accomplishing God's will of curing a patient, but the One who has willed to cure the patient is able to change the tools by which He accomplishes His purpose, or to achieve it without any tool. Again Jesus is able to restore life to the dead, by God's leave. The One who initiates life is able to restore it at any time.

God further reminds Jesus of His favours when He extended His protection to him against the Israelites who, when he produced all these miracles, denied him claiming that they were plain sorcery. On the one hand they did not wish to deny the miracles, witnessed by thousands of people, and yet they were too stubborn to submit to the message they imparted. God protected him and they were unable to kill or crucify him, as they were keen to do. God simply gathered him and elevated him to Himself. Another reminder to Jesus speaks of how God inspired the disciples to believe in Him and His Messenger, Jesus, and they do so, appealing to him to bear witness to their acceptance of the faith and total self-surrender to God. *"And when I inspired the disciples to have faith in Me and in My Messenger; they said: 'We believe; and bear you witness that we have surrendered ourselves [to God].'"* (Verse 111)

All these were favours God, out of His grace, gave to Jesus to serve as clear proof of his status and message. Many of his followers, however, used them erroneously, deviating from the truth and fabricating falsehood. Here Jesus is reminded of all these in the presence of the Supreme Company and in front of all mankind, including those people who exaggerated his status and attributed to him what was not his. When these favours are held in front of him, those who gave him a status far beyond his own humanity will see and hear, and, in consequence, they will be humiliated in the full sight of all humanity.

Favours Granted to Jesus's Followers

In addition to the favours bestowed on Jesus and his mother, the *sūrah* relates some of the favours God granted to his followers, and the miracles with which God supported him, as seen by his disciples.

> *The disciples said: "Jesus, son of Mary! Can your Lord send down to us a repast from heaven?" He answered: "Fear God, if you are truly believers." Said they: "We desire to eat of it, so that our hearts are reassured and that we know that you have spoken the truth to us, and that we may be witness of it." "God, our Lord," said Jesus, son of Mary, "send down upon us a repast from heaven: it shall be an ever-recurring feast for us – for the first and the last of us – and a sign from You. And provide us our sustenance, for You are the best provider." God replied: "I am sending it down to you. But whoever of you disbelieves after this, I shall inflict on him suffering the like of which I have not inflicted on anyone in the world."* (Verses 112–15)

This dialogue reveals to us something about Jesus's people, and the élite among them, i.e. his disciples. What we find is that they differed greatly from our own Prophet's Companions. Those were the disciples inspired by God to believe in Him and His Messenger, Jesus, son of Mary. They did so and called on Jesus to witness the fact of their faith. Yet even after all the miracles they saw Jesus performing, they still requested another miracle so as to reassure themselves about his truthfulness and to bear witness about it to those who would succeed them.

Muḥammad's Companions, on the other hand, never asked him for a single miracle after they had accepted the faith and submitted themselves to God. Their hearts were full of faith, once they had experienced the happiness and joy of it. They believed God's Messenger and asked him for no more proof of the truth of his message. They testified to his truthfulness with no miracle shown to them other than the Qur'ān.

Such is the wide gulf between Jesus's disciples and Muḥammad's Companions (peace be upon them both). Theirs are two widely different levels; yet both have submitted to God, and both are accepted by Him, if He so pleases. But their levels remain wide apart.

The story of the Repast, as told in the Qur'ān, is not mentioned in Christian Scriptures. It is not reported in the Gospels written long after Jesus. Thus, they cannot be taken as a reliable statement of the truth revealed by God Almighty. These Gospels are only reports by saints of the story of Jesus. They are not the text of the Gospel, or the *Injīl* that God revealed to Jesus.

However, these books include a different report on the Repast. In 15: 32 of Matthew, the following report is given: "Then Jesus called his disciples to him and said, 'I have compassion for the crowd, because they have been with me now for three days and have nothing to eat; and I do not want to send them away hungry, for they might faint on the way.' The disciples said to him, 'Where are we to get enough bread in the desert to feed so great a crowd?' Jesus asked them, 'How many loaves have you?' They said, 'Seven, and a few small fish.' Then ordering the crowd to sit down on the ground, he took the seven loaves and the fish; and after giving thanks he broke them and gave them to the disciples, and the disciples gave them to the crowd. And all of them ate and were filled; and they took up the broken pieces left over, seven baskets full. Those who had eaten were four thousand men, besides women and children." Similar reports are given in other Gospels.

Some scholars of the generation following the Prophet's Companions, i.e. *Tābi'īn*, like Mujāhid and al-Ḥasan, believe that the Repast was not sent down. They say that when the disciples were afraid at hearing

God's statement, *"I am sending it down to you. But whoever of you disbelieves after this, I shall inflict on him suffering the like of which I have not inflicted on anyone in the world."* (Verse 115), they no longer asked for it to be granted.

In his commentary on the Qur'ān, Ibn Kathīr quotes several statements by scholars. He quotes Mujāhid as saying: "This was merely a parable given by God, but nothing was sent down." Another quotation by Mujāhid says: "They were offered a table full of food, but they refused it when they were told that they would be severely punished should they disbelieve. They did not want to have anything to do with it." Al-Ḥasan also expresses the view that it was not sent down. He is reported to have said: "When the disciples were told, *'Whoever of you disbelieves after this, I shall inflict on him suffering the like of which I have not inflicted on anyone in the world,'* they said, 'We have no need for it.' Thus, it was not sent down."

The majority of early scholars, however, agree that it was sent down, because God said: *"I am sending it down to you."* God's promise always comes true. We, therefore, take only what the Qur'ān has stated concerning the Repast.

Thus, God reminds Jesus, son of Mary, of His favours when he stands in front of his people on the Day of Judgement, with all creatures looking on: *"The disciples said: 'Jesus, son of Mary! Can your Lord send down to us a repast from heaven?'"* (Verse 112) The disciples, the closest to Jesus of all his followers, were aware that he was a human being, born to Mary. They address him according to his status, which they knew very well. They knew that he was neither a son of God nor a deity, but a servant of God. They also knew that it was his Lord who accomplished all those miraculous events through him. He himself could not do any of them by his own initiative. Hence, when they requested a further miracle, they did not ask him to accomplish it himself, because they were aware that he could not do so. Their question was: *"Jesus, son of Mary! Can your Lord send down to us a repast from heaven?"* (Verse 112)

Interpretations vary as to the nature of their question. How is it that they would use such a form of question when they had already declared their belief in God and asked Jesus to witness their submission to Him? One interpretation of their question is that it did not seek to know God's ability, but rather whether He would give them the repast. Another view considers the question to mean, "would your Lord respond to you if you were to request Him to send down a repast?" Other interpretations are also given.

The Miraculous Repast

Be that as it may, Jesus warned them against asking for miracles, because believers do not ask for them: "*He answered: 'Fear God, if you are truly believers.'*" (Verse 112) But Jesus's disciples repeated their request stating their reasons for requesting it and what they hoped to achieve, should it be granted. "*Said they: 'We desire to eat of it, so that our hearts are reassured and that we know that you have spoken the truth to us, and that we may be witness of it.'*" (Verse 113)

What they wanted was that they should eat of such food which no human being on earth could ever taste. They would have heart-felt reassurance as they would see the miracle being enacted in front of their eyes. They would know then that Jesus had told them only the truth. This would make of them witnesses to the truth of this miracle so that none of their people could ever deny it. All these reasons confirm that the level of those disciples was well below that of Muḥammad's Companions, who were of a totally different mould.

At this point Jesus addressed his appeal to his Lord: "*God, our Lord,*" said Jesus, son of Mary, "*send down upon us a repast from heaven: it shall be an ever-recurring feast for us – for the first and the last of us – and a sign from You. And provide us our sustenance, for You are the best provider.*" (Verse 114)

We note in Jesus's supplication how he makes his address with all the humility of a servant whose Lord has honoured him. He first makes it clear that he recognises Him, saying, "*God, our Lord!*" Then he states his appeal, requesting Him to give them a repast that would bring them joy and goodness, so as to be like a festival for everyone of them. He acknowledges that it would all be provided by God, the best of all providers. Jesus is thus shown to recognise his own status as a servant of God and to recognise God's status as Lord of all the worlds. This is shown in front of all mankind, particularly his people on that great and eventful day.

God answers the prayer of his good servant, Jesus son of Mary, but with the seriousness that befits His majesty. They asked for a miracle, and He will give them the miracle they requested, on condition that He will severely punish anyone who continues to disbelieve after the miracle is granted. Indeed that punishment will surpass in severity any other punishment inflicted on any other of God's servants. "*God replied: 'I am sending it down to you. But whoever of you disbelieves after this, I shall inflict on him suffering the like of which I have not inflicted on anyone in the world.'*" (Verse 115)

This seriousness is important, so that requests for miracles are not made as idle talk. Moreover, those who ask for proof and continue to disbelieve after they have been given what they have asked for must not go unpunished. It has been God's law, applicable to all past communities, that those who continued to deny the messages preached by God's messengers after the miracles were given them were annihilated. In this instance, however, the statement may mean that they would be punished here in this life, or in the life to come.

Did Jesus Claim Divinity?

The *sūrah* does not follow the account of the Repast after stating God's warning. It moves on to deal with the central issue of Godhead and Lordship, which permeates the whole passage. We go back now to that great scene which continues to be held up for all onlookers. We listen now to a straightforward questioning about the Divinity claimed for Jesus and his mother. The person now interrogated is none other than Jesus, facing those who worshipped him. They listen to him as he, surprised and amazed, disclaims before his Lord all knowledge of such a grievous sin they attach to him. He is, indeed, innocent and it is all fabrication:

> *And God will say: "Jesus, son of Mary! Did you say to people, 'Worship me and my mother as deities beside God?'" [Jesus] answered: "Limitless are You in Your glory! I could never have claimed what I have no right to [say]! Had I said this, You would certainly have known it. You know all that is within myself, whereas I do not know what is in Yourself. Most certainly, it is You alone who fully knows all that lies beyond the reach of human perception. Nothing did I tell them beyond what You bade me [to say]: 'Worship God, who is my Lord and your Lord.' I was witness to what they did as long as I lived in their midst. Then when You took me to Yourself, You have been watching over them. You are indeed a witness to all things. If You punish them, they are Your servants; and if You forgive them, You are indeed Almighty, Wise." (Verses 116–18)*

Limitless is God in His glory! He knows very well what Jesus said to people. But this worrying interrogation on that fearful day is intended for people other than the one to whom it is addressed. Putting it in this form adds to our abhorrence of the attitude of those who attributed Divinity to Jesus, God's noble and great servant. For anyone of God's servants to claim to be God, knowing that he is no more than a servant of God, is indeed a horrible offence that no normal human being could perpetrate. Is it conceivable, then, that one of God's messengers who were granted the strongest resolve should perpetrate it? Or is it even conceivable that this perpetrator should be Jesus son of Mary, when God gave him all those favours before and after he was chosen to bear His message? How does he feel when questioned about this claim of Godhead, when he is a good servant of God?

Hence, his answer is tinged with awe and fear. He starts by glorifying God and follows this immediately with an absolute denial of any such thoughts or of any such claims: "[Jesus] answered: 'Limitless are You in Your glory! I could never have claimed what I have no right to [say]'!" (Verse 116) In his own defence, he seeks God as witness to his innocence of such claims. He owns to his humble position of being only a servant to God who has all attributes of the Godhead. "Had I said this, You would certainly have known it. You know all that is within myself, whereas I do not know what is in Yourself. Most certainly, it is You alone who fully knows all that lies beyond the reach of human perception." (Verse 116)

Now, after having made this long praise of God, he is able to state what he did and did not say, declaring that he said nothing to his community other than calling on them to worship God alone, and stating that, like them, he is no more than God's servant. "Nothing did I tell them beyond what You bade me [to say]: 'Worship God, who is my Lord and your Lord.'" (Verse 117)

He then disclaims any responsibility for what they did after the end of his time on earth. Taken at face value, the Qur'ānic text means that God gathered Jesus then elevated him to Himself. Some reports indicate that he is alive with God. In my view, there can be no contradiction between the two situations; for God may have determined that Jesus had completed his term of life on earth, and He may have taken him so that he be alive with Him. Martyrs die and finish their lives on earth, but they are alive with God. We do not know what form their life with God takes, nor do we know what form of life Jesus has; but he says here to his Lord that he does not know what they did or said after he was gathered from life on earth: "*I was witness to what they did as long as I lived in their midst. Then when You took me to Yourself, You have been watching over them. You are indeed a witness to all things.*" (Verse 117)

He concludes with leaving the fate of his people absolutely to God, stating at the same time that they are His servants and at His disposal. God is able to forgive them or to punish them. Whether He decides on one course or the other, that decision is based on His wisdom, which operates in the same measure whichever fate He determines for them. "*If You punish them, they are Your servants; and if You forgive them, You are indeed Almighty, Wise.*" (Verse 118) This is all that Jesus, a model servant of God, says in this awesome position.

But where are those who invented such grave falsehood about Jesus in this whole scene? The *sūrah* does not mention them once. They may be feeling their ignominy and wish not to show themselves. We, therefore, leave them where the *sūrah* has left them. We will only look now at the final part in that remarkable scene:

"*God will say: 'This is the day when their truthfulness shall benefit all who have been truthful. Theirs shall be gardens through which running waters flow, where they will abide forever. God is well pleased with them, and they are well pleased with Him. That is the supreme triumph.'*" (Verse 119) The appropriate comment on the falsehood fabricated by liars against the noble Prophet Jesus, concerning the most serious issue of all, i.e. the issue of Godhead, is to state that truth will be of great benefit to its upholders on that awesome day. "*This is the day when their truthfulness shall benefit all who have been truthful.*"

This is God's word at the end of that interrogation beheld by all creatures. It is the final and decisive word. It is coupled with the reward that befits truthfulness and those who are truthful: "*Theirs shall be gardens through which running waters flow, where they will abide forever. God is well pleased with them, and they are well pleased with Him.*" (Verse 119) Each of these phrases represents a grade above the previous one: the gardens with running waters, the everlasting abode there, the fact that God is pleased with them, and their pleasure with what they receive from Him. Hence the description, "*That is the supreme triumph.*" (Verse 119)

We have looked at this scene as it is portrayed in the unique style of the Qur'ān and we have paid attention to the final word. We say that we have seen and paid attention because the Qur'ānic method of portraying scenes and images does not leave it as merely a promise to be fulfilled or sentences and phrases to be read or heard. The Qur'ān makes of it something to excite feelings and something to behold as if it were taking place now. However, if it is, as far as we human beings are concerned, a future event to be witnessed on the Day of Judgement, it is, for God's perfect knowledge, a present reality. Time and the screen of the future apply to us, not to God.

The Final Note

At the end of this passage and in contrast to the greatest falsehood ever perpetrated by the followers of any messenger, i.e. the falsehood of Christ's Divine nature, which he himself denounces and leaves all decision about which to God alone, a statement of truth is made. It provides the final note in the *sūrah*, declaring that dominion over the heavens and the earth and all that they contain belongs to God, the Lord of the universe who has full control over all things. Nothing limits His power: "*To God belongs all sovereignty over the heavens and the earth and all they contain. He has the power over all things.*" (Verse 120)

This is the finale that suits the great question around which that terrible fallacy has been woven. It is an ending that fits that majestic scene where God is seen to be the One who has all knowledge, Godhead and all power. To Him alone all messengers turn, putting all matters in His hands. Indeed, to Him Jesus son of Mary assigns judgement in his own and his people's affair. He is Almighty, Wise, the Sovereign over the heavens, the earth and all they contain. It is a fitting conclusion to the *sūrah* which discusses the meaning of religion, showing it to be the implementation of only God's law, receiving guidance from Him alone and judging only on the basis of His revelations. Since He is the Sovereign, He is the One to judge, for final judgement belongs to whomever has sovereignty: "*Those who do not judge according to what God has revealed are indeed unbelievers.*" (Verse 44)

It is all one and the same issue: Godhead, the Oneness of God, and judgement on the basis of His guidance.

Index